TASTING VICTORY

TASTING VICTORY

The Life and Wines of the World's Favourite Sommelier

Gerard Basset

unbound

First published in 2020

Unbound

6th Floor Mutual House, 70 Conduit Street, London W1S 2GF

www.unbound.com

Text Design by Ellipsis, Glasgow

A CIP record for this book is available from the British Library

ISBN 978-1-78352-860-8 (hardback)
ISBN 978-1-78352-861-5 (ebook)

Printed in Great Britain by CPI Group (UK)

1 3 5 7 9 8 6 4 2

Dedication

There are so many people I could and should dedicate this book to, who helped me on my journey. To my friends and colleagues, please forgive me for not naming you all. However, I must thank Jancis Robinson, Raymond Blanc and Felicity Carter for all of their help and guidance – this book would not exist without their help – thank you, all three.

There are two more special people I must mention: my wife Nina, without whom none of this would have been possible. And the other is my son, Romané, who has given me such joy and made me so proud. This book is for you, Romané. I love you now and for ever, Papa. Xxx

With special thanks to
Jackson Family Wines
Michael Hill Smith MW

Gold Supporters
Sarah Abbott
AXA Millésimes Gestion Bordeaux
Nina and Romane Basset and Anthony Howe
Paolo Basso
Lewis Chester
Chewton Glen Hotel
Mayu Saito
Martin and Brigitte Skan
TEXSOM

Contents

Preface
Windsor Castle, 2011

We'd been briefed on what to do, but I didn't want to commit a faux pas. I watched what the person in front of me was doing.

Finally, I advanced and took my place in front of Her Royal Highness, Princess Anne. I bowed as I had been told and then Princess Anne talked to me in excellent French. She congratulated me on my career and even referred to some specific events I had been involved with. I was surprised and full of admiration that she could remember so much, as I was not the only one to receive an award that day.

She put the OBE medal on my jacket. A minute later I was quietly guided through some corridors to sit silently at the back of the room, to watch the rest of the ceremony. My family was in one of the front rows and I would only join them when the ceremony was complete.

The organisation was a perfect example of true hospitality. Over in one corner, for example, the musical quartet played well-known songs, including a few French ones. I was touched that they had added some French songs to the list, which I imagine they did because I, one of the recipients, am a Frenchman.

It was ironic that I was there, being born French and not being interested in English royalty for a long time. When I first came to live in the UK, I could not understand why the royals were so popular – after all, in France, we had guillotined our king! Over the years my views changed and I had come to admire the work they do for different charities. In addition, I had become British in 1990, so by the time I received this honour I was fully committed to both Great Britain and the royal cause.

Thursday 20 October 2011 was a magic moment. Yet I could reflect with a certain melancholy on the long journey it had been, from grim beginnings in Saint-Etienne all the way to Windsor Castle.

One

Humble Beginnings

There is nothing wrong with Saint-Etienne, where I was born, but nothing special about the place either. A medium-sized industrial town near Lyon, it was the birthplace of Casino, a large French chain of supermarkets. It also boasted a two-star Michelin restaurant that we never visited, some universities of great national prestige and 'Les Verts', once France's best football team. But despite all these achievements, the Saint-Etienne of my youth could feel bleak. It is very cold in winter owing to a continental climate exacerbated by its high altitude, and it can be very stuffy in the summer. Its beauty lies in the surrounding countryside, whose hills inspired me, making me feel like a racer in the Tour de France as I cycled over them.

My family did not lack money, as my father's father had been a successful local architect and my mother's father had been a partner in a small but flourishing factory. We had a nice house, thanks in part to our grandparents, who helped with family finances.

What the Basset family lacked was harmony. My mother Marguerite, a qualified midwife who had never practised, married my father, Pierre-René, a factory draughtsman, because their two families wanted them to. Both sets of grandparents, unfortunately, were oblivious to the fact that my parents couldn't stand each other. Despite their mutual loathing, my parents produced three children – my sister Antoinette, thirteen years older than me, my brother Jean-Henri who is eight years older, and then me. By the time I was five my sister had gone to work and live in Lyon, and my brother left home by the time I was ten.

They left me in the company of parents who were odd, to say the least. They did not have many friends, as I don't think they knew how to interact with people very well. This is not surprising as they could hardly interact with one another. Neither learnt to drive, so we always had to use public transport, rarely went anywhere and were stuck with each other.

We never had holidays abroad, as my father used to maintain that people go abroad on holiday when they hardly know their own country. Unfortunately, he didn't feel it necessary to explore French regions either, so we simply stayed in the area. At least we had a holiday home in the countryside, thanks to my grandparents, which was twenty-five kilometres away from home. My mother, my sister, my brother and I went there during the school holidays and some weekends; my father would join us on weekends and during his month-long holiday. It is a shame to say this, but it was better when my father was not there, as we could enjoy the small, simple house in peace.

There was a farm next door, where Remi the farmer lived with his dog and I was allowed to play among the cows and goats. It's also where I had one of my first, formative food experiences. One day, Remi grabbed one of his chickens, knocked it dead and then pierced the head with a sharp knife. Remi filled a glass with the blood, which he left to thicken in the fridge for a few hours. Later, he pan-fried the solid chicken blood in small cubes with parsley and garlic. I had a portion of the finished dish, which is called *sanguette*. While I felt sorry for the chicken, the result was delicious.

But my parents sold the holiday house when I was six, along with the family home, so they could afford a new house. From then on, until I was sixteen, we were trapped at home together and without a television.

My father was against us having a TV, because he said programmes were infantile and not good for education. He may have been right, but television was good for social bonding. In France in the 1960s there were only two national TV channels with two big evening shows, which everyone else at school would watch and talk about the next day. It was frustrating not to be able to enter into the conversation. My father's odd beliefs were turning me into an oddity too, excluding me from my peers.

I had another source of shame as well.

My parents argued continually, and it sometimes spiralled into violence. When I was six, I saw my brother try to separate my parents, only to have his arm slashed by the knife one of them was holding. He was cut badly and still bears a large scar today. There were times I saw my parents fight so badly, they both ended with bloody faces.

At school we were given books of family stories, textbook examples of how things should be. I didn't recognise the situations. For me, returning home each day filled me with dread, because I never knew if I would find my parents alive and well or not. Luckily for us, we lived in a detached house – if we had lived in a flat, like most of my schoolmates, we would have been expelled for causing a disturbance. My parents shouted insults and threats to one another so loudly that the neighbours could hear everything. I felt the humiliation deeply. Every time I turned the corner to my home street, the tension forced my head down to look at the pavement. From 200 yards away, I would hear my parents shouting at one another. I only ever took friends home if I was totally sure that one of my parents would not be back until late.

They argued constantly about money, although we were comparatively well off. My mother hated budgeting, while my father was strict. Each morning, before going to work, my father would leave on the cupboard a sum of money in cash that he deemed sufficient for the daily shopping; a bit more if my mum needed to buy clothes for us, a bit less if it was for food only. Mum was not allowed to have her own cheque book. Money became a fundamental point of anger and frustration between them.

My parents were not monsters. They did all their damage to each other, not to us. The only time they got upset was if one of us sided with the other parent. I tended to side mainly with my mother, but my father was still quite loving towards me, although I frustrated him.

My father loved reading. He read Flaubert, Hugo, Voltaire, Zola and more; Jules Verne was his favourite author. It was a great source of disappointment to him that I wasn't buried in the classics. I was reading, but my shelf was stocked with *Asterix*, *Lucky Luke* and other comics. I loved the Saint-Etienne football team, while my father considered footballers idiots running after a ball. We only had one thing in common: a love of cycling. My father loved the Tour de France. Maybe this is why he never drove a car, but always went to work by bicycle.

While he was at work, my mother stayed at home. Cleaning was not a priority, but she baked well. I remember the delicious cakes, jams, jellies and other wonderful desserts she made. Her clafoutis, a classic French cherry cake, was really delicious and her egg flan out of this world. I still carry the taste in my mouth. She could make all sorts of fabulous stews and magnificent varied gratins; her endive gratin was my favourite. Otherwise, her cooking was inconsistent. Because I regularly witnessed my mother cooking and often, like most kids do, wanted to help, I grew up quite interested in food, asking my mother endless questions about her cooking. I was hooked! On the other hand, she could serve us some very average fare too. Neither my father nor my mother knew much about wine, although they drank plenty of ordinary wine.

Something else that did not interest them was my schooling. They knew which school I went to, and that was enough for them. It took until the end-of-year report to discover that things were not going well. I was a natural mathematician and began each year by getting the top marks. However, because my parents were not interested in my progress, I became lazy and my marks gradually tumbled lower and lower, skidding to barely acceptable by the end of the year. To relieve the stress of home, I became the class clown. I wanted to make everyone laugh and was regularly reprimanded.

At home we also had cats and dogs. I was besotted with them and used to play for hours with them; they taught me a lot about life. I enjoyed so much hearing my cats purr on my lap, or playing fetch with my dogs, or other made-up games when we were out in a field. Of course, pets are not eternal and so every time one died, I would be heartbroken and cry for days, completely inconsolable. It was so hard to show open affection to my parents when I was growing up that I gave all my love to animals instead when I was young.

I left school at sixteen with only the BEPC, the official national qualification for that age. I still wonder how I managed to pass this quite simple, basic exam, as I was not focused on studying at all.

When dreaming of an adult life with a family of my own I promised myself that it would be a loving atmosphere and that my home would be extremely peaceful. Like many children who grow up with violence, I developed a sharp sensitivity to people. In my case, I felt a need for people to be comfortable, which would prove useful in my future career.

Finally, life had become too unbearable for them both to continue to live in the same house together and they eventually separated when I was seventeen. I left to live with my mother in the home of her deceased parents, in a town close by. My father also moved house, but stayed in the same town, alone and unhappy. I saw him regularly, but found we had nothing to say. He was not a bad father. He loved me in his own way, but the life that had been forced upon him had made him unhappy.

After she left my father and moved away, my mother had some of the happiest years of her life. However, later in life she had dementia and after she had a fall in the street when she was ninety, she declined quickly. She would not recognise me when I was in front of her, but if we showed her a photo of me in a trade magazine she would say: 'This is my son, Gerard.'

At seventeen, however, it was not obvious that I would become someone featured in magazines. I had dropped out of school because of my poor marks, and the only job I could find was in a local clothes shop. I had no clue what to recommend to customers and was sacked after two weeks.

My second job was in a factory, where I had to push a trolley to different areas and collect boxes, which I then had to stack on shelves. This time, I quit before they could sack me.

Next came a job in a luggage factory, where I was supposed to fold a piece of metal, destined to be part of a suitcase, with the help of a machine. After two days I had not even reached a third of my target and my work was so poor in quality that most of it had to be discarded. I was sacked.

I was sacked so often that the officers at the local Job Centre despaired of me. They told me – often – that I was a lazy, useless idiot. And I was, because my mind was on something else: cycling. It was something I was good at and I dreamt that one day I would be the King of the Mountains in the Tour de France. In my dream, I would be pedalling up the tortuous climbs of le Galibier or le Tourmalet, riding towards victory as the leading group behind me exploded with the effort of it. I would stop for a moment and look down below to see the carnage, with all the other riders exhausted and unable to keep up. The huge crowd along the road would be going crazy, shouting my name. I was their cycling idol!

And so the time passed, with me being sacked during the day, while cycling across the hills in the evenings and at weekends, whenever I had spare time.

At the time young Frenchmen of eighteen years old had to do their national military service, but because my parents were separated, my mother did not work and I lived with her, I was exempt as I was deemed to be supporting my mother financially . . . which was not completely true.

At last, a friend of my mother's found me a job as a sales assistant in a hardware store, selling tools to tradesmen, along with domestic appliances. The two young managers, Armand and Marc, taught me the job and I not only learned about hardware, but also how to sell.

Between the cycling and the hardware, life improved. But it wasn't a life that was taking me anywhere. My parents' neglect had left me undeveloped in many aspects of life. I was only modestly educated, I had no professional qualifications, I struggled to hold down jobs and I couldn't even dance or swim. On top of that, I was shy and sensitive, and easily hurt.

Fortunately, life was about to change.

Two

Times of Change Ahead

When I was eighteen years old, my mother decided she needed better climatic conditions for health reasons. She sold her family house and bought a flat in beautiful Aix-en-Provence, so I quit my job and went to live with her there.

I immediately loved my life in Aix-en-Provence. What was not to like? Aix is still ranked in the top five best French cities to live in, with a large student community, full of young people having fun. In 1975, the inner part bustled with great bars, exciting restaurants, cinemas, museums and plenty more. There were also wonderful vegetables, superb fish and meat, great sweets, an array of magnificent shops and great farmers' markets too. The town centre had many listed houses in old streets leading you to the famous Cours Mirabeau, the main avenue, right in the centre of town. In addition, Aix is close to the Mediterranean Sea so the weather was wonderful, just as my mother needed. For an eighteen-year-old boy, it was magic.

Within a week I had found a temporary job in a *calissons* factory. *Calissons* are small candy sweets shaped like diamonds, a famous Aix speciality. There are variations in the recipe but basically, they are made with stewed melon, ground almond, orange peel, flour, egg and sugar, sometimes lightly flavoured with liqueur. All that is mixed and then the top is finished with icing sugar; then they are mildly cooked just to solidify the icing. They are delicious and during the two weeks I worked there, I ate my fair share of the rejected ones, which are just as good as the real ones, albeit slightly misshapen. It was a fun experience, and a tasty one, but again, not a lasting one for me.

M. Favier, the owner of the hardware store where I had worked previously, had kindly written to the few hardware stores in Aix recommending me and so shortly after I left the *calissons* factory, I had an interview lined up with one of them. I started my new job as a sales assistant, and I went on to complete a full year there. I had a job and I liked it. It provided me with a decent income and as I was living with my mum, I only had to pay a modest rent. Life was good and I had cash in my pocket.

I made friends quickly. Jean-Jacques was one of them, working with me at the hardware shop, and like me he was mad about football (but a Marseille supporter). We spent a lot of time together playing football in improvised teams, with groups of people we met on the many local football grounds the city had to offer.

In the early days of starting a new life, away from the place where you grew up, nobody has put you in a box yet. You have a great window of opportunity to assert your personality and write a new chapter, but you have quite a short time to do so, before the new becomes the norm. For me, my new chapter was football. Because my father was not into sport, apart from cycling, I was never encouraged to do much sport. Even at school, in the late sixties and early seventies, sport in France was not taken that seriously and so my opportunities were limited. I only started learning to play football when I was twelve, which is extremely late. Inevitably, I would be one of the weaker members of any team. I remember at school, when the two designated captains were making up their respective teams, each captain choosing members in turn, I was always one of the last ones to be selected.

However, that did not put me off. I trained regularly and played as much as I could on my school days off, or late in the afternoon after school (instead of doing my homework) for hours on end. By the time I was sixteen, my football skills had significantly improved, thanks to all the endless sessions spent practising kicking a ball against a wall. Still, in the eyes of my peers, I remained only a modest player, never taken seriously, and that made me unconfident.

None of that worried me when I arrived in Aix-en-Provence. Nobody knew me. There was no label put on me within the group of people I was playing with. Therefore, I had the confidence to be me. With my excellent dribbling ability in my right foot, I was able to impress my new peers and established myself as a good player. I loved the feeling of being respected.

Having put myself on the map for my football abilities among my new friends, I was not going to let go of the only sport credentials I ever had, cycling.

When riding near Saint-Etienne, at the age of fifteen, I had been privileged to meet an older rider who had done great things in his racing career. The first time I raced him he beat me well and good, but I must have made an impression on him, as he spontaneously offered to teach me the ropes. How to prepare during the week, how to ride in windy conditions or in other extreme weather conditions, and how not to waste energy when riding in a group. By the time I went to Aix, I was fit and skilled.

Jean, my driving instructor in Aix, was a keen cyclist and we quickly became great friends. In no time, we arranged to meet most Sundays, early in the morning, for long rides, spending four to five hours cycling each time.

France has had a long love affair with cycling. Everyone knows that the Tour de France, taking place each July, is the greatest cycling race on earth. In France it is nicknamed 'La Grande Boucle' meaning 'The Big Loop', in reference to its long journey around the country. Perhaps less well known is the fact that a bicycle itself is often and fondly referred to in French literature and French media as *la petite reine*, meaning 'the little queen'. Apparently, this expression was in reference to Queen Wilhelmina of the Netherlands, who was often seen on a bicycle in the early part of the twentieth century.

On the many small country roads, on Sunday mornings, I would meet countless cyclists, both near Saint-Etienne and even more in my new region. Individual riders, as well as small groups of two to five like Jean and myself, rode on the small side roads, ideal for cycling. Very quickly, larger groups of riders, anything from fifteen to twenty-five people, would all meet up and a group would be formed. We rode together at a good speed and in unison for several miles, but when approaching a local hill, two to four miles long, things would change, and everyone was ready for a fight to the top of the hill. Some of those hills had been classified third or fourth category in the Tour de France in terms of difficulty, so not the ultra-hard ones, but nevertheless, quite testing for amateur riders like us.

I took part in many improvised hill races near Aix. One Sunday morning, a chap I had never met before joined the group that Jean and I were riding with that day. Nothing unusual so far, but I could tell that he looked eager to fight on the approaching hill. After two hard-fought miles, only he and I were left to fight for victory. In the last part of the climb, I tried to attack him on a few occasions, but I could not get rid of him and a few hundred yards from the top he left me for dead. I congratulated him, but inside I was furious and upset.

The next Sunday he was part of our group again. It was early in the spring and the weather could be quite cold at that time. A few miles before the hill I noticed that he did not have any gloves, and in the cold weather he was uncomfortable; he kept shaking his fingers and blowing on them, trying to warm them up. I quickly offered my gloves to him on the pretext that I was quite the opposite, too hot, which of course was not true, but I did not want him to have any excuse if by chance I was to beat him on the hill. In any case coming from Saint-Etienne I was used to the cold weather. He accepted and ten minutes or so later, our group arrived at the bottom of the hill. I had been thinking of a plan all week: I would try to lead the group fairly early on, but I would go slowly enough so as not to burn myself out, but speedy enough to eliminate most riders. Then, I would not lead any more while I prepared my attack. I wanted to give him the impression I was at full stretch and possibly getting tired to trick him. Halfway up the hill, only he, another rider and I were left in front. I did not try to attack him or lead any more and simply focused on the last mile of the climb, which I knew was quite steep. Suddenly he furiously stepped up the pace; the other rider could not follow and lost ground immediately. At first I tried to follow, but I realised that I was going to burn out if I persisted; he was just too quick. Reluctantly, I let him go, but I could still see him fifty metres in front of me. I decided that I should regroup and ride at the best rhythm I possibly could in order not to lose the race by too much, a sort of 'saving face' mode. However, two bends further on I realised that he was not gaining any more ground on me, but in fact he was struggling. He had obviously relied too much on his strength and was paying the price for his earlier violent acceleration. By then I had found a second wind and I was not going to miss this opportunity. Slowly and surely, I caught up with him and without even giving him a glance I left him standing, unable to follow me. Minutes later I arrived at the top of the hill, and waited for him and the rest of the group. When he arrived, he mumbled a weak 'well done' and gave me back my gloves.

Sometimes I wonder what would have happened with my cycling if I'd had family encouragement and support from a cycling club. Could I have made it to the Tour de France? Even though my father loved cycling he never believed that it was possible for an ordinary person to be a professional rider. For him, riders of the Tour de France were like superheroes with supernatural powers. Moreover, as he did not spend too much time watching what his kids were doing, he never encouraged me to join a cycling club. I'm not even sure he knew I was a reasonable cyclist.

So, there I was, in Aix, cycling for fun instead. After a few weeks I had my driving licence and bought an old Simca 1100. It was my first car and added greatly to what I was finding to be an exciting life in Aix: freedom.

And my mother got a telephone. France in the seventies was quite antiquated; if you wanted a landline phone at home you had to apply to the French National Telecommunication service, and you had to wait three to five weeks. In Saint-Etienne, my parents never had a phone at home. If we needed to use one, we had to go the post office or to the local shop and ask if we could use their phone, a part of the service local shops generally offered for a small fee. Once in Aix, my mother was determined to have a telephone and two months after moving, we had a landline at home. Suddenly I could call my sister in Lyon, and call my friends who were connected too. It meant even more freedom.

Not only that, it was the great disco period. The Bee Gees' 'You Should Be Dancing', 'Staying Alive' and 'Night Fever' from *Saturday Night Fever*; 'I Feel Love' by Donna Summer; 'Daddy Cool', 'Sunny', 'Rivers Of Babylon', 'Rasputin' and 'Ma Baker' by Boney M; 'Get Down Tonight' by KC and the Sunshine Band; 'Boogie Wonderland' by Earth, Wind & Fire; 'In The Navy' and 'YMCA' by the Village People; 'Born To Be Alive' by Patrick Hernandez; 'D.I.S.C.O.' by Ottawan; or old songs like 'One Way Ticket' by Neil Sedaka and 'Can't Take My Eyes Off You' by Frankie Valli – all those were disco anthems and I loved them.

The world of disco was kitsch, with its highly colourful and extravagant costumes, its necklaces and medallions, its energetic and frenetic dancing, the multi-lit, chequered dance floor and of course, the iconic big glitter ball on the ceiling, in the middle of the room, creating the strobe lighting on the dance floor. I loved it – and I still do. I used to go to discos with my friends and dance long into the night. I still listen to the classic disco songs or even some recent songs with a disco accent.

After working for a year in the hardware store in Aix, I went to work for my ex-driving instructor and bicycle companion, Jean Flament.

Jean stopped being a driving instructor and began his own delivery business. He was subcontracted by a large company selling washing machines, dishwashers, fridges, freezers, cookers, TVs, hi-fi music systems and so on, to deliver the appliances in and around the region of Aix. He needed an employee and I was paid similar rates to my previous job, except we were getting excellent tips on top of it. Working with

Jean was great fun and I was fit and strong. I stayed in that job for three years.

Living in Aix-en-Provence was enjoyable, apart from one low point. Only a few months after I had moved there, my father passed away. I had lived apart from him for a year while we were near Saint-Etienne and then a few more months further away now that I was in Aix. I was due to take a holiday and go back to my previous region, principally to see my sister, but I would have also planned to see my brother briefly and my father too. My father and I were not close, but having not seen each other for a while and living apart had made our relationship slightly better and easier. I think as I had matured, I had begun to start to understand him a little better. Even though his health was not good, his sudden death was still a shock.

My father and mother had an unhappy life together. Neither loved the other and each would undoubtedly have had a much happier life, had they been able to be with different partners, and if their marriage had not been arranged by their respective parents.

After the funeral in Saint-Etienne, I returned to my new life. In total, I had four wonderful years in Aix-en-Provence, partly because I'd taken all the easy options.

But then something happened that was to change my life.

Three

For the Love of Football

Although I lived in Aix-en-Provence, I carried on supporting Saint-Etienne's football team, which was doing brilliantly in Europe; the fact that I was from Saint-Etienne raised my profile with my footballing friends from Aix.

In May 1976, I went to Glasgow to watch the European Cup Final, where Saint-Etienne was playing Bayern Munich. It was the first time in my life I'd taken an aeroplane. The little I saw of Glasgow that day was nice and the few Scottish people I encountered were friendly, but mostly I remember the French supporters from all across France – around 30,000 of them. There were so many Frenchmen flying in that planes had to be diverted from Glasgow airport, and so many people speaking French that being in Glasgow was like being in France that day.

Bayern Munich won, but that didn't dampen my enthusiasm. When Saint-Etienne played Liverpool FC in the quarter-final of the European Cup the next year, I went back to Saint-Etienne to watch.

I decided to go to Liverpool to watch the return match. Liverpool itself didn't excite me much and nor did the English – my impression was that they were all strange. They drove on the wrong side of the road, had a boring cuisine, loved tea instead of coffee, drank beer at room temperature and had policemen known as 'Bobby' who wore funny hats. And they still had royalty, whereas in France we had been a republic for a long time. To top off the list of peculiarities, it always rained in England, or so I believed.

I wasn't totally anti-English, as I liked watching *The Avengers* and *The Prisoner*, and some of their pop music artists were OK, but overall, I thought they were eccentric. My expectation was that I would go to Liverpool, spend time with other French supporters, and then return home, as per previous matches. I bought my plane and stadium tickets through a Marseille travel agency and was ready to go . . . except that two days before I was due to fly, I remembered that not only did I not own a passport, I had also lost my identity card and wouldn't get the new one for another week. All my friends assured me I wouldn't be able to go.

I panicked for a bit and then decided there was no way I was going to miss that match, even if I had to swim the Channel.

Then a solution revealed itself. We had recently delivered some appliances to a high-ranking customs officer, who had been friendly to us. I asked Jean to look back in his paperwork and find me the telephone number of this customs officer. I phoned him, and he told me to come and see him at his home. It was a Monday, two days before the trip. We talked through the situation and after going over it many times, he came up with the only possible solution. He told me something like this: 'I will be on duty that day, so I will look for you. Very discreetly, I will get you through customs, but after that, once you are on the plane you are on your own. I cannot do anything for you, and you must never refer about our arrangement to anyone, especially the British customs. You will have to pretend that you lost your identity card somewhere after going through customs or on the plane.'

It sounded like a brilliant idea – I was just twenty and couldn't see any problems with it. As planned, I boarded the charter plane to Liverpool.

During the flight, perhaps thirty minutes before landing, I went to see one of the travel agents who was there to help us. I explained to him that I had lost my identity card and was very concerned. He and I looked thoroughly around my seat, trying to find the card, but of course we were never going to find it. After landing, he came with me to the British customs and explained that I had just lost my identity card. When I was interviewed by the British customs officer, he translated for me. The customs officer seemed extremely dubious about my story, as well he might, but the agent did a brilliant job of defending me. I said something along the lines of: 'How could I possibly have gone through French customs in Marseille if I did not have an identity card with me?' Also, because it was a charter plane, booked for a special occasion, it was obvious we were only coming to see the match.

So, I got through.

Around midday I found myself with a few friends in Liverpool town centre. Remembering that in Glasgow we had only met French people and never got a feel for the place, I suggested we visit the outskirts of Liverpool. Half an hour later four of us were already walking far from the city centre. We were all wearing green shirts and/or green jackets, the colour of our team, and we were waving the Saint-Etienne football team flag. I had even put some green make-up on my face and I was wearing a green wig! We were singing the French football songs we normally sang at the stadium.

To my surprise, the locals were extremely friendly and came to see us. At that time English football fans were often in the news because of hooliganism, but we didn't see any. We were invited to drink tea, have biscuits and even sandwiches in more than one house and made extremely welcome. One of the Liverpudlians we met was a French teacher and was delighted to talk to us in French. It was all friendly and we had a wonderful time before the match. I really felt ashamed of myself for having been so cold and childish towards the Liverpool supporters two weeks before in Saint-Etienne.

After this unexpectedly enjoyable afternoon, we went to the stadium. The atmosphere was electric. As Saint-Etienne supporters we were seated next to the famous Kop stand. I vividly remember how impressive it was. Every Liverpool supporter in that stand had a red scarf and held it up in both hands, swaying to the right and then to the left in unison with the other fans. It was like watching a giant red scarf moving.

Liverpool FC won 3–1 and although I was a bit sad, I did not feel too bad. I had enjoyed a truly wonderful day among the people of Liverpool and seen one of the greatest European games I had ever witnessed (even to this day), with two superb teams playing attacking football; and the atmosphere in the stadium had been unbelievable.

Later, in the plane heading back home, there were many discussions among us Saint-Etienne supporters. I was relatively upbeat, saying that unlike the year before, in Glasgow, when Saint-Etienne had lost against a German team playing boring and clinical football, at least we had lost against a superb team full of panache, playing hugely entertaining football. However, a dejected Saint-Etienne supporter (in fact a Marseille supporter, but a Saint-Etienne fan for that day), sitting in the row behind me, did not see it that way at all. In a condescending way, he said that football was the only thing they had in Liverpool. I was quite incensed on behalf of the Liverpudlians we had met.

As expected, I had no difficulty boarding the plane back home with the paperwork the British customs officer had given me and, arriving in Marseille during the night, the Marseille customs officers did not even bother to check anyone, probably because it was a special charter flight. A few days later I went to see and thank the kind customs officer who had helped me. I gave him a bottle of Champagne as a small gesture of my appreciation. Little did either of us then realise that he had helped to shape my future.

During the following days I could not stop reminiscing about the wonderful experience I had enjoyed in Liverpool and quickly I made up my mind. I would go and live in England. I had fallen in love with the country. I told my mum, who surprisingly was quite relaxed about the idea. When I told my friends in Aix, at first they thought I was joking, but when they realised that I was deadly serious, more or less all of them said the same thing: 'Are you crazy? Have you lost your mind? Why would you go there?'

Nothing made me change my mind. It was just a matter of when I would go. It was March 1977 when I took this important decision. However, I was in no rush as I was enjoying my life in Aix. I thought that perhaps I could aim to leave Aix within eighteen months or two years. Common sense said I could not go too quickly as I did not speak any English at all. I had studied English at school, but I never paid much attention to it and so my marks were poor. As soon as I left school the little English I may have known had disappeared from my head.

I took some private English lessons with a young student who had advertised her language-teaching skills in the local paper. She was talented, but obviously with me she had to start with the basics. I did work hard on learning English and made some decent progress, but apart from the lessons with the young student and doing some homework on my own at home, I did not have many opportunities to practise.

At the same time, I started saving money for my move to the UK. I had reasoned that if I could arrive in England and have the equivalent of approximately four months of my current wages in reserve, that would put me in a reasonable position to succeed.

But that was it for planning. I should have gone to English classes to meet more people and practised speaking English more often. I should have read about life in England in books and magazines. I could have contacted different organisations set up to help. I could even have tried to find a few French people who had lived in England for a few years to ask them useful questions. I did none of that.

In early April 1979, I told my boss (and good friend), Jean, that I would stop working with him by the end of July. We were normally on holiday for three weeks in August, as Jean spent family time going away with his wife and his two young daughters. My idea was that I would not return after the holidays and that would leave Jean enough time to find a replacement. Actually, Jean told me that he had had enough of life in Aix and had been thinking for a while of moving to Bordeaux; me leaving was the incentive he needed to do it. His wife, Catherine, was pleased to be moving closer to her family, so for him the timing was fine.

I realised my first year in England might be tough, so I decided to treat myself before I went – by then, I had saved quite a lot of money. A Marseille travel agency had an ad for a three-day, all-inclusive trip to New York, so I thought, 'Why not?'

I saw the Empire State Building and the Twin Towers, and did a helicopter flight above the city. I walked the streets of Manhattan for hours, passing by all the famous landmarks: Wall Street, Broadway, Times Square, Central Park, Little Italy and Chinatown. But what I particularly remember was the New York-style breakfast: bacon and eggs in a style called 'over easy', meaning cooked lightly on both sides, with grits, made from corn maize. And lashings of coffee.

When I got back, I wandered past that Marseille travel agency again. This time, they were advertising a trip to Russia, with three days in Leningrad and three days in Moscow, and the timing was perfect – I would get back one week before I left for England.

It was a complete contrast to New York. To begin with, the trip was structured, and it wasn't possible for tourists to wander round on their own. We visited the Hermitage Museum and the Winter Palace in St Petersburg, St Basil Cathedral in Moscow, the Red Square and the Kremlin, and had our nights out at the Bolshoi Ballet. There was another side to Moscow, too: the Russians who lurked in the street around our hotel, wanting to exchange roubles for hard currencies, offering a much better rate than the official one. It was illegal, but I didn't know that, and I handed over my francs.

And then, home. My sister came to spend a few days with my mother and me to see me before I moved. I had a goodbye dinner with my best Aix friends.

England, here I come.

Four

Bound for England and New Adventures

In the middle of August 1979, I found myself with a single plane ticket bound for London, two medium-sized suitcases and some money.

I found a decent but inexpensive B&B, which I booked for just three days, as I thought I would find a job quickly. Although I didn't have much of a clue how to go about it, I found an office marked Job Centre and went to look at the notice boards covered in cards with job advertisements. After I saw one or two that piqued my interest, I would go to the officer on duty and ask for more details, and maybe for an interview.

The first thing I realised is that looking for work in a city is different from being there on holiday. Holidays are for relaxing and new experiences. Looking for work quickly becomes tense and dispiriting, especially if, like me, you haven't organised much in advance.

After three days of walking from the Job Centre to private agencies, I had still found nothing. My situation wasn't helped by my poor English. Although I knew a lot of English words, and I always had a pocket dictionary handy, I wasn't fluent. I only understood half of the answers, and sometimes less.

After a week I began to worry. The night that I had my leaving dinner in Aix, my friends had joked that I would be back in two or three weeks' time, and now it was a real possibility. I was not going to let that happen. At last, I realised that it was Liverpool I'd fallen in love with, so I booked a train ticket for the next day.

In Liverpool, I did much the same thing as in London: booked a few days in a B&B and looked in job centres and agencies, and after two days

I struck lucky. The Job Centre had an advert for a kitchen porter on the Isle of Man, the island in the northern Irish Sea, just three to four hours by boat from Liverpool. The officer explained to me that the position was until the end of the season, and there were six weeks left. It came with live-in accommodation and if I completed the six weeks, the hotel would pay me an extra week's wages. I thought the six weeks would greatly help me improve my English, I would earn some money, and I would avoid losing face in front of my Aix friends. The day after, I took the boat bound for Douglas, capital of the Isle of Man, and then headed to a village in the south called Port Erin.

Port Erin, a coastal seaside village, was picturesque, but it felt cold. When I left Aix-en-Provence the August temperature was averaging between 25°C and 30°C, while the weather in Port Erin hovered between 15°C and 20°C.

The hotel itself was simple, owned and run by a friendly couple; it had around seventy rooms, where guests would come to enjoy the seaside or play golf on the nearby course. I had to share a small flat with two other members of staff, but they turned out to be fun. In any case, breakfast and dinner were extremely busy as all the residents – all 130 or 140 of them – had both meals. We got to relax a bit at lunchtime, when everyone was out playing golf or just eating sandwiches.

Being a kitchen porter meant getting intimate with the dishwasher. When I wasn't stacking or unstacking it, I cleaned the floor and did other menial tasks. It was boring and if there hadn't been the promised bonus for staying six weeks, I would have left.

The food was extremely basic. The dinner menu had a choice of three starters, one of which was orange juice, which I found surprising. The main course was even simpler, because there was only one, which changed every day for a week and then came around again. The desserts were also very restricted.

The break in routine came on Thursday nights – curry nights. On my first Thursday, the head chef served the curry on rice that he'd coloured bright red. The next Thursday, he'd chosen bright yellow. After I told him that my football team, Saint-Etienne, played in green, he made green rice the following week, in my honour.

On days off, I would go out with the chefs and waiters, which helped improve my English, and during afternoon breaks I watched the staffroom TV. When I had spare time, I would learn the past tenses of irregular verbs by heart and finally, towards the end of my stay, the lady who owned the hotel told me my English had improved.

Then the hotel closed for the season and I returned to Liverpool – and to job hunting. Once again, I had no luck, so I hit on an idea. There was no reasoning behind this, only a gut instinct, but it occurred to me that there would be a lot of French tourists in the south of England. The more I thought about it, the better it seemed as an idea – I would go south and get a job, looking after some of these hordes of tourists.

I was completely wrong about that, as those French tourists who came to England would head for London. If they wanted the seaside, they could get a better version in France. But on my first visit to the Job Centre, I found something promising: 'Looking for full time commis waiter in a hotel/restaurant in Lyndhurst, accommodation provided'. Lyndhurst is a village in the heart of the New Forest, now a National Park, about ten miles from Southampton.

The officer had to explain what a commis waiter was, even though the word was French, and I had to explain I had no experience as a waiter of any sort, even a low-ranking one. The officer thought about it for a moment and decided that I had an advantage, anyway, being French. In the England of the 1970s, many of the better restaurants employed French waiters, because waiter is a well-recognised profession in France, so supposedly the French are professional. Not only that, but students who have graduated from French catering schools are encouraged to work for a year or two in England, to improve their English.

The officer warned me, however, not to tell the interviewer that I had never done the job before. Instead, he advised me to make up a story about doing a summer job as a waiter while in France.

Fortified with that advice, I arrived at the Crown Hotel, Lyndhurst at ten o'clock the next morning, ready for anything. The receptionist handed me a form to fill in and said that a manager would come and see me in fifteen minutes.

The form was a classic employment application with ten to twelve questions in total, some asking about me personally and some about my work experience. Those I could understand – only the last question baffled me. 'What are your criminal convictions?' it said.

As someone often looking for work, I'd filled in many such forms, and I knew that employers often threw in random questions at the end, to see what your thoughts were on a current and relevant topic. Today asking these sorts of questions would be impossible, but it was normal in the 1970s. And as it happened, the death penalty was still being hotly debated in France (though it was abolished two years later, in 1981), and many people were discussing their convictions about the way criminals should be treated. So, I wasn't surprised to see a question on such an important issue, but I wasn't sure how to answer it. Such a serious and weighty question required a bit of explaining, and there wasn't enough room on the form. I thought it would be better to discuss the question in the interview, so I just wrote, 'It would be too long to explain.'

The interview went well. The manager was friendly and the fact that I was fairly well dressed, polite and enthusiastic seemed to impress him. I didn't pretend I had done the job before, but simply stressed that I was motivated to learn. In any case, commis waiter is at the bottom of the pecking order, and it's a role where you're expected to learn. So, all was going well – until he read my answer to the last question. His face changed and became grave. 'I am sorry, but you will have to tell me more about that,' he said.

I cast about, not sure how to begin. I rearranged my face into a look of concern, as befitting such a serious topic, and launched into it.

'Criminality is damaging to society,' I started. 'But perhaps there are some better ways to deal with it that society should experiment with.'

This went on for two minutes.

'I'm sorry, I don't understand,' said the manager. 'Have you ever been convicted of any serious criminal offences?'

'Of course not!' I said.

He started laughing and asked me when I could start. I was there the next morning, my two suitcases with me, ready to start working.

Lyndhurst is a lovely village and a popular tourist destination. Back then, the village had many pubs, a few restaurants, some banks, various shops, dentists, a doctor's surgery and other useful businesses, so it didn't feel isolated. The New Forest was proclaimed a Royal Forest by William the Conqueror in the eleventh century and was used by lords and kings for hunting. Now, it is famous for its many ponies roaming the Forest in total freedom. There are also a lot of deer in the forest, and other wild animals. I often found myself walking there, dreaming up all sorts of exciting stories. I loved Lyndhurst.

The Crown Hotel, then owned by two businessmen, was built in the fifteenth century and still has the half-timbered façade outside and great stone fireplaces inside. The forty bedrooms were of a decent quality, though not top luxury, and it also had a classic, fine dining restaurant along with a bar, two lounges and a busy area where a lot of pub meals were served, especially at lunchtime. There were also two function rooms, which were used for business seminars during the week and weddings or other important social functions at the weekend. The food and service in the fine dining restaurant was a bit old-fashioned even then: prawn cocktail, chicken Kiev, beef stroganoff and sherry trifle were still on the menu – but the hotel was trying its best to deliver a great experience. The menu was full of dishes to share such as beef Wellington, a rack of lamb requiring carving and, best of all, crêpes Suzette on the dessert menu, which was flambéed in front of the guests.

This was 1970s fine dining, to be accompanied by Blue Nun, or a bottle of Chianti; I fell in love with it. At the Crown Hotel I went from being someone drifting from job to job, to someone who was on a career path: hospitality.

Of course, the first two weeks at the Crown were hard, as I knew little about catering and the hotel/restaurant industry. Not only had I no work experience, but I had rarely seen the inside of a top restaurant. I'd once been to a one-star Michelin restaurant in Aix for my mum's birthday, but I hadn't taken much notice of the service. I didn't even know what was expected from me as a customer. So, I was starting from a position of complete ignorance.

It was hard work, but by the time a month had gone by, I was really enjoying it. I became obsessed with knowing as much as I could. What were the differences between silver service, gueridon service and buffet service? What was the best way to carry several plates at a time? The best way to carve? To flambé?

The team at the Crown were friendly and patient, the head waiter and his team teaching me as much as they could. I was serious and eager to learn and did not mind doing the less glamorous tasks like vacuum cleaning or moving countless chairs in different rooms as needed for functions – the type of work the other waiters were much less keen on. On my days off, if I was not going out, I would offer to help in the restaurant, just in case the head waiter would perform a flambé or something special and I could watch and learn.

Stephen Greenhalgh, the head chef, was always obliging about answering my never-ending questions. He would also regularly give me tiny pieces of food to try when preparing a new dish or a banquet.

On my days off, I would often go to Southampton to look in bookshops and buy books on catering, to perfect my knowledge. Maybe once or twice a month I would go to London, where, again, I would look in the many bookshops. I remember buying an English book about the daily routine in the three-Michelin-star restaurants of France. The book had a chapter on each restaurant, of which there were about twenty. It was not so much about the cooking, but more about how each restaurant had reached the top, including their philosophy. The book was full of glamorous pictures of incredible-looking dishes, but also of well-dressed waiting staff carving food, using utensils like a silver duck press – where the cooked duck is placed inside and crushed until the juice runs out – and even preparing cigars for guests. It was all new to me and I was hooked.

On one of my excursions to London, I walked past Selfridges and saw a window display that included a table set for two people, with some beautiful crockery, cutlery and silverware. I noticed that the guest's napkins were folded in a particular way. I had a book about napkin folding and had learnt how to do plenty of different shapes and styles, but this one was not in my book. I went into Selfridges and asked at one of the desks if someone could show me one of the napkins. It took a bit of persuasion and I had to use all of my charm, but eventually someone went into the window display and brought out one of the two napkins to show me, then unfolded and refolded it slowly for me to take notes. I scribbled down some drawings of the napkin and the different stages of the folding and when I was confident that I could reproduce it I thanked the store assistant profusely and left the store extremely happy.

Because I was the only French staff member in the hotel's team, some customers were particularly nice to me. However, as France had a great food reputation, customers thought I knew a lot about food and service and were probably convinced that I was a fully trained waiter from one of the many French catering schools. It could be quite frustrating at times, because even though I was learning fast, I still lacked knowledge and experience and I had so many big holes in my service knowledge and skill.

Having learnt as much as I could, I decided it was time for me to go back to France and learn more about the industry I had started to like so much. I had been in Lyndhurst for six months, and spent my first Christmas away from France. I had lived in a beautiful part of the world, had made good friends, learnt a lot and overall it had been a fantastic experience. With my time on the Isle of Man, I had been in the UK for almost eight months. I felt that I could go back home to Aix with my head held high to see my friends. In addition, I was now on a mission to complete my training in catering.

Five

Gastronomy Pleasures and Opportunities

I arrived back in Aix-en-Provence in April 1980. My mother was in good shape and happy to have me at home for a while, and so was her little dog. The dog was called Miquette and was a crossbreed, looking like a small spaniel; she kept coming to me for endless cuddles, which I happily gave her. The first week was fun and I spent most of it relaxing and seeing my friends.

After my week in Aix, my idea was to go to Lyon to see my sister. I thought it would be nice to spend some time with her. In addition, Lyon was always referred to as the capital of gastronomy, so it was a great place to look for a new catering challenge.

Having devoured the pages of the book on the Michelin three-star restaurants, I wanted to experience being a customer in one of them, so I booked a table at Paul Bocuse's restaurant on the outskirts of Lyon. Paul Bocuse was an institution in France. He obtained his first Michelin star in 1958 and the third one in 1965. At the time of writing this book (2017), Paul Bocuse was ninety-one years old and his restaurant still has three Michelin stars. (Since writing this chapter, Paul Bocuse sadly passed away in January 2018. He died in the room where he was born, upstairs, above his restaurant.) He was the leader of the French gastronomic revolution of the sixties and seventies, the originator of Nouvelle Cuisine. Before Bocuse, fine dining meant dishes slathered in heavy sauces. His great insight was that if you used very fresh, very high-quality ingredients, they would do most of the flavour work. He won an incredible number of awards, including receiving the prestigious title of

Commandeur de la Légion d'Honneur from the French President. In addition, Le Bocuse d'Or, created in 1987 in Lyon and run every other year, is regarded as the most prestigious international cuisine competition; it is the Olympics of gastronomy, with top Michelin chefs from all over the world competing for the title.

My table was booked for a weekday at 7.30 p.m. and so I took a bus late in the afternoon from Lyon, stopping not far from the restaurant, the Auberge du Pont de Collonges. When I arrived, it was very much like I had seen in the book. The outside was colourful, a Baroque fantasy painted in bright pink, green and orange. The reception area was crowded with ornaments and books written by the great chef, and then I was led into the grand dining room, whose walls were laden with pictures. Each table was beautifully set, with lovely plates for each person and sparkling cutlery. I was treated with great care and was given a large table just for myself. Perhaps, as I was a lone diner, the restaurant manager had thought that I was an inspector from the Michelin Guide. In any case, the waiting team quickly realised that I was not there to inspect them, but rather to enjoy and watch everything that was happening in the room, like a little boy in a toy factory.

The presentation of each dish was such that I almost didn't want to touch them, to avoid breaking up their beauty. I still remember all these years later what I ate: truffle soup, and sea bass with a lobster mousse, cooked in a sea-salt crust. There was an enormous cheese platter and the desserts were brought to a large middle table in the centre of the room during the evening. I loved the food, but also I was curious about what was happening in the room – my eyes were constantly watching the service at all the different tables in the room for most of the evening. I was entranced. The service was highly professional, perhaps a bit solemn at times, but friendly, nonetheless. Dishes would be brought from the kitchen on large silver trays and carefully taken to the guests by immaculately dressed waiters, who would put them in front of the guests directly or who would carve meats for them. It was like watching a ballet.

Michelin three-star restaurants are the optimum in the industry. Whatever the type of cuisine they offer, classic, fusion, ultra-modern, molecular or others, the fact is that they are all about uncompromising standards, with enormous precision in every detail. The organisation is second to none. Some chefs will be there very early in the morning to receive the different deliveries of fresh products, others to cook fresh bread and so on. Waiters arrive early to organise the dining room and give it a thorough clean so that it is immaculate. It is all about total focus, discipline and passion. The leader on each side, the head chef and the restaurant manager, each has a large team. Before each service they will double-check that all is in order and brief the team. The team is made up of highly trained professionals who must deliver the highest standards; they cannot afford a weak moment. The managers under the two leaders (second chef, assistant restaurant manager, head sommelier and so on) are there to support the team and to stop anything coming out of the kitchen that is not as it should be. The food products are sourced from passionate and dedicated craft artisans, who keep their best products for that type of restaurant. For instance, artisan craft producers might grow some unique varieties of vegetables organically just for them.

Three-star restaurants have evolved a lot since the eighties, but the philosophy of looking for perfection has not changed. I would argue that the difference between a good restaurant and a three-star restaurant was higher in the seventies and eighties than it is now. Most excellent restaurants today have benefited enormously from the work done by three-star chefs, in the same way that our everyday car has benefited from all the innovations made to the top racing cars we see on TV.

Also, I feel that now, most, but not all, new Michelin three-star restaurants are more like culinary laboratories than real restaurants. You might go once in a lifetime for the experience, but once you have enjoyed it, you would not necessarily go back in a hurry.

What hasn't changed is that Michelin three-star restaurants are not always financially profitable owing to the huge number of staff, the luxurious crockery, cutlery and glassware, and, of course, the top quality ingredients, all of which are required for the restaurant to be able to offer the 'wow' factor. The income that comes with a Michelin star must often be supplemented with all of the memorabilia on sale within the restaurant, such as books by the chef and other branded restaurant goods.

I knew none of that then. All I knew was that my dinner at Paul Bocuse confirmed that I was on the right path. That week, I went for an interview at the Lyon Job Centre, to see what my options were. I wanted to work in a Michelin-starred restaurant, of which there were many in the city.

The officer questioned me closely and when he understood that I wanted to improve my catering knowledge, he suddenly announced that there was an opportunity to apply for a sponsored cooking course starting in two weeks' time. It was a five-month course: three months learning how to cook at the catering school, followed by two months working in a restaurant as a commis chef. The course, sponsored by the French government, came with three months' accommodation and 80 per cent of the minimum national wage. France had many such schemes then. The thinking was that it is better to spend some money providing a new skill with career prospects to adults, rather than having them stay on unemployment benefits.

For me, it was an opportunity not to be missed and I applied immediately. To my great delight, I passed the interview and was given a place on the course.

The school was in a small village called Chénelette, in the Beaujolais region, not too far from Lyon. This was perfect for me as on my days off I could go and stay with my sister.

In total we were twenty students, ten of us learning restaurant service and ten learning cooking. We would have our breakfast around eight o'clock and then from nine onwards we would be with our teacher. Those on the restaurant service side would go into the restaurant or in a classroom, to learn the art of service with lectures or demonstrations and exercises to perform. For my part, I would be in the kitchen, listening to our teacher demonstrating a basic culinary technique, which often we would have to reproduce. Some mornings, perhaps two per week, we had formal lectures. At lunchtime we would be served, along with the restaurant students, what we had prepared in the morning. For the meals, usually two student chefs would send the food and four service students would serve it. The afternoon was about more learning and practising and the evening meal was again prepared and served by the students on duty. After dinner we could relax, playing billiards, chess or whatever we wanted, in a nice comfortable staffroom. The village was very small so there wasn't much of a night life outside of the school, but when Friday afternoon came, we were free until the following Monday.

The three months of schooling went by very quickly. The following two months, I was allocated a place in a Michelin one-star restaurant in Lyon called Vettard. It was an old restaurant right in the centre of Lyon serving a mixture of classic, regional dishes, like the *quenelle de brochet*, with a sauce Nantua (pike mousse with a crayfish sauce) and some modern dishes created by the owner and his head chef.

For the two months I was there, I worked on the starter section and while it was difficult, as the standards were high, I found it very rewarding. In addition, the head chef and his brigade were kind to me and quite tolerant. When the restaurant was not yet open to customers, I would go and see the service team to ask them questions and look at how well laid up the room was, ready for service.

At the end of the five months, the students had to find a job for themselves. The week after I completed the programme, I started cold-calling good restaurants before service started, from early morning to just before lunch, and asking to see the head chef, asking if there were any vacant positions. It took a few days, first receiving a lot of negative answers, but in a hotel called Frantel I found an opening. Frantel was a chain with hotels in most major French cities, of an excellent standard and with a great reputation for its cuisine. The head chef of the Frantel Lyon told me he did not have a position for me, but he believed there was one for a commis pastry chef available at the Frantel Marseille. He asked me if I would mind going to Marseille; I agreed because I really wanted to continue working in a professional kitchen with high standards and also Marseille is close to Aix-en-Provence, so it would be perfect to see my mother and my friends. He phoned the head chef in Marseille to check the position was still available and then told me that if I could be there by tomorrow the job was mine.

I learned much later that the head pastry chef of the Marseille Frantel had trouble keeping staff. Most of them would stay just a few weeks, or even just a few days. His superior, the head chef of the Marseille Frantel, told him the day before I arrived that his colleague in Lyon had just found a commis (me) for him. He told him something along the lines of 'We have just found you a new commis, but I am tired of you not keeping anyone for long, so he is the last one. If you cannot keep him, then I am sorry, but you will have to manage on your own.' For sure I would have been the weakest of all the commis pastry chefs he had had working with him, but because of this threat from the head chef, ironically, I was given a lot of support from the head pastry chef.

The Frantel Marseille was a hotel in the centre of the town very close to the famous La Canebière avenue, and only ten minutes' walk from the old port. It was a business hotel with a lot of bedrooms of four-star French National hotel rating quality. On the ground floor there was a huge coffee shop and brasserie, serving a lot of covers, with a few shops dotted around. On the first floor there were the offices, as well as some decent staff accommodation. On the second floor was the restaurant where I was commis pastry chef.

It had a wonderful reputation and was highly rated, with modern food tending towards Nouvelle Cuisine. For functions, we served more traditional food, like the famous local bouillabaisse, a soup or stew made with different fish and served with croutons and a saffron mayonnaise called *rouille*, or another fish soup/stew, *bourride*, thickened with cream or garlic mayonnaise.

I worked in the pastry section for four months. Most of the time, my shift would be from 3 p.m. to 11 p.m. and my role was to do much of the dessert preparation, like making tarts or other large desserts that the waiters would cut into portions for functions. In addition, I was making the desserts for the gastronomic restaurant, some of which I had to do '*à la minute*'. One that was very popular was made of orange segments, with a *sabayon* which I had to make on the spot. For the *sabayon* I whisked an egg yolk with some sugar and some Grand Marnier liqueur over a gentle heat, and when the consistency was creamy enough I would spread it neatly on the plate with orange segments beautifully spread out and arranged, then put the plate under the grill for just a few seconds to give a nice pale caramelised colour and flavour.

After working for four months as commis pastry chef, I was moved to the starter section. It was very interesting as we had to prepare some starters like *terrine de foie gras*. For that I was shown how to take out the main blood vessels of the big lobes of a duck or a goose liver, then salt and pepper the lobes and pour some Armagnac onto them. The lobes would rest overnight and the next day the lobes would be put carefully in a terrine dish. Beforehand, some duck fat had been poured into the bottom of the terrine dish and once the lobes were in the terrine dish, more fat would be poured in to make sure that there were no gaps. The terrine would then be gently cooked in a bain-marie in an oven.

After four months in the starter section I was moved to the coffee shop and brasserie. There, it was more about varied salads, grilled food and simple dishes. I enjoyed the experience, but after just a few weeks I got bored. I asked the head chef, René Alloin, if I could move to another position, but he told me that no other position was available at the moment. To be fair, I had done a decent job in the different positions I was given, but I was not a shining star of cooking, so he probably did not have a strong desire to keep me. I resigned.

Once I left the Marseille Frantel, I stayed in Aix-en-Provence with my mum for a while. During that period, in 1981, I took the National French Cuisine exam called CAP de Cuisine (Certificate of Professional Aptitude in Cooking). It is an exam made up of two parts. On the first day you have some general theory (French, Maths and some Technical Cookery theory) and on the second day comes the practical element of the exam. For the practical session you had to cook under timed conditions, either a starter and a main course or a main course and a dessert. The two recipes were drawn randomly on the day, picked from a programme of ninety-six recipes that each candidate had to learn. Once you had drawn your two recipes you had to go and select the ingredients already laid out on a large table or in the big fridge. Then each candidate had to recreate the recipe. I did not prepare well and did a poor job with my main course as I cut the vegetables in completely the wrong shape for the recipe, and my dessert was slightly overcooked. I failed the practical part.

After this setback, I thought to myself, why not try my luck in Paris? I had only been to Paris once, for a quick trip to see the final of the French football cup that Saint-Etienne won against Reims in 1977. I thought I would find a catering job easily.

I don't know if it was due to the fact that my time at the Frantel had ended in a slightly disappointing way or that I had failed the cookery exam, but I was not in the right state of mind when I arrived in Paris. I completely lost my way. I looked for jobs, but either I was not experienced enough and did not get them, or I refused the offers because I was too choosy. I spent a lot of money staying in a modest hotel, having to eat out every day and occupying myself by going to the cinema and other distractions to kill time, while not working and not earning money. In a short time, I found myself with no money. It is fortunate that credit cards were not widely used then and I did not have one, as I could have been left with no money and also debts as well.

One morning after I had paid for my hotel in Paris I had only a few francs left. I phoned my sister and explained the situation. She sent me some money through a speedy postal system within the post office, and I took a train to Lyon to go and stay with her.

When I arrived in Lyon my sister did not judge me, she was very kind and welcoming, but I felt very ashamed to have fallen so low. I made a promise to myself that I would never do so ever again. I often used to wonder how people became homeless, living a tough life on the streets.

I was lucky to have my sister rescuing me and my mother would have done the same, but without a family behind me, who knows what might have happened to me. That night, I determined that I would succeed.

The morning after, I went to an agency close to where my sister lived and told the agent that I was prepared to do any manual job. For the next three weeks I worked non-stop every day. I assisted a gardener doing the garden for a rich man, digging holes or whatever he wanted me to do. Another time I was sent to help a man whose job was to unblock chimneys, or special chutes in buildings down which people throw their rubbish directly into bins below, and so I found myself on hose duties or on roofs, unblocking the different holes.

Eventually, I worked in a kitchen restaurant in Lyon, but it was nothing really special and I stayed less than a month. I had also had a brief stint in a Michelin two-star restaurant as commis chef, but I only stayed two days, because it had a 9 a.m. start, but we only had a one-hour break in the afternoon before finishing at midnight. Also, there were cameras everywhere in the kitchen so the boss and his wife could constantly check on us. When I resigned, the owner told me I was only suited for working in a post office.

My next job was even more dispiriting: working as a waiter in a restaurant in the Swiss Alps. The day I started, cash went missing from the till and I was blamed. They found the money, but the problems mounted up. On the fourth day, the owner said: 'You are useless, and you will achieve nothing in life; we don't need you here.'

It felt that nothing I did was right.

So, it was back to Lyon, to another brasserie, where I worked on the night shift, serving people coming in after their night at the disco. Then there was a job driving a van, delivering dishwashing-powder samples. I even got a job as an assistant in what was advertised as a 'specialist bookshop' – a bookshop specialising in pornographic books, videos and toys. What I learned from that is that service is service, and you need to treat people well whether you're serving them a salad or a sex toy.

During this period of odd-jobbing, I re-took the CAP Cuisine. This time I was well prepared, having practised at home, and I passed. So, I decided to take the National French Restaurant Service exam as well, and I passed the first time. This did a lot for my confidence: although I had dropped out of school, I now had two professional qualifications, I had some great hospitality experience behind me, and I could speak a modest level of English.

But there was no doubt I was drifting. Not only that, but I was taking advantage of my kind-hearted sister by living with her, even though I was paying a modest rent.

So, I picked up the phone.

Six

New Forest, New Life

In November 1983 I phoned Stephen, the head chef of the Crown Hotel, and asked if he needed any waiting staff. Soon, I was back in Lyndhurst again and it was as if I'd never left.

Shortly after I arrived, however, the management decided to sell the hotel. What I discovered is that during such a transaction period, the people who still own the hotel stop spending money on it unless they really have to.

This was most obvious at Sunday breakfasts, which were not only very busy, but which ran late, because all the guests slept in. To make sure we had enough tables, we worked quickly to re-set them when people had finished. The problem was, we no longer had enough breakfast cups. Crockery is broken regularly in a restaurant, and normally replacements are bought every few months. But the group owning the hotel didn't want to spend money on new ones, so we were running low. During the week this wasn't a problem, because we could wash the ones we had and re-use them. But shortly before the hotel was sold, we laid out more and more tables without cups. The minute someone left a table, we'd make a rush for their dirty cup and wash it immediately, returning it to the restaurant straight away. Eventually, there just weren't enough cups, and it became embarrassing. I hit on the idea of using staff mugs, a disparate collection, many of which were grubby or chipped or decorated with the colours of a famous football team. Unfortunately, I was never able to set my brilliant plan in motion. As soon as I explained my idea to the manager, he bought enough cups and saucers to keep us going until the new owners arrived.

When Mr and Mrs Green took over the hotel in April 1984, they made many changes, including appointing a restaurant manager, Victor Ladonenko, who was given permission to spend money on the wine list. He knew quite a lot about wine and wanted someone to serve the wine, in effect to be a sommelier. One evening, he asked me to take that role. I did the absolute best I could, so I was dismayed when he chose another waiter the following day to do the wine. The reason, he told me, was he wanted to see the waiting staff work in different positions, so he could see what everyone was suited for. Within two weeks I was back doing the wine. I don't think it caused any jealousy – wine was scary for most people, including the waiting staff. I also knew very little about wine, but I was excited by the challenge.

We weren't required to start the evening shift until 6.45 p.m., as the restaurant opened at 7 p.m. Victor would come down around 5.30 to finalise the table plan, put candle holders on each table and vacuum around the two or three tables used for lunch. I began to come down early as well, so I could learn from him. I would make him a coffee, do the candle holders and the vacuuming, and then sit next to him as he wrote the table plan. I wanted to know why he configured the tables in a certain way, or how he chose guests for our best tables. He had a logical answer for everything.

Dealing with guests often required great tact, like the time I listened to a father explain to his sons that the inexpensive sparkling wine I was pouring was exactly like Champagne. Which was not the case at all, so I felt very uncomfortable when he turned to me and said, 'Isn't that right?'

I said, 'Well, sir, you are right, it is a sparkling wine like Champagne, but it is not made in exactly the same way and both the grapes and the region are different; but it is a lovely sparkling wine and it is a great choice you made.' He seemed very happy with my answer.

Sometimes it was dealing with the other staff that required my quick thinking. Although the meat and fish were always plated, we waiters had to silver-serve the vegetables, meaning we had to go to the table with a tray in one hand and, using a large spoon and fork, put the food on the plate of each guest. During one busy Sunday lunch, my friend John gave me a big tray of vegetables for a table of eight. 'Would you mind serving the veg, as I need to go to the pantry urgently to fetch some desserts for another table?' Of course I didn't mind – until I got to the table and was about to serve my first guest. John had left me with two teaspoons instead of a fork and spoon. I took the challenge. I managed to serve the vegetables properly and in good time, without the guests realising anything was wrong.

The week after, we were offering roast pork for Sunday lunch, and the guests would also be offered apple sauce. We had many sauces available; horseradish for beef, English or French mustards for beef or cold cuts, mint sauce for lamb, cranberry for turkey, tartare sauce for fish, mayonnaise for cold cuts, as well as the apple sauce, with each sauce in its own sauce dish. During service I asked John if he could do the apple sauce, and gave him the dish. Except I'd changed the spoon for a fork. Of course, there was no way he could serve the sauce and he had to apologise and go and change the spoon. It was childish, and we rarely did such things, but occasionally it was nice to let off steam.

At the end of summer 1984, I was told that I would be promoted to the position of maitre d'hotel (head waiter) to reward me for my dedication, hard work and excellence in the restaurant. I was over the moon, of course.

And then things changed again. In the autumn, a catering student who was working a few shifts every week came to see me. As I was the head waiter, and I was French (there was an assumption that being French made me a wine expert), she assumed I knew a lot about wine. She told me that in her course she was learning about wine, but she hadn't understood the part about noble rot – a beneficial fungus that attacks grapes and sucks all the water out, which concentrates the sugar – so could I explain it to her?

Unfortunately I hadn't heard of noble rot either. The next day I went to Lyndhurst's only bookshop and bought a wine book that had a lot of information on the basics of wine production. In the next few weeks, I read it from cover to cover. Although I'd learned about the main French wine regions when I prepared for my CAP Restaurant exam, my wine knowledge was very basic. The only wines I really knew about were the ones we served at the Crown Hotel, the majority of which were French, with some German wines on the list as well. I had no interest in becoming a sommelier, because my ambition was to become a restaurant manager, but it occurred to me that if I could increase my wine knowledge, it might help me move up. And I realised I had a way in, because in Firminy, the town next to Saint-Etienne, there was a lady famous for her wine expertise: Danielle Carré-Cartal, who ran her family hotel, had won the title of Best Restaurateur-Sommelier of France, 1978, the first woman to win such a title. So I wrote to Mme Carré-Cartal and told her that I wished to take the CAP Sommelier exam in June 1985, and could she help me prepare for it. She wrote back and told me to visit her. As it happened, Mum was now living back in Saint-Etienne, so I paid her a visit and took the opportunity to visit Mme Carré-Cartal.

She was charming and helpful and gave me the right books to study and plenty of useful advice. I registered my name for the exam the same week and when back in England I did a lot of revising and prep in the months leading up to the exam. I took the exam as planned in June 1985. The CAP Sommelier followed the same formula as the two CAP exams I had done before, and I passed (just).

The improvement in my position as head waiter and my new qualification made me restless. Viktor had no plans to go anywhere, so I couldn't see a way to progress. Although life at the Crown Hotel was enjoyable, it was time to move on and I began writing unsolicited letters to top restaurants.

Soon I found myself working in a prestigious two-Michelin star restaurant in Oxford called Le Manoir aux Quat'Saisons, owned by the talented and eccentric French chef Raymond Blanc. To get that job I had to drop position and be a waiter again, which was a mistake. The young head waiter above me gave me a hard time straightaway, so being very sensitive I left after a week. I have to say Raymond Blanc was extremely nice to me during that week; I met him again later in my career and we remain close friends of many years standing.

Unfortunately, that disappointing week was followed by another disappointing five weeks, in a two-Michelin star restaurant called Chez Nico, owned by Nico Ladenis and his wife in Shinfield, a small village in Berkshire, not far from London. Nico Ladenis had made his name in London in his tiny (off central London) restaurant, where he gained his two Michelin stars. The couple raised some money with a shareholder scheme and bought a bigger place in the country with the idea to be more luxurious and get three Michelin stars, and they employed me as their sommelier. When I arrived, the new restaurant was being transformed in readiness to open in three weeks, so I set up the cellar and put the bottles of wine in place. The wine list had been created by a wine merchant called Bill Baker, a great character, larger than life, extremely knowledgeable and a lovely man.

Like Raymond, Nico Ladenis was a brilliant chef, but very different in style and philosophy. When in London, he was famous for telling off guests if they asked for a steak well done, which he simply refused to cook. When the Shinfield restaurant finally opened it did not take off as Nico had expected. His London guests did not flock in as he had hoped, and the local guests were not ready for Nico's cuisine. The tables were laid up without salt and pepper and often guests asked for them. Dinah-Jane, Nico's charming wife, would have to tell the guests that Nico did not think his cooking needed any adjustment. The first two weeks of trading were extremely quiet and very boring (a year later Nico relocated his restaurant back to London and eventually won three Michelin stars). Shinfield, I am sorry to say for people living there, was not the most exciting place to be. I was lodging in the house of an elderly and very sweet lady, who spent her time watching cricket on TV. After two weeks of this, I quit the restaurant. On my last night I served Bill Baker, the wine merchant who had some business guests with him and he ordered some top and very expensive wines: Château Latour and

Château d'Yquem. He made a point for me to try all the wines for my enjoyment and my learning. Bill Baker was a class act (he has sadly passed away since).

After these two failures I knew I needed to get on my feet very quickly. I promptly contacted some other restaurants for available job positions. One of them, Morels restaurant in Haslemere, invited me for an interview. Morels restaurant was owned by Jean-Yves Morel from Lyon and the head chef of his own restaurant. I really liked the menu of his restaurant as it was modern and I liked the ambition that Jean-Yves had to win a Michelin star, so I agreed to start the week after. I arrived on the Monday to move into my room – in a big cottage with four other staff members – and started work the next day.

The village of Haslemere is in Surrey. A charming town, it had a railway station and so it was very easy to go to London.

Morels restaurant was quite small and could cater for forty covers. The first week went well, but on the very first day at the staff lunch, the food was not very appetizing, so I told them I was vegetarian. I'm not, but I told them I was doing it for health reasons. It was a good thing I did not mention it at the interview the week before because I am not sure he would have offered me the job. It was the 80s and Jean-Yves was a French chef; there was a bit of a macho culture in kitchens and vegetarian meals were thought to be for eccentric people. All went well with the staff food thereafter, as the chefs were cooking me all sorts of vegetarian meals, vegetarian soufflé, some lovely vegetable gratins and of course quite a lot of pasta. The downside was that on Thursday evenings all the staff had a good-looking filet of beef with a lovely gratin of potatoes, a real treat. Not only could I not have the filet of beef, but I had to be careful that nobody spotted me eating meat or fish locally on my days off.

For service, Jean-Yves was in the kitchen with two chefs and one kitchen porter, while I was in the restaurant with two waiters. Jean-Yves's wife would help on very busy services, but she did very little aside from taking coats, answering phone calls, and writing the bills, as they were hand written. She was also very critical and unpopular with the staff. It turned out she was unpopular with Jean-Yves, too, as they divorced a few years later.

While working at Jean-Yves' restaurant, one morning in October, a letter arrived that was advertising for entrants for a sommelier competition. Jean-Yves came to see me with the letter and told me that as just a few months earlier I had obtained my French sommelier exam, I should enter the competition. It was run by Sopexa, at the time a subsidiary of the French Ministry of Agriculture. There were Sopexa offices in the main export markets for French food and wine and Sopexa offices were there to promote and support the marketing and sales of those French products. The competition was only about French wines and spirits and it was part of a strategy to make British sommeliers focus on French wines.

A week after I applied, I received a letter telling me I was qualified for the second round which would take place in a hotel in London and for that I would need to bring my working uniform as there would be some practical tasks. I arrived and faced tasks including selecting the right glasses for some specific wines, opening bottles and serving them to guests, making some remarks about current wine topics, and doing two semi-blind tastings; these weren't too difficult, because the judge would say: "You have three red wines in front of you. Tell us, which one is the Beaujolais?"

Again, a week later a Sopexa letter arrived telling me I would be one of the six finalists. Now I got serious and began to study French grapes and regions. As to the mechanics of being a sommelier, I was a bit lost on how to prepare.

Still, when the day came, I enjoyed it. It was a whole day of written exams, blind tastings, and serving wines to a guest table of judges. At the end of the day was a gala dinner, where they announced that I had been ranked fifth out of six. When I went to collect my certificate, the head judge, Ailen Trew MW said, "Don't be disappointed. You'll win next time."

After my failure to win, I realised it was time to move on from Morels, too. I'd learned all I could, and Jean-Yves' wife was too unpleasant, so I took a break and went to France. Just to fill in time, I took a job in a Lyon brasserie, which turned out to be a totally new experience. I became a 'Limonadier' or more exactly 'Serveur Limona-dier', which meant serving drinks only. It sounds easy, but it's tough to serve drinks all day in a busy brasserie. I had to take the drink orders for two, three or even four tables, non-stop, and then I had to go back to the bar and recite all the drinks to the barmen. The barmen, of course, wanted to hear about the hot drinks first, even if they were for all different tables. For me, it was a strain, but I watched the old pro Limona-diers remember many orders at once, without ever using a pad, and then carrying up to 15 or more drinks on a tray.

Then it was back to England.

Seven

Competitions Pique My Interest

After a short stint at a different restaurant, I went back to the Crown in Lyndhurst. I had kept a good rapport with Victor the restaurant manager, Stephen the head chef and the owners, Mr and Mrs Green, and I was missing the New Forest.

An idea was also growing on me. I wasn't sure I wanted to be a restaurant manager any more. The Sopexa competition had fired me up and ignited a competitive streak that had been lying dormant since my cycling days. I now wanted to win a sommelier competition.

I knew that if I went back to the Crown, I would be serving wine at busy times, so it would be a good place to practise. Plus, the working hours were shorter than at many restaurants, so I would have time to study. On my return, I found the Greens had done a great deal of effective marketing, and the Crown was now a bustling place, with more business functions and dinners. I was to be co-head waiter, in charge of the business functions, and I was to do some staff training.

That turned out to have its own challenges. One waiter had a bit of an attitude and thought he knew everything. After one busy Sunday breakfast, when he'd disregarded my instructions in a way that made it difficult for the team, I politely told him off and he swore at me in return. The general manager was not sympathetic, unfortunately, telling me to deal with it. She had recruited this waiter and quite liked him. Later, this same waiter got impatient with a guest who didn't give his order fast enough, and shouted at him. He was sacked, of course.

Although such moments were irritating, I'd become obsessed with the

45

idea of becoming a top sommelier. I'd also discovered that there was an annual UK Sommelier of the Year competition, dealing with wines and spirits from all over the world. Not only that, there were wine courses and important wine qualifications to think about: the Wine & Spirit Education Trust courses, the Master Sommelier title awarded by the Court of Master Sommeliers and – the Holy Grail – the impossible-to-get Master of Wine.

I had not become a famous footballer or a famous cyclist. But I could do this. I was going to focus only on wine and aim for the very top: Master Sommelier, Master of Wine. Best Sommelier in the World.

I realised that there was a fantastic opportunity just waiting for somebody to come along and take it. Neither the Sopexa competition nor the UK Sommelier of the Year had been up and running for long, partly because the sommelier profession itself was so new in the UK. Nobody had yet established themselves as the top sommelier – meaning the field was wide open. If I could be that person, I would not just be the first, but I would also be the person who defined the profession.

I didn't know then what I was signing up for. For many years afterwards, I would spend all my holidays in wine regions visiting wineries and meeting winemakers. I would spend my days off attending wine seminars or going to trade tastings, practising tasting drills or doing wine exercises. When I had any spare time, it would be spent poring over wine books and wine magazines.

In the autumn of 1987, I enrolled for the latest Sopexa competition. By then I knew how it worked. The first round of sommeliers would be selected from all the applicants and invited to a big hotel. Once there, the competitors were herded into a function room and made to fill in a questionnaire. Then there was a written blind tasting, where the wines or spirits were usually served in a black glass, so you couldn't tell anything about them by looking at them. Once that part was over, we had to go in front of the judges, one by one, and perform a service exercise. Under timed conditions, I would find myself decanting a red or opening a bottle of sparkling wine, or having to give impromptu wine recommendations to match the menu I'd just been handed.

The Sopexa competition was held in business function rooms near Leicester Square, and the first thing I realised was that standards had risen enormously since the last competition. Still, I found myself among the six sommeliers who made it through to the afternoon session. An hour later, I learned that I was a finalist and would participate in the next round, also in London.

It had been a good year. By the end of 1987, I held the Certificate of the WSET (Wine & Spirit Education Trust) programme and had passed the Advanced Sommelier exam, so I could try for the Master Sommelier Diploma. Not only that, but my face had begun to appear in the catering trade press.

One afternoon I received a call at the Crown Hotel from a headhunter called Guillaume Rochette. After congratulating me on my recent performances, he quickly told me that he could not understand what I was doing in a hotel like the Crown and that he had an opportunity for me to work in one of the very best hotels in England. We agreed that I would go the following week to his London office to meet him. I must admit that I was flattered to have been contacted. Guillaume did not tell me during our phone conversation the name of the hotel he was referring to, so my interest was piqued.

The week after, in his office, Guillaume told me only that the family-owned hotel was in the south of England and had a Michelin-star restaurant. Guillaume added that the standards were so high that the bedroom cleaners would go on their hands and knees if need be to scrub the floor with a toothbrush in order to get rid of small marks. He also said that the managing director was very young and dynamic and wanted a second Michelin star for the restaurant. The hotel was Chewton Glen, in Hampshire.

I was not as enthusiastic as Guillaume would have liked me to be. I said to him that I had heard the hours were very long and that would not be for me as I needed to continue my wine studies. But he convinced me to go for the interview with the managing director.

A few days later I met Robin Hutson. As I was not really that excited about working at Chewton Glen, I felt very relaxed at the interview. I told Robin the good points about me, but also the bad, like my short stints in major restaurants. I also stressed that I did not want to work silly hours as people did in most top restaurants, as I had to concentrate on my wine studies.

At first, he did not seem impressed, but two hours later Robin was showing me around the hotel. At the end of the interview we agreed that I could start in the position of head sommelier in early March 1988, which was several weeks away.

In the meantime, I was facing the finals of the UK Sommelier of the Year competition and my time was taken up with preparation. It was quite different from the Sopexa competition, because the final took place in front of an audience and consisted of answering questions under timed conditions. It was just like appearing on the UK game show *Mastermind* and was a tense experience. However, I did quite well, and managed to finish second. That was nice to have under my belt.

I started at Chewton Glen at the beginning of March 1988 and two weeks later I was competing in the Sopexa final in London. By then I was an old hand at sommelier competitions and just enjoyed the day with the other sommeliers, and the gala dinner that night. Except that when the results were announced – it was my name. I'd won.

The timing couldn't have been better. Chewton Glen was a new experience and I was struggling to adapt. It was more demanding than my previous positions and I was a little overawed by working there. I had never been in such a responsible position before as a sommelier and they had never employed a head sommelier before, so we were learning and finding our feet together. Winning Sopexa took the heat off a little. It also helped that a couple of months later, I passed the next WSET qualification and won a scholarship to Burgundy.

Not everything went my way. In June I travelled to Paris to compete against eleven other sommeliers in the Sopexa international final. When I finished eighth, I realised that no matter how well I was doing in the UK, I wasn't at an international level yet.

As soon as I returned to Chewton Glen, I left a letter for Robin, explaining that I only wanted to work dinners, apart from Sunday lunch, because I needed more time for my wine studies. Three days later, I met him and the restaurant manager, Patrick Gaillard. They told me that although they couldn't grant my request, they were keen for me to reach the top, so I could start work at noon instead of ten in the morning. My sommelier assistants would do the 'mise en place' (trade jargon meaning preparation before service), giving me all morning to study; they just wanted me to come one morning a week at ten o'clock to check the cellar and make sure all was in order. In addition, Robin's deputy, Joe, would order the wines from the wine merchants and do all of the wine admin, saving me a lot of time. I just needed to tell Joe what new wines I wanted to have on the list and Joe would deal with it. It was an incredible offer.

The only snag was with some members of the restaurant team, who thought I was too privileged. For the first few weeks, I had a few comments. 'Did you sleep well, Gerard?' said one. 'Are you not too tired with all this hard work, Gerard?' was another. But after a few weeks everyone got used to it, and I was free to study in the mornings.

From then on, I would get up around seven in the morning – which is pretty early when you're working late nights – and be studying by eight. At 11.30 a.m. I got changed and drove to Chewton Glen, five minutes away.

In a way I was fortunate that Chewton Glen had never had a proper head sommelier before me. That meant I could not be compared to a predecessor. I was also given two young sommelier assistants, who in fact had never been sommeliers, but were simply waiters with an interest in wine. I could build a team as I wished without too much interference.

Taking stock, I had achieved quite a lot in a few months: getting some valuable English wine exams under my belt, winning a scholarship, finishing first and second in two national sommelier competitions and arranging some incredible working conditions in one of the very top places in England. I could see that I was on the right track to achieve my dream.

Eight

Chewton Glen, a Turning Point

The Chewton Glen Hotel is situated in New Milton, a small town in the south of England in the county of Hampshire. From the hotel, it only takes ten minutes to walk to the sea and it's ten minutes by car to the New Forest.

In December 1965 two brothers, Martin and Trevor Skan, had bought what was then a small, ordinary hotel of sixteen rooms much in need of repair. Although the brothers had never worked in the hospitality industry before, Martin wanted Chewton Glen to become something really special. In 1972, Martin bought his brother out of the business and kept pushing his vision and by 1975, a decade later, the hotel had doubled its number of rooms and was regarded as one of the finest hotels in England. Its restaurant had entered the era of Nouvelle Cuisine with dishes like salmon with sorrel sauce and pan-fried duck Maigret with aubergine flowers. It had a Michelin star, which were few and far between in the country at the time. As its reputation spread and the awards mounted, the hotel attracted a prestigious clientele from the top tiers of media, sport, business, politics and the arts – and even royalty.

By the time I arrived in 1988, the hotel was regarded as one of the best in the world, with forty-six bedrooms, the famous restaurant, beautiful grounds, a tennis court and a golf course. The wine list was already well stocked with iconic wines from around the world, partly thanks to the input of David Burns, MW, the wine merchant. What made it unusual was that it wasn't dominated by French wines but had representative wines from both Europe and the New World: New

Zealand, Australia, Argentina and Chile. We served our guests Cloudy Bay Sauvignon Blanc from New Zealand, bold New World Chardonnay and rich Shiraz from Australia. Martin Skan was interested in both wine and travel, and whenever he came back from overseas, he brought another suggestion for the wine list.

One change I did make was to the inexpensive offerings, which were mainly from the big producers. I wanted more wines from small quality growers.

There was one aspect of the wine list that did need a major overhaul: the numbering. The numbers listed next to a bottle of wine made no difference to the guest but can be a make-or-break issue for staff. For example, if wine number 282 was a red wine, but wines numbered 281 and 283 were whites, staff would hesitate when the customer asked for bottle 282. Should they go to the red wine cellar or the white wine fridges? Unless they knew the number off by heart, they would waste time going to the wrong place to try and find the wine. So I renumbered the list, leaving plenty of empty spaces in each category, so that there would be space for future wines to slot into. With two volunteer waiters beside me, we started to move bottles to their new homes at 11 p.m. one night. Unfortunately, the night porter decided to help; he was a lovely man in his sixties, but he had a problem with shaking hands. At one point we watched anxiously as he carried a bottle of Pétrus – one of the most expensive wines in the world – to its new home. None of us had the courage to stop him, so we just watched, scared. Fortunately, he didn't drop it and we carried on all night, finishing the job by breakfast time the following morning.

We had an unusual system for buying wines. Ninety-five per cent of the wines came from a local merchant, David Burns Vintners. David had a wonderful portfolio, but it didn't have everything we needed. He would purchase the other wines from some of his colleague vintners as we needed them – and then he would loan them to us. He only got paid when the wines were sold. It meant our accountant was happy, while David Burns got the prestige of supplying such a famous cellar, which made him in great demand from other local restaurants and hotels.

I had a great relationship with David. Because he was a Master of Wine, I was in awe of him, but he was always extremely nice to me. He held regular wine tastings at his offices about ten miles from the hotel and would invite me, which was great for my wine education. Also, every three months we would do an in-depth review of the wine list. David always took notice of my suggestions, which were based on my wine trips, the trade tastings I attended in London or articles I had read in the wine press. I really enjoyed our quarterly meetings.

Chewton Glen proved pivotal for me in another way. In early June 1989, the restaurant hostess Brenda, with whom I had worked closely with for over a year, gave her notice. I was devastated, as professionally we got on extremely well and I was very worried about who would take her place. A few days later, at the end of lunch service, Robin Hutson and Patrick Gaillard interviewed a young woman called Nina Howe in the bar area. Some of the waiters made it their business to walk through the bar because word had got around that she was stunning. I was still feeling the loss of Brenda, so I didn't bother to go and see for myself.

It was a while before I met her. I was on a wine trip in the Loire Valley when Nina started as the new Chewton Glen restaurant hostess and then she went back to Paris on a short trip. I had spoken to her on the phone while on my wine trip, but she hadn't found the person I needed to talk to, and we exchanged a few cross words. I decided I had no time for her. Plus, I had just been dumped by one of the receptionists, so I wasn't feeling well disposed towards women.

However, a few days later, Patrick Gaillard said, 'You know, I think Nina is the lady for you.'

'You must be crazy,' I said. 'She is twenty-one years old and I am thirty-two.' As it happened, during the week I needed a lift as my car was at a local garage for a service and I needed to collect it. As we happened to have the same days off that week, I asked Nina if she would mind giving me a lift to the garage. We had a nice day, and I invited Nina to dinner the week after.

Two weeks later, Nina moved into my flat. All these years later, she's still here, although we have upgraded to larger houses through the years. (She says she moved into my flat because I had a washing machine and she didn't.)

Meeting Nina wasn't just a turning point in my personal life. She did so much for my career as well, starting with her taking WSET wine courses so she could understand my passion.

When I met Nina, I'd just bought a flat a few weeks before. I bought it for £52,000 and took a 100 per cent mortgage on it, which was nothing unusual then. I was confident, because everyone had told me you can only gain when you buy property. Two years later, in 1991, the UK plunged into deep recession and the price of property dropped dramatically. Suddenly my flat was only worth £34,000. Instead of moving somewhere bigger as we had hoped, we were stuck in a one-bedroom flat paying more money to the bank than it was worth.

It wasn't just my flat that was affected by the recession – Chewton Glen was as well, because rich people weren't keen on flaunting their wealth in such difficult times, for good reason. For example, fifteen people from a well-known company came for two days, so they could use the function rooms. While they were there, they had dinner with wine, as you'd expect. Two days later, a friend of mine asked me if I had read the *Sun* that day. Then he suggested I buy a copy, without telling me why. When I opened it, I saw a huge article about directors from a national company spending a lot in a posh hotel while they deliberated on which of their hundreds of employees they should make redundant. The article wasn't Chewton Glen's fault, but it scared other companies away from holding functions in top hotels.

That wasn't the only drop-off we experienced. Normally we had a waiting list for the weekends, but suddenly the hotel had empty rooms. The weekdays were even quieter.

After six weeks all of the staff members – there were about 120 of us – were summoned to an important meeting. Robin Hutson told us that the financial situation was very serious and it could not carry on like that. At the end of his speech, Robin asked for a show of hands, either to have 10 per cent of the staff members made redundant or for everyone to accept a 10 per cent pay cut, including himself. We all voted for the pay cut. It lasted three months and when business started to pick up, we had our full salary again.

Nine

Amazing Experiences

Every month we organised a wine dinner, where the guest of honour was the winemaker from the winery on show that evening, or a Master of Wine, or a famous wine journalist. In October 1989 we held a Château Latour dinner, featuring the Hon. Alan Hare, president of the château, along with Jancis Robinson, OBE, MW and Hugh Johnson, OBE, two of the greatest wine writers Britain has ever produced. The wines included Champagne Louis Roederer Brut Premier for the aperitif and then Pavillon Blanc 1982, the white wine from Château Margaux, Les Forts de Latour 1971, the second wine of Château Latour, Château Latour 1967, Château Latour 1961 served from an Imperial bottle, and the Château d'Yquem 1979 to finish. We had capped the event at thirty-six people as we only had one Imperial bottle.

The star was definitely the Imperial of Château Latour 1961, a mythical vintage in Bordeaux. It was particularly special because it came from an Imperial bottle, which contains six litres of wine, or the equivalent of eight 750ml bottles. Wine ages more slowly in these large quantities.

I had been worried all week about this Imperial, thinking about what would happen if the wine was corked, or if I dropped the Imperial when decanting it. On the day of the event, my two sommeliers and I spent the whole afternoon polishing our most beautiful wine glasses to make them extremely sparkly. In addition, we used a long piece of string to lay the glasses on the table so that the glasses for each wine were in a perfect, super-straight line.

We decanted the Imperial just before dinner; I had three people helping me. I was holding the Imperial bottle with the help of Joe Simonini, Robin's deputy, while Patrick Gaillard held the several decanters we needed and one of my sommeliers took each decanter from him when they were filled up.

Of course, I was privileged, along with my team, to taste all the wines. The Imperial of Châeatu Latour was stunning, but the other wines were superb too. The three speakers did a brilliant job in commenting on the wines; the food was delicious and so the evening was an outstanding success and a most memorable one.

On the other hand, another night with the legendary 1961 vintage went horribly wrong. It was a Friday evening and the couple were late for their booking. However, the gentleman immediately ordered our most expensive white wine, a Montrachet from Marquis de Laguiche. They were a nice couple but demanding, which was no surprise given they were spending a lot of money. They were staying at the hotel for two nights and the gentleman informed me that for their Saturday dinner, they wanted our most expensive wine, the Château Latour 1961. I was very excited and so I went to see the head chef and asked if we could make a special dish just for that couple, to make them feel special. I talked to them and gave them three options that the chef came up with; they selected the rack of lamb. We spoke about how their Saturday evening would unfold the next evening. He told me that they would come down at 7.30 p.m., have some Champagne in the bar and come to the table at 8 p.m. He had ordered a half-bottle of Meursault for their starters, which we had agreed I would serve them at 8 p.m., just before the starters arrived. The Château Latour 1961, which I would have decanted at 7.30 p.m., would be served at 8.30 p.m., a few minutes before their rack of lamb was served.

Unfortunately, we were extremely busy that Saturday and most of the guests arrived late. It was difficult to ask residents spending a lot of money to come down at seven o'clock when service started. The restaurant manager tried as much as he could to control table timings, but if the residents decided to come later there wasn't much we could do other than deal with it.

The starters and the half-bottle of Meursault were served on time at 8 p.m. but then things unravelled. The kitchen struggled to cope with so many main courses to be sent all in a short period of time, and some tables were affected. Regrettably, the couple having the Latour 61 was one of them. When the rack of lamb still hadn't appeared at nine o'clock, the head waiter and I did our best to appease the couple. At 9.30 p.m., when the lamb had still failed to materialise, the gentleman stood up and walked towards me right in the middle of the restaurant. I apologised again and told him I was going into the kitchen to check what was happening. He swore at me and suddenly the restaurant became quiet and people were looking at us.

His swearing saved the day. 'Sir, I understand your anger and I am very sorry for the poor service we have given you this evening, but I respect you, so please may I ask that you remain polite,' I said.

He was taken aback and said, 'You are right, you win!' and went back to his table.

By the time the lamb arrived they had lost their appetite, and even declined the complimentary – but expensive – half-bottle of sweet wine for their dessert. On his way out he apologised for swearing at me and said he was not upset with me, but added, 'This hotel is a joke and I will never come back.'

There are even worse situations that can arise. One Saturday evening, for example, I saw a couple seated at their table, who I realised I knew. I went to the table with a big smile on my face and said a very warm, 'Good evening. How are you?' However, I only got a polite but very reserved 'Fine, thank you' from the gentleman. I was quite mystified by his rather aloof reply, as around three weeks previously, I had had a long conversation with him in the lounge after lunch all about wine. I remembered very well that during our chat he had been extremely passionate about the wines he liked and so I was really surprised by his attitude towards me. I said, 'Excuse me for asking but aren't you the gentleman who works for [famous company] and had lunch here a few weeks ago?'

Of course it was him, and because I'd named the company, he couldn't deny it. But he panicked and said, 'Yes, I am, but you don't know me.'

At that moment, I realised the woman he was dining with was not the same one he had been with three weeks ago. This lady, no doubt, was his wife.

'Of course, I am very sorry,' I said and took his wine order very quickly.

From that day on, I became very careful when greeting guests, to the point that I kept my welcome to a minimum of words until the guests opened up to me.

Fortunately, such incidents are rare, but they are stressful when they happen. And also fortunately, not every mistake turns out to be a disaster.

On another occasion, I was advising a couple on a particular wine for their meal. They had a lamb dish for their main course and I gently convinced them to have a red Bordeaux, in fact a wine from the Pessac-Léognan appellation. It was a moderately priced wine and they were happy with my suggestion. Talking to the next couple I recommended a Burgundian Nuits St-Georges Village to go with their partridge dish.

Every twenty minutes or so, I would stop taking wine orders and go into the restaurant to see how the service was going. If my sommeliers needed help, I would serve one or two tables to take the pressure off them. Then I would go around the tables topping up glasses if needed, and asking the guests if they were happy with the wine I had recommended to them.

When I asked the couple to whom I recommended the Bordeaux, I was discomfited to see they were drinking the Burgundy. Before I could say anything, the gentleman said, 'You were right, this wine is delicious with the lamb!'

Five minutes later, when I arrived at the table with the couple who were supposed to have the Burgundy, they were drinking the Bordeaux and when I hesitantly asked them about the wine, they told me they loved it!

Perhaps it was my French accent and they didn't understand me, or maybe it was because the couples were so deeply in love. Whatever it was, both couples were happy, and I ensured they were both charged the rate of the less expensive of the wines. We only lost a few pounds.

Most of the time, we got it very right. Like the Friday evening I had been chatting to a table of three Frenchmen about wine and was later told to go out and speak to them about their wishes for the next day, when there would be twelve of them.

The gentleman in charge hesitated before he spoke. 'Look, we did not want to say anything, but we trust you. Michel Rocard [then the French prime minister] will come with his family and some advisers for a quiet meeting tomorrow. He chose to be away from France so nobody would recognise him,' he said. 'We are the security detail and so we will keep our table separate, but you will need two more tables, one for his family and one for him and his advisers.'

We were used to serving famous politicians. Indeed, Sir Edward Heath, the former UK prime minister, lived not far from Chewton Glen and he would regularly dine with us. He also had a security agent with him who would have to eat on a separate table and who was always served first. Sir Edward was always very polite, drinking whisky as an aperitif, followed by a white Burgundy and a classed growth red Bordeaux. I used to tease him and joke with him about drinking New World wines, but he always chose to stay with his French favourites.

I wondered how Michel Rocard thought he could stay incognito at Chewton Glen, as at least twenty of the staff members working front of house were French, but we followed instructions. As it turned out, he was very easy to serve. Unfortunately, he was barely interested in wine, and so they only had very simple ones that night.

What I learned while working at Chewton Glen is that when you offer good service, you can get a lot back from the hospitality – like the time a big company hired the entire hotel for two days. They had invited some of their top clients and team members, about fifty people in total; as they were one group, it made it easy for us as well.

For the first evening, they had hired the Royal Naval Band for a musical show before dinner, a superb performance. The second night, the late Paul Daniels, at the time the most famous magician in England, had been hired for an after-dinner performance. He did several of his famous tricks, including making balls disappear and reappear in different cups at full speed and even pretending to do the same in slow motion; or the trick where he asked one member of the audience to lend him a high-value banknote. After a long play the banknote is found inside a walnut, which was itself inside a lemon, and so on. However, for me the best was at the end, when Paul Daniels mingled with the coffee-drinking guests, pretending to be a bit tired. He said to some of the guests sitting closest to him: 'I am quite tired, it must be late, what time is it?' The guests naturally looked at their watches – except they had disappeared. The brilliant Paul Daniels had taken the watches without anybody realising. He was a maestro and it was such a pleasure not only to make the guests happy with our hospitality, but to be able to share the wonder of two such top-class entertainments.

A month before I left the hotel, we had ten city traders – all men – come for dinner. They arrived at around 8.30 p.m. and had a few bottles of Dom Pérignon Champagne for their aperitif. With dinner they enjoyed bottles of Long-Depaquit Grand Cru Chablis, Château Lafite-Rothschild and Château Latour, and then two bottles of Château d'Yquem with their desserts. All the wines were from excellent vintages so all were extremely expensive.

They had a minibus coming to collect them later, at around one in the morning. After their meal they had a few Cognacs in the bar and then asked me to prepare three bottles of Krug Champagne, to be served in the snooker room. By then it was late and, unfortunately, the law was clear: non-residents could not be served alcohol after midnight. The gentleman ordering the drinks wasn't annoyed, but just asked if we had some rooms free. It was the middle of the week and so we had a few unsold. I offered him a discount; he followed me to reception, and signed for a room. He didn't bother to take the key, but just said, 'Can we have the Champagne now?'

My reply? 'Of course, sir, with pleasure.'

They left around 1.30 a.m., and not only paid the very expensive bill, but left a generous tip behind. I felt very proud of myself for having played my part in such a successful arrangement.

Ten

Onwards and Upwards

Throughout my six and a half years at Chewton Glen, I focused a lot on my wine education, gaining as many accolades as I could.

In 1989, I won the UK Sommelier of the Year. This meant I could compete in the Best Sommelier of the World competition, a few weeks later in France. In the meantime, I won a regional show, just to keep in training.

The Best Sommelier in the World competition was not plain sailing. All the candidates and presidents were assembled a week before and sent on a tour of several French wine regions. On the one hand, it was good for my wine education. On the other, we had the problem of each region competing to outdo the others in hospitality. Every lunch and every dinner was an exercise in getting through too much food and too much wine, and then finishing late each night.

The Champagne house Laurent Perrier, for example, kindly hosted a dinner dance and we left at three o'clock in the morning, despite having to get up just a few hours later to go to Burgundy! A few candidates began claiming they were ill in order to miss a few evenings, which was not very popular with the organisers. Out of politeness, I did not miss one evening.

By the time we arrived in Paris for the competition, we were all exhausted, having slept an average of only four or five hours a night. After we did the theory paper, we were taken to see the musical *Cats*, as a special treat. I don't remember the show, because I fell asleep – as did almost everyone.

Anyway, the theory questions were strange, being mostly technical questions, including very specific ones about the chemistry of wine-making. We knew the questions would be tough, and that aspects of winemaking would come up, but we were asked these unusual technical questions to the exclusion of the things sommeliers are normally expected to know: wine regions, grape varieties, viticulture and wine history, along with liqueurs and spirits, cocktails and other relevant topics of the job of a sommelier. I didn't make it through to the finals.

But I'm not sorry. It was won by Serge Dubs, a brilliant sommelier, who had won the inaugural 'Best Sommelier of Europe' the year before. Serge Dubs also deserves huge respect and great admiration for the fact that he remained head sommelier of the three-Michelin-star Auberge de l'Ill, at Illhaeusern in Alsace, for more than forty years.

While I was disappointed about the Paris competition, I did obtain the Master Sommelier qualification that year. It was my second attempt. The examination has three parts: theory, service and tasting, and in the first year I failed the tasting. You get three attempts to get the three sections, so once you've passed one section, you don't have to re-take it. Since I only had the tasting section to re-take, I prepared like mad. This was where Nina was invaluable: every day for weeks, she would pour me several glasses of wine that I had to describe and identify. Thanks to that, I sailed through the tasting.

There was also the qualification round for the Sopexa competition for UK Best Sommelier for French Wines & Spirits 1990 to prepare for; however, as I'd already won, I wasn't allowed to enter again. I sent a letter to the head office in Paris and pointed out that a player who wins Wimbledon or Roland Garros can enter again the year after, so why should it be different in sommelier competitions? They wrote back and said I would be allowed to re-enter the 1992 competition.

By then, I had the bug for competitions. I put myself in for everything and when a new competition came up – the Best Sommelier of Europe – I entered immediately. Unfortunately, there was a problem: you couldn't represent a country unless you were its citizen. I wrote and complained to the organiser, Michèle Chantome, who was subcontracted by Champagne Ruinart, the founder and sponsor of the competition. I pointed out that as a Frenchman working in England, it was very unlikely that the UDSF (Union de la Sommellerie Française, the French Sommelier Association) would want me representing France, as I lived and worked in the UK.

It turned out that was the point of the rule – they wanted to ensure that all the French sommeliers working abroad didn't swamp the competition. Michèle told me that international competitions needed to have competitors from different nationalities.

After thinking about it for a few days, I came to the obvious conclusion: British citizenship. After all, I loved England, was in love with an Englishwoman and would probably live out my life in the UK, where I was building my career. As soon as I discovered that gaining British citizenship wouldn't mean losing my French passport, I found two people willing to write me a reference, paid the money and sent off the forms.

The European competition took place in October 1990, which meant I had to win the UK selection in June. The timing was tight. I phoned Michèle and explained that my British citizenship might not arrive in time. She was very kind and said she would allow me to enter. Maybe it was because I kept phoning her and so she realised how determined I was.

I entered the UK selection, and out of a dozen or so applicants I finished equal first, tied with a very talented sommelier from Scotland called Johnny Walker (yes, that's his real name, just like the famous Scotch whisky). As each European country could present two candidates, that was perfect. And my British citizenship arrived in time for the European competition, so everything was in order.

About the same period as the UK selection, I obtained the WSET Diploma, a two-year course. I still have a tiny bit of regret about the exam, as I rushed to do it. It was an essay-based exam and my writing skills were mediocre at the time; I only passed because of my wine knowledge, not because of the quality of my arguments.

But there it was. My last wine challenge for the year was Best Sommelier of Europe, a very innovative competition. The first part took place in a hotel and the final at the Ruinart cellars. Ruinart is the oldest Champagne House, created in 1729, and it has the most magnificent cellar carved a long time ago from the chalk; because of sites like this, the Champagne region is a UNESCO heritage site today.

The first round consisted of a theory paper, a written blind tasting and some service exercises. The next day, in front of an audience, the three final candidates from the field of about thirty were announced. I was one of them.

However, although I did my best in the final, my inexperience in international competitions showed. I finished third behind Jean-Claude Ruet, the French candidate, and Mikael Söderström of Sweden, the winner. Still, I was delighted to have made it to the final. It was the third time I had represented the UK at an international competition, and if I hadn't made it to the final, the UK selectors might have started to wonder what the point of sending me was. I was moving in the right direction.

In 1991, I also started the Master of Wine programme. The MW programme was (and still is) principally a self-study programme with some mentoring from past MWs. There was also a short official programme to help the students, made up of a series of days in London, every other Monday from January to April, followed by the exam in May. The days in London would consist of a morning blind tasting training session of twelve wines, with an analysis afterwards, then a lunch break and in the afternoons, a presentation by a wine personality. Those days were wonderful opportunities to improve my blind tasting skills and learn more about wine. I greatly enjoyed them, although getting up at four o'clock in the morning to drive to London was sometimes hard after working until late the night before.

I knew that 1992 would be an important year. When I started my career, I was one of a pioneering generation of sommeliers. But now there was a new generation of ambitious and well-prepared sommeliers on the rise. Among them was Bruno Asselin, the young head sommelier of Le Manoir aux Quat'Saisons in Oxford, a rising star, who didn't hesitate to tell everyone that 1992 would be his year. Nick Mobbs, owner of the Imperial Hotel in Great Yarmouth, was also a very serious contender, as were Steven Wilcock and Joël Lauga, a very promising and talented French sommelier.

This time the Sopexa competition for Best Sommelier in French Wines & Spirits in the UK took place before the UK Sommelier of the Year. Thus, in March 1992, after a tough round in the morning, I was among the three candidates to qualify for the final. We were put in a room with the same food the judges would be served for lunch an hour later. We tasted the food and the twelve wines that were on the list for us to suggest and serve to the judges with their lunch. The wines were from different sub-regions of both Bordeaux and Burgundy.

Each candidate would have to serve ten judges. When we started service, I opted to recommend two wines with the starter and two wines with the main course. I told the judges that I was proposing to serve them a light crisp white wine from Bordeaux alongside a rounder, slightly oaky white wine from the south of Burgundy. For the main course I offered a fleshy red wine from the right bank of Bordeaux and a velvety red wine from Burgundy. Each time, I described the wines with great enthusiasm and gave precise reasons for my choice, adding that I would love to hear their comments at the end.

Serving two wines each time for ten judges was a bit more work but it pleased the judges that I did not restrict them to just one wine per course. After the long lunch service, we had different exercises to practise individually in front of different panels of judges, such as a blind tasting exercise and a food and wine matching. I did well overall, except that I was not very inspired. The wines I suggested were all well known and although I presented them with moderate flair, I was a bit flat after all the adrenaline of the lunch service. In such an exercise, the suggestions should consist of a mixture of both well-known and discovery wines and of course the candidate must show a lot of enthusiasm. One of the judges in that section was Nick Lander, the renowned *Financial Times* food critic and husband of Jancis Robinson. I wanted to shine in front of him, but my performance in that exercise was only average. Fortunately, I had done enough to win! Elizabeth Morcom, MW, the head judge, gave me my winner's trophy.

By the time the Ruinart UK Sommelier of the Year 1992 came around, which took place at the Savoy Hotel in London, I was the favourite. There were six candidates and after a tough first round I was among the three finalists announced at a small dinner at the Savoy the evening before the final. All six candidates stayed at the Savoy for the event. On the morning of the final, Nina and I got up very early to work on my blind tasting technique. Nina had brought in a bag filled with six bottles of wine and several miniatures of liqueurs and spirits, and she prepared several wine and spirit glasses for me to practise tasting. After an hour and a half of training we had our breakfast in our room. When the room-service waiter entered our room to deliver our breakfast, he could see plenty of alcoholic miniatures and bottles of wine opened and discarded all over the floor, with the room reeking of alcohol. I am not sure what he must have thought of this spectacle at such an early hour of the day!

In the morning, the three finalists had to do an oral blind tasting of three wines and six spirits; I had practised so much that I could recognise some spirits and liqueurs just by their colour.

In the afternoon, the second part of the final was taking place in one of the Savoy's banqueting rooms in front of an audience. To start, we had to serve a bottle of Ruinart Champagne. I was not especially nervous, but to my surprise I lost control of the cork and it went flying into the air with a big bang. The audience went silent in disbelief – the favourite had just made a huge mistake!

Three years earlier a mistake like that would have shaken me terribly. By then, however, with all of my competition experience under my belt, I quickly recovered by making a joke and served the Champagne in the most stylish way possible. I reasoned that a team can still win a football match, even after conceding a goal.

I won! With Nick Mobbs second and Steven Wilcock third.

I was over the moon. Because I had won the two 1992 UK Sommelier competitions, I was qualified that year for the Best Sommelier of Europe competition in May, the Best Sommelier in the World in September and finally the Sopexa Best International Sommelier for French Wines & Spirits in November. Thankfully Nina was supportive, because all of my holidays in 1992 were spent at home practising.

The Best Sommelier of Europe 1992 was much tougher than in 1990. When the results were announced, I had finished third, just as I had two years previously. Strangely enough, second place went to Jean-Claude Ruet, who had finished second two years earlier too.

In early September, I flew to Brazil for the Best Sommelier in the World competition; Nick Mobbs came as well. We shared a room in the wonderful Intercontinental Hotel in Rio de Janeiro where the competition was taking place and had a fun time together, Nick being a great travelling and competition companion.

The competition started with the candidates having to draw an official number. This number would be specific to us, to put on all our written papers in place of our names, so the judges wouldn't know whose papers they were marking. We had to keep this number secret and not lose it, because if we qualified for the final round, it would be the number announced, not our names. I put the number in a small wallet and kept it on me at all times, even when I was in bed.

There was a theory paper, a written blind tasting and a service exercise. I was mildly happy with my performance in the written papers, but not ecstatic, when I was called for the service exercise. The judges played the role of guests, and we were given the following scenario: 'Please present a bottle of Alsace Riesling and serve a Cabernet Sauvignon from Brazil to this couple. You have three minutes!'

These exercises are tough, because it's a new environment. Candidates don't know the place, the layout, or have a feel for the material and equipment provided, plus it's all done under strict timing, with no questions allowed.

I presented the Riesling, but did not open it, and then I opened a bottle of Brazilian Cabernet Sauvignon and served it, but regrettably I was unable to complete the exercise fully. The bell rang just as I was pouring the host some Cabernet Sauvignon so I could not fill up his glass to the exact right amount. Three minutes is not a lot of time. Many candidates served the Riesling and thus had no time to serve the Cabernet, or they decanted the Cabernet and then ran out of time to serve it.

Both Nick and I thought it was unlikely we would be among the five to get through to the final. So, on the day of the final, which was due to take place at three o'clock, Nick and I went for a stroll. About eleven o'clock we stopped in a bar and had two beers, something I would never have done if I thought I was a finalist.

We came back in time to get changed and join the group photo. Then we trooped into the banqueting room. Just as I entered, two lovely Brazilian women came to see me. They had stayed at Chewton Glen the year before and at that time I told them that I was hoping to qualify for the world championship in their country; they told me that they would come and watch the competition. They had kept their word!

The numbers of the finalists were announced slowly, which added a sense of heightened drama. We did not know the numbers of the candidates, so when a number was announced we all looked to see who was getting up from their chair to go on stage. Three finalists had been announced already and one of them was the favourite; then suddenly I heard my number. The last finalist was called, French sommelier Philippe Faure-Brac, and so the final could start.

My performance was patchy; excellent food and wine matching and a good effort serving the couple pretending to be restaurant guests, but an average blind tasting. Philippe's performance, on the other hand, was excellent.

After the final we went back to our rooms, had a shower and relaxed a little before the gala dinner, when the results would be announced. During the aperitif, many people came to me and said they thought it was a competition between me and Philippe Faure-Brac; so many, that I dared to hope that I might be the winner. At the end of the meal, Jean Frambourt, the president of ASI (Association Sommelier International), gave the results. The candidates from Canada and Luxembourg were equal fourth, Didier Fiat representing Ireland was third, and then Jean Frambourt took a bit of time before announcing the second position and the new world champion. After some interminable seconds I heard my name for second place, and the camp of French followers erupted. This meant that Philippe Faure-Brac was the Best Sommelier in the World 1992.

Of course, I was disappointed, but I recovered. I had started the day with no expectation of even being a finalist, so being second was a great result and it meant I was progressing in the international standings. Besides, Philippe's performance was superb.

Then there was a two-month interlude before I was off to Paris for the Sopexa Best International Sommelier for French Wines & Spirits, where I would be competing against twenty-one candidates from twenty-one countries over two days. There were no elimination rounds.

The day before the competition, Nina and I got together with the UK team for dinner in a classic French brasserie. I ordered a seafood platter, complete with oysters and other shellfish and suddenly noticed everyone looking worried – of course, it wasn't the ideal thing to have ordered, as I could have eaten a dodgy oyster. I kept eating, the food was delicious, and I didn't throw up during the night, so everything worked out.

This was the competition where I hit my stride. I decanted the bottle of red wine without a problem, matched the food and wine and got through the blind tasting. Then came the lunch service. The table I had to serve happened to have the international president of Sopexa on it, along with an official from the French Ministry of Agriculture. Towards the end, I took over the service of the cheese trolley as the waiter in charge of the table was not very confident. I carved the cheeses at the table and gave a long explanation as to why the wines I was recommending would go well with the cheese; I believe I impressed the judges.

Of course, while I was happy with my performance, I had no idea how the other competitors had done. To add to the uncertainty, my colleagues from Chewton Glen had all come over to attend the gala dinner and hear the results. Finally, the Sopexa president got up to announce the winners: Markus del Monego from Germany was second, and Eric Beaumard of France was also on the podium in third place; Gerard Basset of the UK was first.

'God Save the Queen' began playing and Jean Frambourt, president of the ASI, quietly remarked to me that it would be better if it was 'La Marseillaise'. But I was so proud it was 'God Save the Queen'. After all it was in the UK that my sommelier career had started. I kissed Nina and then was hugged by the whole Chewton Glen contingent. The celebration carried on well into the night. Champagne Laurent Perrier was one of the sponsors and I remember drinking quite a few glasses!

What a year. In 1992 I had entered five competitions, finishing once third, once second and winning the other three. And I had ended the year with a big win.

Winning didn't mean money, but it did mean I'd won trips to several different wine regions – and most of them were trips for two people. Finally, I could repay Nina for all her help with coaching and take her to some lovely places. Other invitations began to arrive for far-flung wine regions, including California.

In the days following my win, journalists came to interview me. Tim Atkin, MW, a very well-known wine journalist, wrote an article about me in the *Guardian*, nicknaming me the 'Red Rum of Sommeliers', after the legendary thoroughbred that won the National three times.

But the journalists were surprised by what I had to tell them: it was the end of my sommelier competition career. Now I had another focus: I wanted to get the most coveted wine qualification of all. The Master of Wine.

Eleven

An Exciting Proposal

I first heard the term 'Master of Wine' while working at the Crown Hotel in Lyndhurst in 1984.

Just as at Chewton Glen, David Burns Vintners was the main supplier of wine for the Crown Hotel. David Burns had established a great reputation and a stronghold in the New Forest area. He was one of the first Masters of Wine, as the MW examination was first held in 1953 and he passed it in 1956.

The first time I heard about David Burns, I asked who he was and remember the awe with which I was told he had an MW, because there were so few around. In 1987, when I started the WSET Certificate, at the time the very basic exam of the WSET programme, I asked the woman in charge of the course enrolment what I would need to do to become a Master of Wine. She smiled at my question and thought I was being funny – after all, I was just about to start at the very bottom of the ladder, and the MW was right at the top.

As I progressed in my wine career, I began to meet more MWs. In the late 1980s and early 1990s, the head judge of the UK sommelier competitions was always an MW, while many of the wine books I read had been written by MWs, such as the highly renowned Jancis Robinson, MW, but also other big names of the wine trade, such as Serena Sutcliffe MW, Rosemary George MW, Michael Broadbent MW, David Peppercorn MW and Clive Coates MW. It was very clear to me that being an MW was not only a huge accolade, but also the ultimate reference point for wine expertise. I discovered, however, that the pass rate was extremely low and many candidates simply abandoned the project after several unsuccessful attempts.

The UK has historically been an important country for the business of wine. The first papers of the Vintners Company of London (one of the twelve great livery companies) date back to 1363 and the wine trade has been a key business in England for a very long time. Many famous wine regions, including Bordeaux, the Douro in Portugal and Jerez in Spain, owe much of their renown to the English wine trade.

In 1953, the Vintners Company and the Wine & Spirit Association created this now mystical exam, partly to raise the prestige of the UK market even further. In 1969, the Vintners Company and the Wine & Spirit Association were again involved in setting up the first Master Sommelier (MS) examination, in conjunction with other UK wine bodies. It's quite remarkable that both the MW and MS examinations have originated in England and set the global standard. Since 1992, the MW examination has become truly international, with the exam being delivered on three continents: Europe, Australasia and North America. By 2018 there were MWs from twenty-eight countries and the Institute of Masters of Wine had 370 members worldwide.

By the late 1980s, while I was working very hard to establish myself as 'The Sommelier' in the UK by winning as many sommelier competitions as I could, I understood that to be really taken seriously I needed to become an MW.

It was certainly not an easy task, as I had left school at sixteen with only a very modest level of education and my mastery of written English was really sub-standard. Knowing that the theory part of the exam requires many well-structured essays to be written, and that plenty of the candidates who abandoned the programme were university graduates, my prospects for attaining the MW were not brilliant.

Despite this, after obtaining the WSET Diploma in 1990, I was free to apply for the Master of Wine programme, even though I had passed the WSET Diploma with an average grade. I knew of the reputation of the MW exam, but did not quite realise how far I was from the required level.

In the 1990s, the Master of Wine could be done in a year. The applicants took an entrance exam the year before the programme began, consisting of a morning blind tasting and some essays in the afternoon. Depending on their results, candidates were either accepted onto the programme or not. Then, from January to April, every other Monday, there was a series of training sessions in London. In the morning we would have twelve wines blind. In the afternoon, a wine professional of renown, who could be a grower, a winemaker, an owner of a winery or a wine marketer, would come and talk for an hour, and that was followed by a question and answer session.

The exam took place in the first week of May and lasted four days. The first three mornings were blind tastings of twelve wines each session: white wines the first morning, red wines the second and a mixed bag the third morning. The first three afternoons and the fourth day were for essays on wine production (comprising topics such as viticulture, winemaking, wine maturation and wine handling), the business of wine (including contemporary issues) and a philosophical essay on wine.

Successful candidates had to obtain at least a 65 per cent pass mark in each part. Candidates who passed either the whole blind tasting section or the whole theory section, but not both sections, were entitled to keep the successful part. In the following years, they only had to do the missing part and they were entitled to five more attempts.

I still don't know how I managed to be accepted after the entrance exam, but when I started the programme in January 1991, it did not take me long to realise that I was miles from being able to pass. That did not bother me too much. I was busy with planning hard for several sommelier competitions in 1992, so I had other priorities. As I said before, I used the MW programme for improving my wine knowledge and tasting skills, so it was a very useful support for the sommelier competitions.

Early in the summer of 1993, Robin Hutson asked me if I would go with him to a private wine tasting the following week at Bibendum, a well-known London wine merchant. I was surprised as Robin did not normally go to trade wine tastings. He explained to me that David Burns, our existing main wine merchant, would probably retire soon and it would be useful to sound out some other serious wine merchants, just in case.

We arrived at Bibendum and Robin and I were presented with a relatively large selection of wines to taste in order to give us an idea of the quality of the range. After the long tasting, two Bibendum employees took us for lunch in a local restaurant. The restaurant would now be referred to as a gastro-pub. The decor was rustic and artisanal, but quite trendy. The service was relaxed and the food, although simple, was modern and tasty. The emphasis was more on the taste, thanks to the quality of the ingredients, than trying to be clever. Back then, this place stood out as being very different, innovative, trendy and fun.

On the train back to New Milton, Robin asked me what I was planning for my future. I told him that I would like to obtain the Master of Wine exam in the next two or three years and stay another two years at Chewton Glen after that. Then, Nina and I would quite like to move to California, to the Napa Valley. We had enjoyed our Californian trip in 1990 so much that we had discussed going to work there for a few years in the future. I thought that if I was to obtain the Master of Wine, coupled with my sommelier credentials, I would be able to find a position as brand ambassador for a leading wine producer.

A week later, on one of my days off, Robin rang, asking me if he could pop by to see me in the afternoon. A few hours later Robin was in my flat explaining that what he was going to say had to remain strictly confidential.

Robin told me that he had it in mind to start his own business. He wanted to create a hotel/restaurant that was very different in style from Chewton Glen. The lunch we had in London with the Bibendum directors the week before had inspired him further. His idea was to create a mid-market hotel/restaurant, but of great quality. It would cut down on the high luxury items and the range of services offered, but offer a great venue, excellent food and professional, friendly service. He did not have the complete picture of what it would look like and exactly how it would be, but he was already quite advanced on some aspects of the project. After completing his presentation, Robin asked me to be his business partner in this new venture.

I was taken aback. My first reaction was to point out to Robin that I had no savings. In addition, Nina and I could not even sell our flat to raise money to invest in such a project; being in negative equity we would not only make no profit but, even worse, we would have to complete the shortfall to pay back to the bank. Robin replied that money would not be an issue as we would find some shareholders, borrow from the bank and do a share scheme that would allow us to start a business with little money input from us. Robin told me to reflect for a few days.

At the time, Nina was a hotel/restaurant inspector for the AA Guide, so she was away three to four days every week, staying in hotels in her allocated work patch. Normally, Nina was not working on my days off, but it was not always possible to have days off each week together and that particular day, even though I was not working, Nina had to work and so she was away from home. That evening, I spoke with Nina and told her of Robin's unexpected proposal.

Without hesitation, Nina told me that we should go for it. I was less enthusiastic as I really wanted to carry on focusing on my wine career. Nina, however, was trained as a hotelier. She had spent four years at the Hotel Management School at Westminster so the idea appealed to her greatly. Thus, with her persistent persuasion, I agreed.

A few days later, I told Robin that, in principle, I was up for it. However, I added that before we committed to anything, it would be useful to spend some time going through all the aspects of this possible venture to see if we really shared the same vision and understood fully what we both wanted to achieve. The week after, Robin and I spent a whole day discussing all sorts of ideas and at the end of the day we were reassured that we should go for it as a team – and I was more excited by the idea.

From that moment, we would try to meet as often as we could. Robin would often pop to my flat and on my evenings off Nina and I would go to his house for a simple bite to eat, to discuss our exciting project with Robin and his wife Judy.

We knew what we wanted to create: a mid-market hotel, quite trendy in style and great value for money. We wanted to be different and the best in our category. Our philosophy was to have lovely bedrooms with comfortable beds, great bathrooms, each with a big bath and a powerful shower, a busy restaurant offering tasty food, but unfussy in style. The service would be friendly but quite relaxed. The wine would be served properly – at the correct temperature and in excellent quality glasses – but all in a relaxed manner. If the guests wanted to pour their wine themselves then no problem, we would let them do so. Mid-market hotels with all those facilities seem quite obvious now, but in the early nineties it was a very different situation, and nothing like what we wanted to create really existed, especially in provincial towns.

We did not have a name for our new concept, but after a brainstorming session we came up with 'Hotel du Vin', partly because of my wine credentials and also because wine would play a big part.

Having completed the Master of Wine one-year programme three years in a row (1991, 1992 and 1993) and never attempted the exam, after the 1993 programme ended in May I decided that I should give the exam a go in 1994. This was to be the first year that the exam included a dissertation and each candidate had several months to write it before the exam week. So, late in 1993, we were given five dissertation titles to choose from. I selected 'An organic vineyard in action'.

Organic wine was not mainstream then and only a very few wine professionals were talking about it. In fact, in the 1990s, unlike now, the term 'organic wine' was not officially legal, but instead it was referred to as 'a wine made from organically grown grapes'. While I thought it was an interesting topic, it was very difficult to locate much information, as I could not find any really serious books on the topic. There were only two small guide books: *Thorsons Organic Wine Guide* by Jackie Gear and Jerry Lockspeiser and *The Organic Wine Guide* by Charlotte Mitchell and

Ian Wright. Those two guides explained briefly what an organic wine was and listed several wine producers who adhered to an official organic body, such as Nature et Progrès, FESA or Terre et Vie, the Soil Association, Demeter and a few others.

I knew Jancis Robinson well, so I phoned her and told her what I was doing, asking her if she had some advice and some information on the topic to share with me. I was in luck, because Jancis was working on completing the first edition of *The Oxford Companion to Wine*, known in the wine trade as the 'Bible'. It is an enormous book with entries on an incredible number of wine topics. Jancis Robinson is both the main author and the editor of the book, but in addition, many of the entries have been written by several wine professionals, each a world expert in a particular wine field. Jancis kindly sent me all the material on organic vineyards and the wines made from them that she had gathered for her book, several months before the book was published. It was wonderful to have access to it. The content was both superbly written and well organised and that gave me a lot of information and ideas on how to prepare my dissertation.

In the following weeks I contacted many wine producers that I found in the two organic guidebooks. A lot of them were in France, but I also contacted producers in Australia, New Zealand and the USA. As the internet was not well developed back then in the early 1990s, it was a case of phoning or faxing, but I mostly used the phone as it was easier for interviewing people. I had a shock when my phone bill came, as it was three times the usual amount, and so was the next bill.

I also went to visit Sedlescombe Vineyard in East Sussex, one of the few organic vineyards in the UK at that time, and spent all day with the owner trying to understand as much as I could, bombarding him with all sorts of questions.

At the time I was also taking weekly private English lessons with a lady called Monica Morgan-Watson. She kept an eye on my progress with the dissertation, ensuring that I did not make silly mistakes. However, she did not try to change my overall style as I really wanted the dissertation to be my work and not someone else's.

In 1993 I still did not know how to use a computer. Therefore, I wrote all my dissertation on sheets of paper and every so often Nina would type up my work on her computer. Nina copied my dissertation onto a floppy disk that, coupled with a paper version, I would eventually send to the Institute of Masters of Wine when it was completed. Quite incredible now to think I wrote it all on paper.

It took me four months to complete the dissertation and I was quite happy with the results. Of course, I did not think it was a masterpiece, but still, I had structured it in a logical manner and I had explained well all the important aspects of organic viticulture and the resulting wines, backed up by a lot of relevant examples that I gathered from different parts of the world. The dissertation was several chapters long and more than 7,000 words. I sent it off in January 1994 and hoped for the best.

This deep research of mine on organic viticulture and its wines did not make me a world expert on the topic, but certainly I had a far better understanding of it than before. It was especially rewarding to know quite a lot about it at a time when it wasn't yet greatly spoken about in the wine trade. In addition, I really enjoyed doing all that research.

By the autumn of 1993 we had identified a site that would be ideal for our Hotel du Vin project. It was only thirty miles away from Chewton Glen, in the historic town of Winchester. The Southgate Hotel was a lovely Georgian building, albeit rather faded in its glory, very close to the centre of the town. It needed to be totally transformed. It had nineteen small bedrooms, though not all were en-suite, a pub/restaurant area, a lounge, a cellar and, very importantly, a relatively large car park for a hotel right in the centre of the town.

The Southgate Hotel was up for sale for £750,000 and Robin had estimated that in addition we needed around £500,000 for the refurbishment and other opening costs. We knew it would be tight and so our budget was really made on a shoestring. The bank was happy to lend us £750,000 if we could raise £500,000 on our side. After several weeks, we managed to raise £500,000 by bringing in fourteen shareholders.

Robin had said that while he and I would not have to put large amounts of money in, it was still important that we could come up with a minimum amount of money to keep an important percentage of the shares. We could not match the amount of money we would raise from the shareholders, but Robin came up with a scheme. He and I would put in £25,000 each and we would also have some partly paid shares. Both of these together meant that we would have just above 50 per cent of the shares in our business.

I sold my car, Nina's parents lent us some money and Tony, Nina's dad, gave me his old business car to ensure we could remain mobile. Robin lent us the shortfall, so we were able to come up with our £25,000.

On his side, Robin had done most of the work to find the shareholders as he knew many wealthy people through his network of contacts. The fourteen shareholders were each bringing anything from £10,000 to £100,000. In addition to their shares in the business the shareholders were entitled to a few perks in the restaurant. The shareholders were mostly local businessmen who knew Robin and me from Chewton Glen. There were also some of Robin's family; and finally we had managed to convince two celebrities, the F1 racing driver Derek Warwick and the McLaren F1 boss Ron Dennis, to invest too. It was a great mix, and having fourteen shareholders gave us fourteen ambassadors, all happy to promote Hotel du Vin.

By April 1994, roughly seven to eight months after Robin and I began work on the project, we had finally raised the £500,000 we needed to get the £750,000 loan from the bank: £450,000 from shareholders and £25,000 each from me and Robin. We bought the hotel. We had planned that the transformation of the Southgate Hotel into Hotel du Vin would take around six months and so we were looking at opening at the beginning of October 1994. The Southgate Hotel closed in April and the builders moved in.

During this same period, in early 1994, I had started, for the fourth time in a row, the series of training Mondays with blind tasting sessions and speaker's presentations as part of the MW programme. On the blind tasting side, I would experience some lesser and some better sessions, but that was to be expected. Normally, the way the blind tasting sessions worked was that we would each taste the twelve wines on the day, write our answers, have a break, and then be interrogated at random on each wine by the two Masters of Wine running the session. So, for instance, two or three students would be asked to read in turn their answer for wine one, other students for wine two and so on. When interviewed, each student had to give the grape or grapes, country and region, the vintage of the wine, explain its methods of production and, more importantly, demonstrate how he or she had reached those conclusions.

In March, roughly seven or eight weeks before the exam, I went to the very first seminar, introduced to better help the students with their preparation for the exam. It took place in a business hotel belonging to one of the big supermarket chains. It had some great facilities, with rooms of an excellent standard, a large restaurant and several conference rooms with great equipment. It was situated fifty miles north of London in the countryside and it had a green park around it, so the place was quite relaxing, ideal for studying and training.

Normally in the mornings we would taste twelve wines blind under exam conditions, but we might also have some tastings in the afternoons, or a famous speaker. I remember that one day we had Dr Richard Smart, an Australian and a highly respected leading scientist on viticulture; another day we had Nicolas Joly, a Frenchman and, at the time, the most famous biodynamic wine grower (the most extreme form of organic viti-culture), who had written several books on that subject and who pro-duced a famous wine, Savennières La Coulée de Serrant, in the Loire Valley. We could not have had two points of view so dramatically dif-ferent, but that is what made it so interesting. The rest of the afternoon might be devoted to essay writing and essay techniques or more tastings. The day before leaving, we had a mini-exam and feedback was given to us the morning before departure. That week turned out to be very enjoy-able, but more importantly extremely beneficial in view of the exam.

For me, a major turning point was to occur in the middle of the seminar week during an afternoon blind tasting of eight red wines. Of the forty students or so, I was the only one to have all the wines . . . wrong! I was totally devastated. Even more so because the wines were fairly classic and one of the students whom I knew well, and was seated close by me, had nailed all the wines and was quietly boastful about it.

It was one of those awful moments that all tasters experience once in a while, a bit like an excellent football team being absolutely hammered by a team well below their level. It doesn't happen often, but just occasionally it does. I must say I get really annoyed with wine tasters when they only mention their positive experiences but deliberately forget those days when everything went wrong. I have taken part in countless blind tastings with inferior right through to great results, but I have also judged a huge number of highly talented colleagues and equally witnessed massive failures and amazing successes from the same individuals. Once a talented sommelier in the final of an international competition found the five wines (grape and region for each), and witnesses of the event were talking of this sommelier as a genius who had an amazing palate. Five months later, in another international competition, that same sommelier could not identify any of the wines in the final! I could give many similar examples.

Anyway, at the end of the week, when I came home, following a lot of thinking, I took a radical decision. There was less than two months left before the exam. I did not want to pull out as I had worked so hard on the dissertation and I knew that the following year I would have very little time to prepare for the exam because of the opening of Hotel du Vin. From the feedback of the MW seminar, I knew that at that moment my overall level meant I would probably fail both parts of the exam. The last thing I wanted was to get 55 or 60 per cent in both parts and have to redo them both the next year. I knew that it was impossible for me to catch up in just less than two months. Therefore, I decided to focus on the blind tasting part only and completely forget the theory. At the seminar we had several blind tasting sessions and yes, I had done extremely badly in one of them, but in the others, without being exceptional, I had had some decent results. Thus, I thought it was possible to be ready for it, if I spent a lot of time preparing and focused on the blind tasting part.

I put all my wine books away except the few related to wine tasting, and started to work exclusively on all the aspects of blind tasting.

In the Master of Wine exam, candidates get a lot of marks for the identification of the wines, but also for the reasoning. To succeed, candidates must excel in both identifying the wines and demonstrating how they reach their conclusions.

In the period that I had followed the MW programme, I had collected some unofficial papers given out during training sessions of what were thought to be great examples of blind tasting answers, with great reasoning. Until then I had never spent too much time looking at them, but this time I started studying them with the greatest care, to decipher how the reasoning was expressed. I spoke with many friends who were already MWs about the topic to glean as much information and advice as I could. For a week, I only worked on building a strong and very logical methodology with the most precise vocabulary I could think of.

Once I was happy with the methodology I had put together, I practised different exercises every day. I would write typical answers for the three classic wines that I imagined tasting, to ensure I was working only on the reasoning — I wanted it to become second nature that I would write great answers.

While I purchased a lot of wine, friends of mine kindly gave me some and David Burns Vintners, the Chewton Glen wine merchant, also generously contributed some bottles for my training. I had around 600 bottles at home.

Each morning, I would taste twelve wines blind. When Nina was away from home working, I had to prepare the wines myself. I developed a technique. All my bottles were wrapped and well taped up in newspapers with the capsule (the protective cover on top of the cork) taken off. I would pick a bottle among my pile in the corridor, carry it to the kitchen sink and open it without looking at the cork (a Screwpull was great for that), then I would pour some into a tasting glass and write my answer. Once I had finished, I would tear off the newspaper around the bottle and check how badly or how well I had done. I would repeat that eleven more times each morning.

In addition to the official Master of Wine Monday sessions, some Masters of Wine very kindly ran unofficial blind tasting training sessions in London. I attended a few of them. I remember at the last one I was sitting next to my friend Fiona Morrison (now Fiona Thienpont, MW). In our break, we compared what we had answered. For the first three wines I had given Chardonnay as the grape and it turned out to be correct; furthermore, I had done well on identifying the regions of those three wines. However, for the fourth wine I had given a different grape in my answer. Fiona was surprised and said something like, 'Gerard, it can't be, it has to be Chardonnay because the text of the question clearly says that the first four wines are made from the same grape!' Fiona was right and I was really annoyed with myself. I did not read the text of the question properly, as if I had, I would not have made such a silly mistake.

Laurent Metge-Toppin, a French winemaker who at that time was selling wine in London, was also doing the exam. We had struck up a good friendship during the programme, so I proposed to Laurent that we should spend a whole weekend, just the two of us, tasting wines blind. Laurent had a relation living in Hastings on the south-east coast of England, who kindly lent us his house while he was away. We each brought around seventy or eighty bottles. Laurent had followed my instructions religiously in taking off the capsules and wrapping them all in newspaper. When we met at his friend's house, we mixed our two lots of bottles, all well wrapped.

For the whole weekend we blind-tasted around 150 wines. This time, we were not working on the reasoning, but simply on sharpening up our identification skills. For two days we tasted all the wines blind, both in turn giving our opinion on what the wine in each bottle could be before unwrapping each one to discover the identity of the wine. We also re-tasted each bottle a second time, but this time knowing what the wine was. Once we had blind-tasted a lot of wines, we would simply compare similar wines (same grapes, but different regions), to see what the taste differences were. It was a sort of boot camp weekend, but in a friendly atmosphere. Not only did we do some serious and great work on our blind tasting ability, but we had a lot of fun too.

The weekend before the exam, I felt ready. I knew I had absolutely no chance of passing the theory part of the exam. However, with all the hard work on blind tasting, coupled with the huge number of wines I had tasted blind in the last two months, I had given myself a real chance to get the tasting part of the exam.

But my blind tasting training was not complete. Very early on, I had put aside thirty-six bottles to taste just before the exam. They were very classic wine styles that I wanted to make sure I would recognise if they were in the exam.

In 1994, the exam took place during the week of the Bank Holiday Monday. Tuesday morning was the start of the exam and Friday the final day. On the Bank Holiday Monday, Nina and I went to stay at Nina's parents, who at the time lived in Uxbridge in north-west London. On the Monday evening Nina opened twelve bottles of white and I tasted them blind. I did not write any notes, just tasted them to work on my identification skills.

Each morning, the exam started at ten o'clock and we had to be in the exam room by nine thirty. Nina would drive me every morning from Uxbridge to central London where the exam was taking place. To make sure I was on time, each morning we would leave very early, a bit before seven, but not before I had tasted again the wines opened the day before.

On the first day of the exam, we blind-tasted twelve white wines. I finished in time and I was happy with what I had written for each wine. However, as we would not be told what the wines were until the Friday lunchtime, I could not be sure if I had done well. Once the tasting was completed, as I was going to my lunch break, I found myself walking next to the colleague who had done so well in the blind tasting two months before, when I had done so badly. I did not want to talk to him in case he had answered differently from me, as that could have demoralised me. However, I could not avoid hearing him mentioning to another candidate what he had answered and many of the wines were different from mine, quite different. I thought, 'Oh my God, here we go again!'

During the theory part in the afternoon, I did what I could, but I knew that the essays I had written were mediocre to average at best. In the evening, at my parents-in-law's house, Nina prepared twelve red wines for me to taste blind, and again early in the morning before we left the house.

The second day unfolded in a very similar way, except that I managed to avoid my 'friend' who had shone during the seminar!

On the Thursday morning, after I had re-tasted the mixed bag of sparkling, rosé, sweet and fortified wines, we left Uxbridge. Halfway through our journey in Nina's car I suddenly panicked. I told Nina: '*Oh là là*, I have forgotten to taste a sparkling rosé recently. Quick, we must find one before the exam just in case!' Ten minutes later, it must have been just after 8.30 a.m., we saw a supermarket. We quickly stopped and parked the car and ran inside towards the wine department. I saw a bottle of Cava rosé, we bought it at once and left the shop in a hurry. In the car park, in no time, I took one of my wine glasses (for the exam each candidate must arrive with twelve wine glasses) and tasted the Cava rosé on the spot. A few people looked at me and must have thought I had a serious problem to be drinking so early in the morning. When I entered the exam room and started to pour the twelve wines (which had been transferred into neutral bottles as usual) into my glasses . . . there were no sparkling rosés in the exam.

As usual in the afternoon I wrote essays without much conviction, just going through the motions. The Friday morning was the last session of the exam. The tasting part had been completed during the previous three mornings, so that morning was reserved for a philosophical essay on wine. We were offered the choice of a few essay titles and we had two hours to write just one essay, so a longer answer was expected than the previous days. The title I selected inspired me and I enjoyed writing the essay.

Once every student had handed in this last essay, we would be given a sheet of paper with the names of the thirty-six wines we had tasted blind during the week. At the same time, we were offered a most welcome glass of Bollinger Champagne to celebrate the end of the exam.

Sipping my Bollinger Champagne, I reviewed the names of the wines and compared them with my answers. The more I went through the list, the happier and more excited I got. Indeed, my success rate was extremely high for each day of the blind tasting part. Thirty minutes later I joined Nina, who was waiting for me outside the exam room. I remember telling her, 'Well for sure I have not passed the theory part, but if I don't get the tasting part then I don't know what else I can do!'

Around three months later, I received the results letter from the Institute of Masters of Wine. As expected, I had failed the theory part, but I had passed both the dissertation and the tasting part (officially called the Practical). I was over the moon, having passed two sections at my first attempt. It meant that I could now focus solely on the theory part of the exam and I had five more attempts to complete it. My strategy of concentrating only on the tasting part had paid off.

However, the task ahead was never going to be easy, as we were about to open the Hotel du Vin Winchester and my life was going to change.

Twelve

Hotel du Vin

Robin and I had not yet told Mr and Mrs Skan, the owners of Chewton Glen, about our project, but now it was time to do so. As managing director and right-hand man at Chewton Glen, Robin wanted to tell them personally.

The day before Robin was due to meet the Skans and give them the news, the final of the UK Sommelier of the Year 1994 was taking place at the Dorchester Hotel. Mark Walter, my assistant at Chewton Glen, was in the final. Mark had been working with me at Chewton Glen for three years and in 1992, when I was preparing for all the different sommelier competitions, he would occasionally help me, setting up some exercises for me during our afternoon break. In addition, in 1993 and 1994, as Mark was entering the world of sommelier competitions, I was there to train him. Early in 1994 he had qualified for the final of the UK Sommelier of the Year 1994. That year, for some reason, a lot of experienced sommeliers who had participated in the competition in previous years did not re-enter, so it was mostly a new generation taking part. I thought that there was an incredible opportunity here for Mark if he put in the right amount of effort.

I set up a lot of wine tastings and exercises for Mark. In addition, I made Mark work on his mental strength, telling him how to approach the different challenges with some tips on how to control stress. I wanted Mark to avoid the big mistakes I had made in the past. He worked very hard and took a lot of my advice on board, and thus it wasn't all that surprising that he qualified for the last part in one of the two UK national competitions. Mark was talented, but certainly not the favourite to win the UK Sommelier of Year 1994. However, as there were many new sommeliers and not much left of the old guard, nobody knew how the competition would pan out. Furthermore, having nothing to lose, Mark was only mildly stressed. On the afternoon of the final, he was up against Mourad Dine of the Dorchester in London, one of the favourites and one of the few candidates to have some real competition experience. The other candidate was Philip Dougherty from the Grosvenor in Chester, who, like Mark, was not experienced in competing in national finals. Philip Dougherty did a decent final but was obviously not totally ready and finished a credible second. Mourad Dine missed a golden opportunity, because his nerves got the better of him and he could only finish third. Mark performed steadily, did not make many mistakes and so, to the surprise of everyone, won the competition.

I was over the moon, as it was the first time I had spent so much time training someone and to see him win was rewarding. In addition, it was great timing as when Robin told the Skans the next day that in a few months we would both be leaving Chewton Glen, there was already an excellent replacement who knew Chewton Glen well and had just won a big sommelier title.

As planned, the day after Mark's competition win, Robin told Mr and Mrs Skan of our project. They were a bit shaken but took the news quite well. They had a few months to find a replacement for Robin, and already had a head sommelier in waiting in Mark Walter. The agreement was that Robin and I would stay working at Chewton Glen until the end of August 1994, roughly a month before we would open Hotel du Vin.

The months from April to August were exciting. We now owned a hotel and could talk freely about it. The refurbishment work was taking place and so we could start implementing our strategy for real, not just on paper. Next, we had to build a team, starting with a talented chef who would understand the type of food we wanted to serve. For several weeks we interviewed young chefs who had been introduced to us by trade colleagues. Often, they were working as sous-chef (second in command) in their restaurant and were looking for an opportunity to become number one somewhere else.

Several of them came to see us and cooked for us and we also went to visit quite a few in the places where they were working. However, we could not find the right person. Either we were not impressed with the quality of their cooking, or they cooked well, but not in the style we wanted, or we could not afford to pay them the salary they wanted. The weeks were passing, and we started to worry. The restaurant (more properly, the bistro) would be such an important part of our future business that the food needed to be excellent.

We had already found a few other staff members. Franck Massard, a junior French sommelier who had started to work in my sommelier team just a few weeks before we announced our project, was a bit upset. He had come to work in England specifically to train with me, so he was not happy that I was leaving so soon after he had arrived. He asked me if he could come and work with me at Hotel du Vin. I went to see Mr Skan to get his permission and he very kindly agreed to let me take Franck.

James Martin, a young chef working in the pastry department of Chewton Glen, also wanted to come. He had worked in London in the kitchen of Anthony Worrall Thompson, a famous chef at the time, and Robin and I offered James the role of second in the kitchen. However, as the weeks passed and we still had not found our head chef, we asked James to cook a few dishes for us. After tasting his dishes Robin and I were impressed. It was very much in the style we wanted, and while not everything was perfect, it was nonetheless an excellent standard. There ensued a quick discussion between Robin and me and fifteen minutes later we offered James Martin the position of head chef of Hotel du Vin, which he accepted immediately.

Slowly we started to recruit a few more team members. However, all the people we employed understood that they would only begin to work for us two or three weeks before we opened as we did not want to start spending unnecessarily on wages before we had to.

During this period of planning an utterly unexpected event occurred.

We heard on the radio in the summer of 1994 that Rosemary West, the infamous murderer who, with her husband Fred West, was accused of murdering several children, was to be judged at Winchester Crown Court, and the case would begin in October 1994. Her husband Fred had committed suicide before the trial so only she would be judged. Obviously, it was an appalling case, but it attracted a great deal of international media attention. Winchester Crown Court was only a short walking distance from Hotel du Vin and our large car park backed onto the court. This unexpected (and horrible) court case came to play a big part in the success of our early months of trading.

On the financial side, we obtained a small amount of money from the local authority to help restore our old building. We also raised some through a sponsorship scheme, inspired by Mosimann's Club in London, which had some function rooms sponsored by famous luxury brands. Each of our bedrooms would be named after a winery, in exchange for a sponsorship fee of between £4,000 and £6,000, depending on the size and location of the bedroom, for a three-year contract. In exchange, the sponsoring companies would get the use of six bedrooms free each year and a 20 per cent discount when using the restaurant. They could bring their own wines for an event and not have to pay corkage. Furthermore, we would have a minimum of two of their wines on our wine list, though it was our choice and we did not have to give them any exclusivity; if I had a Californian sponsor, I could still list many other Californian wine brands on the wine list. I was in charge of finding the sponsors, as obviously I had a lot of wine contacts. Robin had contacted a few potential sponsors he knew personally very early on and three had said yes already, so I did not start my hunt for sponsors from nothing at all.

It was not an easy task to convince wine producers to part with some money, as Robin and I had no real track record as businessmen. The London International Wine Trade Fair of May 1994 seemed the perfect opportunity to meet many potential sponsors and present them with the details of our project. On the first day of the Fair, I did around twenty-five presentations. My spiel lasted ten minutes, and then I handed over a document to anybody interested. By the end of the day I was exhausted, and I had just four or five potential sponsors who told me that they would think about it, so not a great outcome. Nevertheless, I decided to do one more presentation before the Fair closed for the day, and as I was near a Chilean wine stand, I thought I would do it there. On the Chilean stand I recognised a famous winemaker called Ignacio Recabarren and thought I would do my presentation to him, as he was a high-powered professional. A lady greeted me and asked me if she could help, but I said, 'No thank you, I really wanted to speak with Ignacio.' She was upset that I did not want to engage with her and told me sharply that I would have to wait until Ignacio was free, as he was talking with someone. It was not that I did not want to engage with her, but that day I had done several presentations to so many wine people, just to be told many times over, 'Sorry, it is not my department, can you please recount to my colleague here what you just told me'!

I really did not want to do another spiel, only to be told at the end of it, 'Sorry, it is Ignacio you should speak to.' Anyway, after ten minutes, Ignacio came to see me, and I presented our project to him. At the end, he thanked me but said that actually the person I should do the presentation to was the lady I had just rejected, as she was his boss. I felt so stupid. Ignacio called her over and so I redid my spiel just for her, but her body language was telling me all the time that she would not do business with me as she had felt snubbed, and of course, at the end of my presentation she declined my offer with a certain pleasure. I couldn't blame her, and I had not wanted to upset her, but it was simply the end of a long day.

Fortunately, I did enjoy several successful outcomes. Five months before we opened Hotel du Vin, I was in Milan with Nina for the final of the Sopexa Italian Sommelier competition. As the winner of the International Sopexa competition 1992, I had won a wine trip for two people to the country of my choice, and I had selected Italy. The week of my Italian wine trip corresponded with the date of the Italian Sopexa

1994 final and so I had been invited to be a guest judge. In the evening at the gala dinner I found myself sitting next to the CEO of a Cognac house, Cognac Renault, which was only well known in a few countries. During the evening I happened to mention our project to him and also the sponsorship scheme, without thinking he would be interested; also, I really wanted wine sponsors, not spirit sponsors, so I was certainly not trying to make a sale. Nevertheless, he told me that he could be interested and asked me to send him a contract to consider. I did, reasoning that, after all, Cognac is made from grapes, and if we had one spirit sponsor among all the wine sponsors it would not be the end of the world. To my surprise he returned the contract, signed, and quickly paid the fee.

A month before we opened, I finally had a full set of sponsors – sixteen in total, covering the thirteen bedrooms, a lounge and a function room; I even managed to get a sponsor for the statue of Bacchus. The Roman god brought a lucky combination of agriculture, wine and fertility to the corridor close to the entrance to the hotel. We raised around £70,000 and that proved hugely helpful. Among the different sponsors we had Beringer from California, USA; Brown Brothers from Australia; Castello Vicchiomaggio from Chianti, Italy; Laroche from Chablis, France; Marqués de Cáceres from Rioja, Spain; Villa Maria from New Zealand; some Champagne Houses including Pol Roger, Veuve Clicquot and Pommery; and more.

As D-Day approached, our team was taking shape.

Food was at the heart of our business, so we had to get it right. At the time, Winchester only had a small number of excellent restaurants. Right at the beginning, Nina, Robin, his wife Judy and I had set out to eat in all of the restaurants we thought were of any worth – all four of them. Winchester had been an affluent town for a long time, and we were convinced that there was room for one more restaurant, providing it was excellent and different. In the final weeks before the opening, James, Robin and I worked on the menu, making sure the dishes would be popular, easy to produce and costed at the right price. It was very stimulating, and we would look at different cookbooks to get some inspiration, especially those specialising in modern bistro food like fish-cakes and lamb shanks.

The wine list was also exciting, as I was starting with a blank canvas. I had to make sure I had at least two wines from each sponsor, but I could do what I wanted with the rest, although I could not spend a fortune on stock. I needed a well-balanced list with plenty of affordable wines of different styles and regions. As wine tastes had become more sophisticated, people were growing confident about trying new things, from Chilean Cabernet to the increasingly popular offerings from South Africa. We also had some great classics and a small range of very fine wines. To save money, Robin and I decided to lend to the hotel a few bottles of some of our own best wines, as both of us had a few lovely bottles at home.

September 1994 came around and we left Chewton Glen so we could devote all of our time to the project. Most of the refurbishment work was completed two weeks before the opening date, and we were beginning to take receipt of everything from furniture to cooking equipment, to computers and televisions, to cases of wine. It dawned on us that we didn't have any night-time security, and it would be easy for thieves to raid our hotel.

To prevent that, we decided to sleep at the hotel. As the beds hadn't yet arrived, Robin and I, and sometimes Nina, slept on the floor on improvised camp beds. It was fun – Robin slept in the room next to mine, but we left our doors open so we could communicate. It was an old building, and even with the recent repairs, we could hear creaking and other strange noises during the night. We weren't always sure it was the building, so occasionally one of us would wake the other up and say, 'Did you hear that funny noise, was it you?' 'No, it wasn't me,' and then we would get up, each armed with a broom and a torch in our hands, going down the stairs to do a full inspection of the hotel. Often, after our security round, we had a cup of instant coffee and then went back to sleep, ready for Nina to arrive in the morning with fresh pastries for breakfast.

We also had to organise an opening party for Saturday 1 October. Owing to the size of the hotel we weren't able to have a huge number of people, just 100 or so. The list included the fourteen shareholders and their partners, a representative of each of the sponsors, a few suppliers, a small number of journalists we knew well, our PR team and quite a few key players from Winchester and the surrounding area, plus a few close friends and family members.

The party started at seven o'clock with a glass of Champagne on arrival. During the evening we provided a buffet of mostly finger food, but plenty of it. We had also set up a drink buffet and to save on costs I had asked all of our sponsors if they would kindly donate six bottles of one of their wines for the occasion. Around 9.30 p.m. we had a few short speeches, principally to thank everyone, and by 11 p.m. the party started to die down. Although, Robin, Judy, Nina and I, along with a few brave people, carried on partying for a few more hours, it turned out not to be a great idea, as we had to start trading the next day.

As we only had thirteen rooms, we could not accommodate everyone for the party, so we ended up booking a dozen rooms in a hotel not far from us. One of the sponsors, a director of Cognac Renault (not the CEO I had met in Milan, but a colleague) asked if she could come a day earlier, as she could get a plane landing at Southampton Airport on the Friday but not on the Saturday. We happily accepted and I went to get her from the airport, even though it was a manic time. She was a very chic French lady with real class – an aristocrat. I took her luggage and we went to my car, happily chit-chatting. When we finally arrived at the car, I put her luggage in the boot and very gallantly opened the door for her to sit – and my heart sank. I was giving a lift to a very sophisticated lady wearing beautiful clothes, in my very tatty old car. Not only was it an old car, but as Tony, my father-in-law, was a welder, he had put all sorts of materials in the car and the seats were damaged and not very clean. Anyway, she did not say a word and twenty minutes later we arrived at Hotel du Vin. We had managed to get her room just about ready. However, as the team was getting on with all the jobs in readiness for the party and everything else, we did not have time to cook for her that night. Totally disorganised, I had not booked anywhere and the only place I could find was the local pizza restaurant, serving mediocre food and playing very loud music all evening. Nina was not impressed by my lack of thinking. I am sure the French lady must have wondered why on earth her CEO had agreed to sponsor our hotel.

Among the many mistakes we made, the biggest was not to have invited Mr and Mrs Skan to the opening party. The Wednesday and Thursday before the party we had done some dry runs or 'soft openings', meaning that some chosen guests were invited, allowing the team to get some practice. On the Thursday we had invited Mr and Mrs Skan to dine and stay over and all went very well.

However, when we were putting together the list of invitees for the party, we stupidly assumed that inviting the Skans for a dry run evening was enough. Perhaps because we had so much on our minds at that period, we were unable to grasp the magnitude of our mistake.

The Thursday of the week following the party, *Caterer* magazine, the UK publication for the hotel and restaurant trade, did a four-page feature on the opening party of Hotel du Vin with a few photos. To make it worse, on the photos you could see a few staff from Chewton Glen who had come on their days off to help us for the opening party. Upon seeing the *Caterer* feature, Mr and Mrs Skan were quite rightly furious and wrote a polite but strongly worded letter to Robin, telling him how disappointed they were with the way our opening party had been handled by us, both using some of their staff without their permission and then not having the manners to invite them. They saw Robin as the leader in our business partnership and so I escaped their wrath, even though I was as guilty as Robin. Happily, we were able to overcome such an oversight on our part and we remain firm friends with the Skans today.

We made plenty of mistakes. Overall, though, we were on time. It was on with the show.

Thirteen
Adapting to Being an Hotelier

In retrospect, it was not wise to open the day after the opening party as we could all have done with a rest day. We had agreed that Robin would stay on after the party, sleeping on the sofa; he would oversee breakfast. I left the party with Nina around three o'clock on the Sunday morning, went home (forty-five minutes' drive) to sleep a few hours and was back at the hotel for 11 a.m. I was in charge of lunch and dinner that day.

That first day of trading was the hardest working day of my life. Lunch was a nightmare, even though we only had half of the restaurant taken. It was the hiccups that caused the stress: we had devised a Sunday lunch menu, but it was boring. That wouldn't have been so bad if the execution had been first-rate, but it wasn't. Our team was too exhausted.

A guest I knew well from Chewton Glen, and with whom I had been on fairly good terms, had booked a table for himself and his wife. I went to see them while they were eating their main course and he told me, aggressively, that the food was very poor and our restaurant a complete joke. I apologised, but I was upset. We had a few other complaints, either because people had waited too long or because the food was not great. None of the guests could say anything positive and I ended up not charging some of the items on several of the bills as a goodwill gesture for our shortcomings. I felt quite deflated and fairly demoralised.

In the evening, the kitchen team raised their game and produced a much better level of food. Nevertheless, it was not a pleasant service. As most of the Winchester restaurants were closed on Sunday evenings, it followed that the owners, managers and head chefs of those restaurants had booked tables in our restaurant. That evening, half of our fifteen tables were occupied by competitors. The atmosphere was awful. They hardly talked to me, but as they all knew each other well, I could see some of them leaving their tables from time to time to talk at another competitor's table, obviously comparing their thoughts about our food and our restaurant. They whispered so I could not hear what they said, which in a way made it worse. I felt very stressed and despondent. Fortunately, around nine o'clock, when every guest who had booked a table was seated and eating, Thierry, a maitre d'hotel from Chewton Glen and a lovely guy, entered the restaurant and asked me if it was too late for him to have a quick bite. I was so pleased to see him – at last, a friendly face!

Despite the atmosphere of that evening, we had an excellent rapport with our competitors, as Robin and I had met all of them in the weeks leading up to our opening. However, as we had made a lot of noise through a strong marketing campaign before we opened, they were perhaps irritated by all the attention we had already generated and understandably they were worried that we would take business from them. Thus, they were not especially warm towards me that evening. However, over time, people started to talk more about the Winchester restaurant scene and everyone ending up profiting from it.

The day after the opening, on Monday morning, Robin and I debriefed and considered how we could correct some of the early mistakes. We did not have much time to ponder, as the lunch service was starting at noon and incredibly, in the space of thirty minutes, the restaurant was full. The atmosphere was buzzing and while it was hard, it was extremely stimulating and exciting to be that busy so early on.

The pattern did not change, and every day was busy in the restaurant. It became even busier two weeks later when the Rosemary West court case started. Not only was the restaurant busy, but suddenly our bedrooms were full too. As we were a brand new hotel in Winchester and close to the Winchester Crown Court, all the journalists wanted to stay with us. We had thirteen bedrooms but could only sell twelve as we did not have a night porter (we could not afford one), so either Robin or Nina and I would stay in the hotel each night. From Monday to Thursday evening we sold ten rooms to journalists, keeping two for other guests, and at weekends we had plenty of tourists staying, so the level of room occupancy was very high. Among the journalists we had one from each of the main UK newspapers, *The Times*, *Telegraph*, *Guardian*, *Daily Mail*, *Sun* and a few others. The case began in mid-October and, aside from a two-week break at Christmas, lasted around three months; the journalists stayed with us all of that time.

Not only was it great to have all the journalists spending well in the hotel and in the restaurant in the evening, but it also brought other positive effects. Some of the journalists told their colleagues in charge of the restaurant review section about us, and we quickly had food critics coming to visit.

The most important review occurred very early on. During the fourth week after our opening, Jonathan Meades rang and booked a table with us. Jonathan Meades was the food critic for *The Times* on Saturday and the most powerful food critic in the UK. He had a full page in one of the supplements of the newspaper and rated restaurants out of ten. It was not unusual for him to give some restaurants he did not think much of some very low marks like one, two or three. We were very worried in anticipation of his forthcoming visit.

The day before he came to review us, we spent a lot of time working with James on the menu, making sure it was balanced. We also read through Jonathan's columns. We knew he liked hearty food, so we made sure we had a few hearty dishes on the menu that we hoped he would enjoy.

When he arrived, we welcomed him in a friendly manner, but did not overdo it. Robin stayed most of the time in the kitchen to check, double-check and triple-check each of the dishes before they left the kitchen, not just the dishes for Jonathan, but for everyone, as we knew he would look closely at what was being served to other tables around him. On my side, I stayed in the restaurant and ensured that the service was very smooth and faultless. I spoke a bit with Jonathan, but not too much, as we did not want him to think he was getting special treatment.

Three weeks later the review came out – and the full page was extremely complimentary about our new business, both the food and us. In addition, he gave us six out of ten, which was perfect. A six from Jonathan Meades was an excellent mark, especially when we were a bistro and not a fine dining restaurant. In fact, had he given us a seven or an eight that could have been dangerous for us, as it would have raised guest expectations too high. We were already a very busy place when his review came out, but I remember that for several days the telephone never stopped ringing, with people having read his review all wanting a table.

When a new business starts there are some employees who love it and thrive in the evolving environment, while others do not like it, cannot adapt and quickly quit. We had our fair share of staff departures, but overall it was not too bad and most of our key members stayed with us for more than just the early months. We would be very proud in the following years of how many of them developed so well, even those we didn't always expect to do so. On our second Sunday of trading, during the afternoon I was sitting at the reception desk for an hour ready to answer phone calls when I saw a young woman with her mother entering the hotel. They saw me and the young woman, who was in her early twenties, told me, 'I graduated from university a few weeks ago, I live in Winchester and I am looking for my first job.'

I looked at her and said, 'Fine, if you are happy to work in the restaurant come tomorrow at 10 a.m. We can give you a try.' Her name was Megan Lloyd Davies, a tall, attractive young lady, who was well educated and smart with a beautiful smile and lot of energy. In the first two weeks she found it hard to adapt to a working life, the long hours of the business and the fact that Robin and I were looking for high standards, which for her was initially difficult, having never worked in catering before.

Megan moaned and complained a lot. Three weeks after she started, I took her to one side and I told her that unless she stopped moaning and focused on her job, she could go and work somewhere else. Within a few days of our chat Megan was getting on with the job and very quickly became the star of our restaurant. The customers loved her and a few months later we promoted her to restaurant manager. Megan left us two years later, as she went to do a journalism course, and is now a very successful author, having written many books. All these years later, I am delighted to say we are still great friends and Nina and I remain very fond of her.

While the early months had gone well in terms of trading, it took a little while before Robin and I adjusted to our new positions. Robin had been my boss for six and a half years at Chewton Glen and occasionally he would carry on behaving as if he was still my superior; conversely, I would often refer to him to seek his approval, because I lacked confidence when taking some decisions. Slowly, we each adapted in our new roles and our business partnership worked well.

Nina worked with us for the first year, doing all sorts of jobs Robin and I did not have time to focus on. She was helpful in the restaurant, oversaw the housekeeping department and often helped in reception. I remember one day Robin was off, and Nina and I were in charge. The boiler stopped working and Nina managed to sort it out using a screwdriver and pliers while speaking on the phone with a technician telling her what to do.

After eight months of trading we decided that it was time to employ a night porter. Until then we had only been able to sell a maximum of twelve rooms each night as Robin or I still needed to stay in the hotel. It could be complicated at times, as occasionally some residents would have dinner outside the hotel, so if we missed giving them a back-door key we had to wait until they came in. On rare occasions some came back very late and we had to wait up for them, which made for a very long day.

From a financial point of view, the first year had gone well, although we had a relatively big mortgage for a small hotel. In 1995, the official

UK interest rate was 6.75 per cent, but the bank was charging more on top, so the monthly repayments were quite hefty. Robin had taken a pay cut when compared to his Chewton Glen salary, while I had a rise, as my Chewton Glen salary was not very high, but Nina worked unpaid for the whole year at Hotel du Vin. In addition, we had quite a lot of staff.

Looking back, there are many reasons why Hotel du Vin took off so fast. The period over 1995 and 1996 was an excellent time to start a business in the UK. The economy was beginning to do well again. Winchester was in need of an excellent hotel and there was room for more quality restaurants. Our concept was modern, with tasty food and a wine list with plenty of choice that was very reasonably priced. The bistro had a lovely retro style, with plenty of memorabilia to look at. We had a mishmash of tables and chairs and no tablecloths, a very relaxed atmosphere. The staff were friendly and the service, while professional, was unstuffy. Robin, Nina and I spent a lot of time on the floor to make sure the food and the service were of a high level and that the team was led by example. Judy, Robin's wife, was instrumental in ensuring that Winchester and then the later hotels were all stylish and comfortably quirky. Her decor was quickly adopted by others, which was a big compliment to us all.

Of course, mistakes were made, but because Robin, Nina or I were there, we could apologise, rectify and compensate if needed. Also, even when all went well, not everyone liked our concept. Because we were very busy the bistro could be quite noisy, and some people did not like it. Fortunately, there were enough people who liked us and kept coming back.

One guest, Mike Martin, a skilled technician who was working on a building project locally, stayed with us for a very long period. Every weekend he would go home, north of London, but as the local project lasted around eighteen months, he took up residence with us during the weekdays for all of that time. While his case was exceptional, we had many regulars, both for the bistro and for the hotel.

I learned a lot from the experience. For example, just prior to opening, we had begun taking bookings. Renovations were still going on, and while Robin, Nina and I tried to be as organised as we could, working from a building site is not always conducive to perfect administration and a few mistakes occurred. One day, going through future bookings, we realised that we had double-booked our function room for two evening events. Both parties were of a similar size of around twenty-five to thirty covers each. The evening was less than three weeks away, the second week after our opening. Had we had no restaurant bookings that evening we could have given the restaurant to one of the parties, but we already had four tables booked. It was too late to call the organisers of both parties and ask one of them if it was possible to change the date. Similarly, we could have phoned the restaurant customers and told them that unfortunately we had to cancel their restaurant bookings, but it would have been bad PR, especially having just opened. We decided there was no choice but to honour all of the bookings. We thought long and hard and came up with a plan. First, we stopped taking any more bookings for the restaurant in order that the kitchen could cope with all the diners that evening. Secondly, we realised that one of the two organisers had never been to see us and all details of their event had been dealt with on the phone. Therefore, the guest had no idea where the function room was, or even if we had more than one function room. Our lounge was a strange shape, but if we were to remove all of the sofas and other furniture, it could just about accommodate thirty people for dinner. For that evening we hired some banqueting tables and chairs and set up our lounge as a banqueting room. When the guests of the first party arrived, it was a bit chaotic as they had to have their pre-dinner drinks in the corridor/reception, instead of the lounge, but they did not seem to mind. Fortunately, the two parties were not booked at the same time, so by the time the guests of the second party arrived, those of the first party were seated, so again we could serve the pre-dinner drinks for the second party in the corridor/reception. It was a tense evening, but everyone in our team worked extremely hard and we managed to pull it all off. Both organisers were happy and the party in the lounge never realised they were not seated in a function room.

Then there was the midweek dinner service that was particularly busy. The service was going well, and the customers were happy. It was probably around 10 p.m. and all the main courses had been served. I mentioned to Robin that I was going to the cellar to check the stock quantity of some of our wines. Robin looked around and told me that the team seemed in control so he would come with me. Nina was in reception checking some bills, so I told her that we would be in the cellar for ten minutes and if we were needed just to call us. The Hotel du Vin Winchester cellar was underground and while not big, it had great character, with a few alcoves and lovely corners. In one alcove, I had put some really special bottles that were not even on the list yet. Robin was looking in that section and asked me to give him some short comments on some of the wines. I took a bottle of Clos de La Roche Domaine Dujac 1989 and started to tell him how great this wine was and why. Suddenly Robin suggested that we should open the bottle and try it. I was surprised, but he did not need to tell me twice! I went to grab some clean glasses, opened the bottle and served us some wine. It tasted wonderful, perhaps a bit too young, but nevertheless beautifully perfumed, incredibly silky on the palate and fabulously delicious. We sat down on some wine boxes and reflected on how well our new business was going. We were enjoying this stunning wine and as a completely improvised moment it was pure heaven. An hour later we were still in the cellar finishing the wine when we heard Nina calling us from the top of the stairs and, without seeing us, asking if we were all right. We laughed and answered that we had almost finished the work we were doing and would be back soon.

On another Saturday evening we had a group of nice young men, seemingly well educated and quite well mannered, staying with us. However, they were going to a wedding outside the hotel and so were not having dinner with us. As it was still the period when we did not have a night porter, we gave the leader of the group a back-door key. Nina and I finished the bistro work late, around one o'clock on the Sunday morning, but the young lads had not come back yet from the wedding, so we went to bed.

Around three o'clock Nina woke me up and said, 'Can you hear the noise in the corridor?'

As I was really still asleep, I vaguely said, 'What noise?'

Nina shook me awake and said, 'The young lads! They are back and they are mucking around having an improvised party in the corridor. They are going to wake up the other residents. Go and sort them out!'

I said, 'You are crazy, in the state they are, they will not listen to me, you go!'

So Nina did. She went into the corridor, in her pyjamas, and asked them in her most authoritative manner: 'What's going on? What are you doing raiding our linen cupboard? I give you two minutes to sort yourselves out, stop all that noise and go back to your rooms! Aren't you ashamed to behave like that and disturb so many of the other guests?' Anyway, these young lads, all built like strong rugby players, were embarrassed in front of my wife, who stands at just five feet, and retreated very sheepishly and peacefully back to their rooms. Had I gone myself I would most probably had received a bloody nose! They said sorry the next morning and all apologised to Nina for the disturbance and for making such a mess of the linen cupboard.

Dealing with the wine trade was always interesting, as some wine merchants have huge personalities and characters, as for example, the legendary Bill Baker, or Robin Yapp, who did so much for small growers from the Loire Valley and the Rhône Valley in the UK at a time when those areas were not so fashionable. As we were called Hotel du Vin, we needed to have an excellent wine offering and thus we dealt with many wine merchants. Franck Massard, my first head sommelier, and I would meet them, and these encounters occasionally brought us some exciting moments.

One particular wine merchant made a great pitch to us and after a few dealings with him, I realised that he had the knack of upselling. He was a young Frenchman and he represented some excellent wines, mostly from small to medium-size growers of excellent reputation. We always bought from him a few more cases than we should have had. One of his tricks was that once we had tasted and given our order for a particular wine that we liked, he would say in a very serious tone: 'His wines are so in demand, we could only secure twenty cases for the whole country!' If I really liked that wine, I used to feel a sense of panic and begged him to let us have one or two extra cases, to which he would reply: 'Let me see . . .' and he would look at his stock sheet and 'umm' and 'aah' for a moment. 'I don't know . . . Well, fine, as you buy a lot of wines from us!'

Another merchant, with whom we were dealing for the first time, presented some lovely wine to Franck and we ordered ten mixed cases. Then I noticed from his list that he was selling Henschke, Hill of Grace, a cult Australian wine that was not yet that well known in England. I asked him if we could buy a few bottles of it, but he replied in an apologetic tone that sadly he did not have much and he had to keep it for his regular customers, which was fair enough. It was almost midday when we finished dealing with him. As he was leaving, he turned back towards me and asked if he could have a table for a quick bite to eat. I said: 'We have a lot of bookings, but if you are gone in an hour and I can have your table back then, with pleasure.' During his main course, a rib-eye steak, I went to see if he was enjoying it, to which he replied with a genuine smile, 'Delicious.' So, completely out of the blue I said to him: 'Right, your meal is on me, if you let me buy a few bottles of Henschke, Hill of Grace.'

He looked at me and said, 'Deal!' and we shook hands, thus proving that there is nothing that a delicious meal cannot sort out.

We also carried on the wine dinner formula from Chewton Glen. As we had a banqueting room that could accommodate forty-eight people, we had an ideal setting, so we held them once a month, on a Sunday evening. Sundays can be a quiet time for hotels, because the weekend guests have left and the majority of business people come on the Monday. This leaves many rooms unoccupied. Creating an interesting event can be one way to generate revenue, plus it gives the head chef an opportunity to design a special menu, while the sommeliers benefit from the chance to discover new wines and hear different guest speakers.

These dinners were so successful that later on, when we had several Hotel du Vin outlets, I would organise one wine dinner each Sunday in rotation within the different hotels.

One of the most unusual we had was a dinner with Jane MacQuitty, the wine correspondent for *The Times* on Saturday. In one article she had reviewed the main, big commercial wine brands and given each of them a mark out of twenty. I don't remember all the scores, but most of those famous commercial wine brands had obtained marks well below ten. I thought that was interesting, so I asked Jane if she would mind coming to the Hotel du Vin to do a wine dinner at which we would serve some of these 'dinosaurs' of the wine world, and we would put alongside them wines of similar prices, but that we thought had much more character. Jane accepted with great enthusiasm, and we quickly agreed on the famous commercial wine brands and the alternative wines, mostly from small producers. Normally when I was organising a wine dinner, I dealt with wine merchants and arranged for the wines to be delivered a week in advance. However, in this case I found myself in the wine aisle of my local supermarket, filling my shopping trolley with a dozen bottles each of Blue Nun, Mateus Rosé, Piat d'Or and similar very well-known wines. Walking towards the checkout, I met two neighbours, who stopped to say hello and have a chat. I could have died with embarrassment, and I did not know what to say or do. I can easily imagine what they must have thought when glancing at the contents of my trolley: 'Here is our supposed wine expert neighbour. Look at what he is drinking at home!' After a quick (very, very quick) chat with them, I paid the cashier, but also prayed that I would not meet anyone else I knew on the way to my car.

The early years of Hotel du Vin went better than we could have imagined, and not only from a financial point of view. In our second year, Hotel du Vin Winchester won a Catey Award – the Oscars of the catering and hospitality industry – for Newcomer of the Year.

Things were happening fast.

Fourteen

Exciting Challenges

When we started Hotel du Vin, Robin and I weren't sure how it would go and so we did not have a grand plan for the future. Our main concern was to ensure that our business survived and then became established. It is often suggested in business that people starting a new project should have an exit strategy in mind from the moment they start conceiving their project. This makes a lot of sense, as it focuses the owners' minds on who the business could appeal to and so provides a clear direction from day one. However, like everything in life, there are two sides of the coin. The danger can be that owners are so concerned with the future that they make everything fit within the exit plan, even if it doesn't suit the business, thus endangering its success right from the start. In our early days, we had no such strategy, but we did develop one of sorts, over time.

As we began our second year of trading in 1995 one of our shareholders, Ashley Levett, made a very enticing offer to the other shareholders and they agreed to sell him their shares. Consequently, the structure of the shareholding changed, and out of this new deal our partly paid shares became fully paid. It had been great to have fourteen shareholders, all of whom were excellent ambassadors for the hotel, but having only one was easier.

One of the ex-shareholders, Bob Niddrie, was a retired accountant and early on in our project he had been a non-executive director with us. He remained in that role after the restructure. It was extremely useful to have Bob on the board as he would point out some of the possible dangers when we were a bit over-enthusiastic with our ideas. In addition, he knew I was not confident about reading official accounting statements and so he always made sure I fully understood the financial situation. We named him Uncle Bob.

After the restructuring, we bought the derelict house and piece of land adjacent to the hotel. The ground floor of that house was converted into a bar and a small extension of the bistro and the first floor was transformed into two bedrooms. On the piece of land, we built four bedrooms, each with a little patio terrace. Having a separate bar solved many problems, and the extra six rooms increased our revenue nicely, giving us the ability to deal with larger functions that required bedrooms for most of their guests.

In January 1995, I started the Master of Wine programme again, but of course I was not required to attend the blind tasting sessions. In the four months leading up to the theory exam I did what I could, but regrettably, because of the huge amount of work with the Hotel du Vin, I had little time to spare. When the exam took place, I had made very little progress on my essay-writing skills and so I failed my second theory attempt.

The rest of 1995 continued to be extremely busy at the hotel and so I had no time to plan for the exam for the following year. Therefore, when in January 1996 I restarted the theory programme, I was not much more advanced than the previous year and so in 1996 I failed my third theory attempt. With hindsight, with all that was happening in my professional life, it was a waste of time to have tried to complete the exam in those two years of 1995 and 1996.

Indeed, by 1996, we were more organised at the hotel. Thus, once having taken the exam, I could have carried on working on my essay techniques in provision for the following year. However once in early May of 1996 I had taken the exam, I then gave all my attention to the competition for Best Sommelier of Europe 1996.

My wine competition career had not, after all, ground to a halt. After my great competition year of 1992, I had shifted my focus to the Master of Wine qualification and was convinced that I would never compete again for a sommelier title.

Indeed, in the latter part of 1994, the Best Sommelier of Europe 1994 was taking place in Reims, Champagne and not for one second had I considered applying for it; when the Best Sommelier in the World 1995 took place in Tokyo, I ignored that too.

But in 1996, the year of the next Best Sommelier of Europe, it was different. After I'd won UK Sommelier of the Year in 1992, I'd won a trip to Champagne Ruinart, which included a dinner with the CEO of the company, Roland de Calonne, and his charming wife. Champagne Ruinart were sponsors of a number of sommelier competitions, and the founder of the Best Sommelier of Europe. M. de Calonne asked me to re-enter the competition. Before I could answer, he looked me in the eyes, and said, 'Gerard, we are all citizens of Europe now. The European Union is getting bigger – Europe is the future! You must do the competition again!'

I politely and diplomatically agreed with him, but without great conviction. M. de Calonne had been the CEO of Ruinart for a long time and was a very charismatic person. He was a gentleman and a very imposing personality, so when he spoke, even if you did not always agree with him, you took notice.

In life we can all experience something important without straightaway realising how important it is. This suggestion by M. de Calonne was one of those situations. His words did not seem that significant to me then, but I would remember them for a long time to come.

When in early 1996 the question arose of who would represent the UK for the Best Sommelier of Europe competition taking place in the autumn of 1996, those words came back to me with force.

By now, we had been running the hotel for more than a year and while we did not have it all completely sorted, Robin and I were getting better organised. Megan had become an excellent restaurant manager and that took a bit of pressure off me. Some days I didn't have to appear until mid-afternoon, and so I had time in the mornings for competition preparation.

The Best Sommelier of Europe 1996 was going to be in October, so in May I calculated I had just enough time to prepare. It was a bit of a gamble, as really for such a competition you need more than just five or six months of preparation, but I reasoned that I might just be able to pull it off. I was also on the Master of Wine programme, which was helpful in some respects, particularly for the information it offered about viticulture and winemaking.

The Academy of Food and Wine Service, the official body representing the UK at the Association Sommelier International, wanted to send a strong UK candidate. When Jeremy Bennett, the then president, heard that I was considering applying, he called me and we met. He told me that I would be the best person to represent the UK and he and his board members had agreed to select me if I wished to go.

In addition, I was lucky because the two most recent winners of the UK Sommelier of the Year, Henri Chapon in 1995 and Franck Massard in 1996, were French; unlike me, they did not hold British nationality and thus could not represent the UK in Europe. Champagne Ruinart, the European sponsor, only wanted competitors of the nationality of the country they represented. That made the case for my selection even easier.

I quickly formed a plan. I asked Henri Chapon, with whom I had become friends, to help me by setting some service, food and wine and tasting exercises once a month. I'd met Henri during my Chewton Glen days. When he was preparing for the UK Sommelier of the Year in 1995, I set up several training sessions for him. So, I knew Henri would enjoy helping me in my quest to win the Best Sommelier of Europe 1996.

The next thing I did was to contact Le Creuset, the kitchen utensil company. I knew their managers well, as their head office was not far from Winchester and many of the Le Creuset team held meetings at Hotel du Vin. I asked the managing director if Le Creuset would be happy to sponsor me. I wanted to buy a lot of bottles of wine for my blind tasting training sessions and sponsorship would help cover other costs. He quickly agreed and we set up a photo shoot with me recommending their range of Le Creuset Screwpull corkscrews.

In preparation for the tough and very wide-ranging theory section of the competition, I spent the first six weeks updating my files. I made sure I had the latest information about the different wine regions of the world. I redid some of my many wine maps; I completed, as needed, my files on viticulture and winemaking, and the same for wine history, wine laws and regulations, liqueurs, spirits, sake, beer, mineral water and even tea and coffee. I was ready to learn (and re-learn) it all.

Among the many exercises I did was to sit down and reproduce all the wine maps, complete with all the facts. When I checked my attempts against the original, I would re-do it all over again if I made a single mistake. I got up early every day to practise memory drills; eventually, I was so exhausted that either my eyes would begin watering, or I would fall asleep at my desk. But I didn't stop.

For the blind tasting part, I bought a lot of wines, as well as plenty of miniatures of liqueurs and spirits. Every morning Nina would serve three wines, along with a series of six liqueurs and spirits in black glasses, so I had no clue as to what the liquid might be. One day I would give an oral summation of one wine, while writing about two; the next I would do the opposite, giving an oral summation of two wines, while writing about one. In the final months we increased the number of wines to six each day. My goal was to develop a deep tasting vocabulary that was well structured but not robotic. I had worked out my own way to describe the wines, but I wanted enough vocabulary variation so that I wouldn't sound repetitive. This is a tricky task, as it becomes difficult not to double up on words when comparing similar wines.

Nosing liqueurs or spirits from black glasses can sometimes be easier, because the colour of the beverage can be misleading. To ensure that I did as much blind tasting as I could, one of my sommeliers would prepare for me a series of liqueurs and spirits, and one or two wines.

In the summer of 1996, a young French sommelier called Vincent Gasnier had come to work with us. Vincent was passionate about wine competitions and on his days off would come to the hotel or to my home to set blind tasting sessions for me. He always gave me his honest feedback and even though he was young, he often had some very valid, constructive criticisms. One day at home in my kitchen Vincent had selected and prepared for me a series of six wines blind to assess orally. By the end of the session, I had acquitted myself relatively well on the identification side of the wines, having uncovered grapes and regions for four of the wines, but annoyingly missed them for two of the wines. I asked Vincent, apart from the identification aspect, what he thought of my presentation. Vincent commented that while my vocabulary for describing the wines was excellent, he thought I was not speaking with a voice of authority and so not engendering great confidence, even if my vocabulary was extremely precise. He added that I was looking at the glass too much when I was talking. Instead, I needed to stand upright and look at the audience like someone with plenty of self-assurance. I was surprised at first, but really grateful for such useful feedback. Vincent was right – I needed to project an aura of authority without being arrogant.

For both the service and the food-and-wine-matching sections, I was practising regularly thanks to some tasks set up by my sommelier team at the hotel, and once a month, for a full day, I would be put through my paces by Henri Chapon. We would work on service aspects such as my decanting skills, trying to improve the technique and the speed. The goal was for my skills to become second nature to me, so I could execute them perfectly while thinking of other issues, the way an experienced driver doesn't think about the brakes or gearbox, but instead focuses on the road and the traffic. Henri would also imagine some tricky scenarios to make it more challenging. For instance, if we were doing a food-and-wine-matching exercise, he could come up with a menu suited to white wine, but the instructions might be that the guests only drink red wine, to see if I could think of an imaginative, credible and suitable answer. We both found the exercises very stimulating.

The competition was held in Champagne and three days before Nina and I left home early in the morning to drive to Reims. We would be arriving mid- to late afternoon. I wanted to arrive early in order to relax and be really well prepared. Because we were driving, I could take all my training equipment: my theory folders, books, four cases of wine, a case full of liqueur and spirit miniatures, some tasting glasses, my uniform, a tricky decanter with a small opening and a wine basket, so I could practise decanting in my room.

You can't make much difference by practising in the last two days, but it was psychologically comforting to have all those items with me. All forty-eight of the bottles did get opened, thanks to Nina setting up blind tastings, and I did a lot of nosing with the miniatures.

The day before the competition, a dinner was organised for the candidates, presidents of national sommelier associations, followers and journalists. We had to come dressed in our uniforms two hours before the dinner, as official photos would be taken. It is always an exciting moment when you suddenly discover who the other competitors are. I knew a few of them from past competitions, but many were new to me as I had been out of the circuit for four years already.

There was a pre-dinner drink (a glass of Champagne Ruinart), then the dinner, with a welcome speech from Roland de Calonne. Ideally, as a candidate you would want to have a light dinner and go to your room early, but regrettably it was not possible – Champagne Ruinart had put on a superb dinner. In addition, all the important instructions for the competition day were issued at the end of the dinner, so we had to stay until the last moment.

The dinner was delicious and the different cuvées of Ruinart served with it were sumptuous, but like most of the candidates, I ate moderately and hardly drank the Champagnes as I wanted to be in perfect condition the following morning.

The day after, we all met in the lobby of our hotel around nine and were taken for a tour around the Ruinart cellars. The visit lasted two hours and was followed by a tutored tasting of the latest Ruinart range with Jean-François Barot, the head winemaker, Chef de Cave of Champagne Ruinart. Although my mind was more on the competition that would start in the afternoon, I knew that it was important to pay attention to the visit and the tasting. Indeed, it was perfectly possible that in the theory paper there might be a question related to what we had seen and been told during the visit, and similarly it was possible that among the several wines for the different blind tasting exercises, one Ruinart cuvée would be used.

The visit and tutored tasting were followed by a light lunch for the candidates and then around three o'clock we were taken to the room in which the questionnaire and the written blind tasting would take place.

We drew our candidate numbers. Then, finally, we were told to take the questionnaire on the table, open it and start writing. We had an hour and a half to work through around thirty pages of questions. I read the questions very studiously and answered as well as I could and by the end I was satisfied with my work. Of course, it doesn't matter how much you prepare for it, there are always some questions that you cannot answer, and you never know how well the other competitors have done.

The next task was the written blind tasting. I wrote some excellent comments and I did well on the identification of the wines. For a first day of competition I felt reasonably happy. In the evening we had to attend another Ruinart event and again I did not indulge much, in order to be sharp for the practical tasks.

The second day consisted of two tasks: a food and wine exercise and a decanting task. I did well on the food and wine task as I had a lot of original ideas to match the food and wines and I was full of confidence while talking to the judges. However, when I entered the other room to perform the decanting, I suddenly felt very nervous. I recognised the judges straightaway, one of whom was a sommelier I had competed against a lot in 1992 and for some strange reason that destabilised me. That was stupid of me, but in any case, I felt very uneasy and lost my assurance. I managed to perform the task required correctly and in time, but with little panache, and I was very stiff in my demeanour. I thought to myself that it might not stop me qualifying for the final, as I knew I had done so well everywhere else, but I was still worried I had blown the chance of a place.

As usual we had a Ruinart dinner that evening, and speculation abounded as to who would be the three finalists. The room was abuzz with rumour and comment. I had relaxed since the decanting task and was trying to enjoy myself. The final would take place the next afternoon so we would have the whole morning to rest and psych ourselves up in preparation for taking part in the final.

In the morning, Nina prepared me a last blind tasting training session of wines, liqueurs and spirits. I cannot remember if it went well or not, but it was more a question of going through the ropes one more time and feeling mentally ready in case I was in the final. After lunch we were taken in buses to the Reims Congress Centre, where the final would take place.

After a long wait for everyone to be seated, all the candidates were introduced to the audience. Then the three finalists were announced: Eric Duret from France, Roberto Gardini from Italy, and myself. The unsuccessful candidates were asked to leave the stage and take a seat among the audience. Then the three finalists drew their numbers for the final. I drew number one so I was the first to go, Gardini would go second and Duret last.

Sommelier competitions all tend to be run in a fairly similar way, but there are always variations from one to the other. That year the final would be run in two parts, with an intermission between them.

The first part included the service of a bottle of Ruinart Champagne to a small group of guests. It was followed by the decanting and service of a bottle of red wine to a table of four people; then the correction of a wine list that contained mistakes. I did a decent performance, but I did not feel I had mentally entered into the competition, and when I had completed the tasks I was not very happy with myself. As I was first to go and obviously could not change my performance, I was able to watch the other two candidates. Roberto did an excellent service overall and while we could not know his marks, in my head I had him ahead of me. When he had completed his turn, he came to join me, and we watched Eric's performance. I thought Eric was brilliant on certain aspects but a bit stiff on others. Nevertheless, again I placed him ahead of me. That meant that in my mind I was third, and to have a chance to win I had to perform brilliantly in the second part of the final.

The second part included the wine matching of a long tasting menu and then the blind tasting of three wines and six liqueurs and spirits. I relaxed very quickly and did, in my opinion, a superb food and wine matching. I moved on to the blind tasting of the wines and by then I was very comfortable, completely in a zone. I described the wines with passion and great technique; furthermore I did well on the identification aspect. When I started the liqueur and spirit section, I literally felt on fire! I was in total control and having nosed so many liqueurs and spirits for the last few months, I felt super-confident.

Roberto collapsed technically, not at all as smooth as he had been in the first part. He made some important mistakes and did not control his timing well, so in my mind he was out of contention. However, Eric did reasonably well. Now it was a question of whether I had done enough to take the lead. I was sure Roberto Gardini would be third, but I have to say I did not have a clue who was to be the winner. I asked Nina and a few close friends who had seen the final, but they all said that it would be close between Eric and me.

Before the gala dinner we all gathered in the cellars of Ruinart for a glass of Ruinart Champagne. The cellars were absolutely magnificent and Ruinart had organised a lot of their employees to be in cellar uniform, carrying flaming torches. The candidates were even collected from the hotel in vintage cars! There, in the very picturesque atmosphere, Roland de Calonne announced the winner.

The problem was that he made a very long speech in French about why Ruinart believed in the art of *sommellerie* and then when he had finished, and we all waited in anticipation for the name of the winner to be announced, he said he would give his speech once more, but this time in English. It was torture. Not only that, but an official camera crew was filming us and I felt that the camera was often directed to Eric Duret, so I whispered to Nina, 'You see Eric must have won as the camera is often on him!' Nina told me not to be paranoid and to stay calm, but I could not as I was very agitated inside.

After what felt like an interminable time, M. de Calonne concluded the English version of his speech. He then received a sealed envelope from the head of the judges and said that he would soon reveal who the winner was. I kept looking at the cameraman, who was focusing in turn on the three finalists, but I was convinced he spent longest with the camera trained on Eric.

'The Best Sommelier of Europe 1996 is: Gerard Basset, United Kingdom!'

As I went on stage, Eric Duret was announced as second and Roberto Gardini as third. Once the Union Jack had been put up and the national anthem had been played, we could finally all go upstairs for dinner and this time Nina and I were sure to enjoy ourselves.

After the long and enjoyable Ruinart gala dinner, a friend of mine took us to a club and we had a few more glasses of Champagne to celebrate. There was not much of the night left, but while the competition was over, the activities were not. The next day, the Association Sommelier International had organised some official visits to other Champagne houses and we were all expected to attend. Nina and I had no more than two hours' sleep, but it did not matter. I had achieved my goal, so being very tired for a whole day was a small price to pay for such a reward.

In addition, my prize for winning the competition was a week for two in a European country to visit one or more famous wine regions. I chose Spain and a year later Nina and I, along with Michèle Chantome as our guide, spent a wonderful week visiting the Rioja and Ribera del Duero regions.

By the end of 1996, we were entering our third year at Hotel du Vin in Winchester, and Robin was itching to start a new hotel. We decided to do a series of hotels, each with a different theme; we registered a holding company called The Alternative Hotel Company Ltd. We wanted to create a Hotel des Arts, a Hotel des Sports and so on. We started looking for a second property and began negotiating on a hotel in Richmond, but the deal was quite complicated, and the hotel did not have a car park. We ended up rethinking the whole expansion plan.

I liked the idea of having several hotels, each with a different theme, as it would bring diversity and also give the trade press a lot to talk about. However, Robin remarked that in the future it would be easier to sell a group of Hotel du Vin outlets; I agreed. From that moment on we focused on replicating the Hotel du Vin Winchester in other appropriate provincial towns, particularly those in wealthy areas, some of which had cathedrals, just like Winchester.

Robin and I came to an arrangement. I would focus on the Winchester Hotel du Vin to begin with, especially the very important bistro. Hotel du Vin Winchester was where it had all started and was our head office, so it was crucial that standards were maintained. We had a general manager, so he could handle the day-to-day administration side of the hotel, freeing me up to focus on the bistro and to train the sommeliers, barmen and restaurant staff for future outlets. For his part, Robin would focus on talking to estate agents around the country and be in charge of planning and developing the new sites. Closer to the time of a new opening, I would get involved with staff recruitment and training.

In January 1997 I restarted the theory programme for the Master of Wine. I was at a very similar level to the previous years. That was starting to depress me a fair bit and I began to think that I would join the ranks of the many people who never managed to complete the MW exam.

Nevertheless, in the months leading up to the 1997 exam I found more time to study and I made some real progress. I had bought a lot of books on essay writing and I spent hours absorbing the techniques. I developed systems for writing great introductions and powerful conclusions, as well as linking the different paragraphs of the body of the essay in a logical sequence, with a very precise and varied vocabulary. I became obsessed with writing well-thought-out arguments that strongly and concisely answered the questions, without waffling, and all in a balanced manner.

In effect, I was working hard to put into practice the unofficial motto of the MW exam: 'Investigate like a fine detective and argue like a brilliant barrister.'

On the advice of several MWs, I read *The Economist* magazine as we were told the style of writing in that particular weekly magazine was excellent and very much what essay writing should be. I remember that every week I would select two or three articles of medium length, of, say, less than a page, and read the first two paragraphs, then go directly to the last two paragraphs to see how the journalist had answered the issue set up at the beginning. Then for each of those articles I would read the whole content to appreciate the writer's style of building a strong argument.

When the 1997 exam came, I was in much better technical shape. I had some decent results for some of my essays, but not quite enough to pass the whole theory section. However, when I completed the theory exam in May 1997, I did not wait until August, when we would get our results, to restart preparing. I knew I would fall short and that I would need to take the exam again, so I took a two-week break from studying and by the end of May 1997 I started to prepare again.

One day, early in 1997, Nina took me to one side and asked me if I had any sommelier competitions coming up. When I said no, she said, 'Then let's get married! You won't need to do much, I will organise everything, except the wine.'

'Let's go for it,' I said.

We'd been together for eight years and had only once talked about marriage. After I came back from the Best Sommelier in the World 1992 in Rio de Janeiro, we were at Nina's parents' home when I went down on one knee and asked her to marry me. She said yes, but we did nothing about it. Five years had passed, and Nina decided the time had come.

She kept her word and organised everything; I just had to look after the wine. Robin organised my stag night for the Sunday two days before our wedding. He asked me who I wanted to invite, and I gave him around twenty names.

We had dinner in the function room of the hotel, of course. We provided the dinner and the Champagne aperitif, but the guests each had to bring one great bottle of wine.

Robin added a twist to the evening. As the four-course meal started I saw two waitresses I didn't recognise. We were employing quite a few part-time staff to help with functions, so it didn't surprise me – until the middle course arrived and they took off their jackets and served us with their bras fully displayed. For the main course, they dropped their bras and for the final course they dropped their skirts, serving us just in their knickers, stockings and suspenders. Then they left. I have to say, they were good strippers, but they were also excellent waitresses.

Two days later, on Tuesday 3 June, the whole of Hotel du Vin was reserved for our wedding. We had the ceremony at a small church in the centre of Winchester. Then we came back to the hotel for a light, late lunch for around forty people, just family and close friends, and in the evening we had around 120 guests for a buffet dinner, with a band for everyone to dance to. Robin was my best man. He did an excellent job and made a lovely speech, and so did Tony, my father-in-law. In fact, Tony's speech was especially funny, as being a welder by trade, he started his speech wearing welding goggles. Even the vicar seemed to have particularly enjoyed the Champagne, as his very joyous mood indicated. My sister Antoinette and her partner Jean Max were with us for the wedding, along with my great friends Christian and Renée from France. In a quiet moment of reflection, I realised how far my life had come from when I was a little boy living within a family that was so dysfunctional. Now I was part of a loving circle.

Nina had done a brilliant job of organising it all. In addition, the weather was warm and sunny, the food and the wines were delicious, the service superb and the band excellent. When, late in the evening, I reflected on the whole day, I realised how wonderful it was that my beloved Nina was finally my wife and I genuinely thought that day had been the best day of my life.

My mum wasn't very well and couldn't come to the wedding, so we went to France to see her the following week. She arranged a small Champagne and canapés reception for twenty people at the Town Hall. Even a schoolfriend with whom I had lost touch was there. Unexpectedly, Michel Thiollière, the mayor of Saint-Etienne, presented me with the medal of Saint-Etienne. It was quite a homecoming.

Fifteen

Business Expansion and Personal Development

By 1997, we had identified a few towns as possible sites for our second Hotel du Vin and we finally selected Tunbridge Wells in Kent. Like Winchester, Tunbridge Wells was a prosperous place and close to London. It was in the south of England, but far enough away from Winchester that it wouldn't compete, without being so far that it would be difficult for us to get to. A hotel in the centre of the town was for sale, bigger than the Winchester hotel and extremely well situated. The back of the hotel looked out onto Calverley Park and as the hotel was high up on the hill, it provided a great view for the bedrooms at the back. The hotel had a smaller car park than the Winchester one, but there was a commercial car park just over the road, so residents' parking was not an issue. It was in need of repair, though.

With the money from our shareholder, a bank loan and a small input from a new partner, we bought the hotel and closed it immediately to start the refurbishment, so that it would be open for the Christmas period.

The new partner was Peter Chittick, a Canadian. Peter was a qualified lawyer and also had an MBA from the famous INSEAD Business School outside Paris. He owned a lovely hotel in Provence, but as his wife was now working in a top position in London, he wanted to come back and live in England. Peter became a full partner of our small group of two hotels. He would be in charge of Hotel du Vin Tunbridge Wells and responsible for its day-to-day running. Robin and I would visit Tunbridge Wells once or twice a week to give Peter some support and we often stayed over. To help Peter with the running of the restaurant we had enrolled Henri Chapon, the winner of the 1995 UK Sommelier of the Year and head sommelier of the two-Michelin-star Le Manoir aux Quat'Saisons in Oxford. Henri was a friend of mine, but actually I was not keen for him to work with us, as I did not want to mix business and friendship. While Henri was undoubtedly very talented, I knew that he did not have quite the same way of thinking as Robin and me on certain service aspects. Nevertheless, Robin convinced me that we should employ Henri, so finally I agreed. Peter and Henri opened Hotel du Vin Tunbridge Wells, but sadly their partnership did not really work as well as we had all hoped. They often disagreed and could rarely come to a good solution.

We started Tunbridge Wells with twenty-five bedrooms (later it would become thirty-two bedrooms), two function rooms – a large one, capable of accommodating eighty covers and a small one, for fifteen covers – a large bar and large lounge, as well as a snooker room. Tunbridge Wells did not take off as rapidly as Winchester did, but the performance slowly improved and after a year we were happy with how it was doing.

To make sure Hotel du Vin Tunbridge Wells would have a great team from day one, we had sent some of our Winchester staff there, and we made the Winchester sous-chef the head chef of Tunbridge Wells. It was a great idea to have some Winchester staff going to our new hotel as they would bring our philosophy with them and play a big part in establishing the hotel in the way we wanted. The downside was that it suddenly weakened Hotel du Vin Winchester and for a few weeks we felt it. I had to spend a lot of time training the new Winchester members to get back to the level of service we wanted.

Another important turning point occurred in 1997. Through our time at Chewton Glen, we had got to know Ian McGlinn, the business partner of Anita and Gordon Roddick, founders of the Body Shop. Ian came to see us in Winchester and liked both what he saw and our vision. He agreed to talk to Anita and Gordon, to see if they might be interested in becoming involved in our business.

When we met Anita and Gordon, we all got on well, and they agreed to come on board and put some money into our business; they became shareholders along with Ian McGlinn. They were really wonderful people and over the years we would realise what a privilege it was to be associated with them. I have really fond memories of the two wine trips I organised for Ashley Levett and Gordon Roddick; it was great fun to tour the vineyards of Burgundy and the Rhône with them both.

Of course, each time we restructured, it diminished our share percentages, but we understood that it was better to have a smaller percentage of a big pie than a bigger slice of a small pie. In any case we had little choice, if we wanted to continue to grow the business.

By January 1998, I was mentally ready for the Master of Wine theory exam. Of course, the last few months leading up to the exam are very stimulating because we meet many other students and can share some new ideas. Furthermore, as well as the official programme there are some small working groups to provide extra help. Therefore, when I sat the exam yet again in May 1998, it was the first time I thought I had a real chance to pass the theory and complete the qualification.

The four days (three afternoons and one morning) of writing essays went fairly well, I thought, and much better than in the past. Each day I would think back and was happy with what I had written. Three months later I received the envelope from the Institute of Masters of Wine. My hands shook when I opened it – and then I jumped in the air.

The French boy who had dropped out of school at sixteen, and who had been told he was fit for nothing but working in the post office, was now a Master of Wine.

Of course, I did not do it alone. I had been privileged to meet so many wonderful people who helped me, from Jancis Robinson and David Burns to the many wine producers who opened their wineries and cellars to me.

A few weeks later, at the magnificent Vintners Hall in London, I received my diploma alongside the other successful candidates. In addition, owing to my high score in the 1994 practical (the blind tasting section), I had won the Bollinger Medal for tasting excellence. Funnily enough, in 1990 I had won a travel bursary competition giving me a week in Champagne with Nina. That week included a visit and lunch at Bollinger Champagne. During the lunch, I had told Christian Bizot, the CEO, that I was hoping one day to take the Master of Wine exam. M. Bizot was very interested because in 1988 Champagne Bollinger had created the Bollinger Medal specifically for the MW exam. I remember him telling me that it would be wonderful if I passed the MW and in addition won the Bollinger Medal! Fast forward to 2018: for the 30th anniversary of the Bollinger Medal, Jérôme Philippon and Etienne Bizot (son of Christian Bizot and great-nephew of Madame Bollinger), both senior directors of Champagne Bollinger, organised a superb lunch and ceremony for all the Bollinger Medal winners at Mark's Club in Mayfair, London, which I was honoured and privileged to attend.

When the 1998 MW ceremony at the Vintners Hall was finished, Nina and I went to enjoy a celebratory dinner at Le Gavroche restaurant in Mayfair, along with Robin, his wife Judy and a few other friends.

It had been a long, long road, but I got there.

After I became an MW, I wasn't sure if I would ever take part in a sommelier competition again. Not only were the hotels doing well, but by early 1999 I had another project on my hands: I had decided to write a book on wine tasting, as I was fascinated by blind tasting. After some consideration, I was not sure I would have enough to say just about blind tasting, so I decided to do the book about wine tasting overall, devoting just one chapter to blind tasting. However, on reflection, I should have stuck to my original idea and written a book only on blind tasting, as it would have been unique at that time.

It was the first time I had written a book, and I made a number of mistakes when I set out to take on the challenge. The first problem was that although I found a publisher willing to publish my book, I did not know how to use a computer. I also hadn't written a single line, despite having sold the concept. In February 1999 I agreed with the publisher that I would finish the manuscript by the end of the year. The publisher was Kyle Cathie and my book would be called *The Wine Experience*. The title was suggested to me during the course of writing the book, and I thought, why not? It just goes to show how little I was prepared for everything involved in writing and publishing a book.

I went to some evening classes to learn how to use a computer and that proved very useful, but still it took me a little while to get to a decent computer-literate level.

Meanwhile, following the successful launch of Hotel du Vin Tunbridge Wells, we went on to buy a derelict building in Bristol that had once been a sugar refinery. It was a departure from our two previous projects, as they had been conversions of existing hotels. This time, a completely different type of building in a real state of disrepair would have to be transformed. The building had been derelict for many years and was in a very poor state. Indeed, when we were inspecting it, we had to be careful where we were walking, as a lot of the wooden flooring was rotten, and it was inhabited by large flocks of pigeons. One day Nina, who was heavily pregnant, was with us. I could see how worried Robin was about taking us round the building, regularly telling Nina to be extra careful, especially as she bravely climbed the ladders to see the top floors.

We had obtained planning permission to create a hotel before we even purchased the building, as the Bristol local authorities were so happy to have the building used – the ruin was such an eyesore.

On 17 May 1999, a few months before we opened Hotel du Vin Bristol, Nina gave birth to our son Romané. We didn't know in advance if it was going to be a boy or a girl, and we'd discussed a variety of names. One day I was putting away a bottle in our home wine rack when Nina saw the label; it was a Vosne-Romanée from Domaine René Engel (now belonging to François Pinault and renamed Domaine Eugénie).

Nina thought that Romanée was a lovely name and she knew that a wine-related name would please me, especially as we already had a dog called Merlot! Therefore, we decided that if we had a girl, her name would be Romanée with two e's, but if we had a boy, his name would be Romané, the masculine French ending. Our son is now nineteen years old; he is very proud of his name and why we chose it. At the time of writing, he has just received a Distinction in his WSET certificate, so maybe his name determined his future.

In the early years of motherhood, Nina stayed at home, while I focused on my role with the growing Hotel du Vin Group. From the very beginning, we took Romané with us to activities or events, as we wanted him to be accustomed from an early age to our busy social life in the hospitality industry. In June 1999 I was invited by Champagne Bollinger to receive the prize I had won the year before, the Bollinger Medal for the best taster in the Master of Wine examination of 1998. The CEO of Champagne Bollinger suggested that he would give me my medal at a ceremony at their stand during Vinexpo, the huge inter-national wine fair that takes place every other year in Bordeaux. When we arrived at the Vinexpo entrance, we had Romané in a pram as he was barely a few weeks old, and that sent the security people at the wine fair into a real panic – no one under the age of eighteen may enter. The se-curity staff were adamant that Romané would not be allowed to go through the barrier. I told them to call a manager and that there was no way I was going to attend my prize-giving ceremony if my wife and son were not allowed to come with me. After a long discussion, Nina and Romané were allowed to enter, but without the pram. Romané slept through the whole event in Nina's arms, even during the post-ceremony lunch, when Nina wrapped him in a blanket and put him under the table, warning all the other guests to be careful of their feet. Every couple of minutes one or other of the guests checked on him while we all enjoyed a delicious glass of Bollinger Champagne and a lovely lunch.

By August of 1999, with everything that was happening in my life, I realised that I could not complete the book by the end of the year. The publisher was very understanding, and we agreed to a May 2000 deadline for the manuscript, so that the book could come out in September 2000. It was a reasonable compromise.

Hotel du Vin Bristol opened in the autumn of 1999. It had forty beautiful, mostly large bedrooms. The bedrooms were quite different from our other two hotels and much more trendy, with some loft-style ones. The inspiration for the bedrooms came from Babington House, the Somerset hotel that Nick Jones had created and opened in the first part of 1999. Nick had come to see us in 1998 seeking advice on certain aspects of his business, so we went to Babington House quite a few times in its early days. Hotel du Vin Bristol also had two function rooms, a smallish lounge, a large, very vibrant bar and a cigar room. It had a small car park, but again there was a large commercial car park very close by. The hotel was not right in the centre of Bristol, but very near. It was successful and very profitable early on.

By then it seemed that nothing could stop us – we felt invincible. Soon we were working on opening Hotel du Vin Birmingham. Like the Bristol hotel, it had not previously been a hotel; it was an old eye hospital, which had been closed for a few years before we bought it. It was in the centre of the city and it was transformed into a sixty-six-bedroom hotel, our largest, with a roomy bistro/restaurant, two bars, a lounge, three function rooms and a small gym and spa.

In the meantime, the question of who would represent the UK in the Best Sommelier in the World in October 2000 came up. The UK body AFWS (Academy of Food and Wine Service), a member of ASI, the International Association, wanted me to go. It was understandable as I had won the last two international competitions I had entered. I had finished second last time I did the Best Sommelier in the World in 1992 and I had also become an MW. On paper I was the perfect candidate.

I was flattered, and also my competitive streak was re-igniting. The only international title missing on my resumé was the big one: Best Sommelier in the World. If I were to get it . . . I would complete the big competition grand slam.

I figured that if I completed the manuscript of my book by May 2000, I would have part of May, June, July, August and almost the whole of September to prepare for the competition. The schedule was extremely tight, but I thought with my wine level and my experience I could do it. I had not really considered Nina or my new son in this scenario, but I was driven to succeed. In March 2000 I agreed to be the UK representative, to compete in Montreal.

I completed the manuscript of my book by the end of May 2000, two weeks later than I hoped, and found I was exhausted. I had not had a holiday since March 1999. I had taken a wine trip to South Africa with my friend Franck Massard; then Romané was born in May 1999 and I had had to adapt to fatherhood. On top of my work for Hotel du Vin, I had spent all of my free time writing my book.

The pressure was on. By the end of May, the publisher knew I would be competing in the Best Sommelier in the World in Montreal in early October. The book was due to come out in September so, as I was one of the favourites for the competition, she managed to convince a Canadian book distributor to buy a certain number of copies.

As soon as the manuscript was finalised, and the editor was happy with it, I took a weekend off to relax. Then, in June 2000, it was back into preparation. As I had very little time left, I updated my files superquick. Not only did I have to revise all the previous information, but the wine world was constantly changing and there was so much more new detail and still more information to learn.

To prepare for the blind tasting side of the competition, I bought a fair amount of wine and some spirit miniatures. The Hotel du Vin group provided me with some bottles of wine too and Le Creuset, through their brand Screwpull, sponsored me again to help me buy more wine.

I used a similar training method as I had when preparing for the Best Sommelier of Europe 1996. I regularly blind-tasted wines and spirits at home. As Nina was not working (albeit she was adapting to becoming a new mum) and was at home she could prepare most of the blind tasting sessions for me. I would spend time memorising all the facts in my files and also drawing wine maps. At work I took every opportunity to blind-taste wines and spirits with the help of several sommeliers. All my days off and holiday periods were devoted to preparation.

In 1996, I had been working the floor – physically working in the res-taurant – of the Winchester bistro. By 2000, I was off the floor. I spent most of my working time training the barmen and sommeliers of the Group, as well as organising wine events and doing managerial duties. I did ask some of the sommeliers to set up service tests and I practised decanting quite a bit.

Decanting is an important part of the sommelier's job. Although a simple task, it needs to be done very precisely. As a fine red wine ages, some of the elements of the wine begin to precipitate out of the liquid, as sediment. Decanting is done to rid the wine of its sediment; if not done precisely, the sediment will mix with the wine. A steady hand is needed to keep the bottle horizontal, above a source of light, while the liquid is poured very slowly and steadily. It's important to stop pouring when the sediment reaches the neck of the bottle.

During a competition, nerves can make even this simple exercise into a huge challenge. Still, on the whole, I did not allocate too much time to it. After all, I had only a relatively short period to prepare so I had to prioritise. I had been a waiter and sommelier for many years, and so ser-vice was second nature to me.

I had become friends with French sommelier Franck Thomas, who was preparing for the Best Sommelier of Europe 2000. In February 2000, Franck came for a week to train with me in Winchester and a few weeks later he won the European title. As he was not competing in the Best Sommelier in the World, he was free to help me. He gave me some of his latest findings for me to learn and also some new ideas on the service side. Franck lived in the South of France, near Cannes, and in the summer of 2000 I went to spend three days with him, and we had a useful training session together. I did well on the theory and tasting side, but not so well on the service side. For some reason, that did not alarm me too much – which it should have.

From June to the end of September I trained non-stop. The competition was to take place in early October, with the final on 7 October, but the competitors were required to arrive in Montreal on 29 September.

When I arrived in Canada, in Toronto, it did not take me long to realise that I was the number one favourite to win the competition. Most of the people connected with the competition, presidents of associations, journalists, followers and even most of the other candidates thought I was going to win. People would tap me on the back and said things like: 'Ah Gerard, soon the title will be yours!' or, 'We are rooting for you, Gerard. You are going to do it, you are the best!'

What these people did not know is that I was physically tired and mentally drained. Too much had happened in the last eighteen months, with no time to relax and recover. I was simply not prepared for the competition and all it entailed, and I had some serious gaps in my preparation, especially on the service side.

As usual for the Best Sommelier in the World, the organising country wanted to impress all the people who were part of the trip. The early days before the competition were spent travelling in different parts of the country, and activities with some of the sponsors. We went from Toronto to Niagara on the Lake, then Ottawa, then Quebec Ville, then the Charlevoix Region, then on the Saint-Laurent River to watch the whales, then the Laurentians Region and finally to Montreal. To do all that we had several long coach journeys, one long train journey and one long boat ride. In addition, each evening we had a long and late dinner, which was often not close to our hotel, so there was no way to escape. It was great if you were a follower, a journalist or a president of an association, but completely crazy if you were a candidate. After all, you would not ask athletes the week before the Olympic Games to take part in all sorts of busy activities and lose sleep. To be fair, I understand that organising a world contest with many people is an expensive business. Sponsors are needed and they need to be looked after, so for the organisers it is a difficult balancing act. In fact, the Sopexa competitions for French wines and spirits do not exist any more because around the late 1990s the

French government, which was the major financial contributor to those competitions, did not have the budget for them. It just shows how important sponsors are.

On the afternoon of day six, the competition started. We had the usual draw for our secret candidate number, and I drew number one! I was shocked and devastated to have drawn number one. Straightaway, I thought I would have to be the first candidate to go in front of the judges in the service section of the semi-final. That stressed me a lot as I imagined that the early candidates, and especially the first one, could never get a top mark as the judges would want to keep a bit in reserve in case they witnessed an amazing performance from a candidate later on. That was quite ridiculous and more an indication that I was not very strong mentally during that time. I felt quite paranoid about it.

We started with the questionnaire and the written blind tasting of wines and spirits. When we had finished I felt happy with my performance. Of course, we were not given the answers to the questions and neither were we told which wines and products had been in the blind tasting. In addition, as a candidate you would not know how your colleague candidates had performed, so we were all in the dark. Still, I felt relieved.

Day seven was dedicated to an excursion and on day eight we had the second part of the semi-final, with the food and wine exercise and the practical service section. I did fine in the food and wine section, which was a written exercise, so we did it all together. We were given a plate of cold smoked fish and two different wines. We had to select the wine we thought went best with the dish and write the reasons why.

For the service section, I was first. The scenario was that we had to greet some guests who were joining other guests already seated. As the restaurant manager was busy, we had to deal with the situation and then take their drinks order and serve them whatever they asked for. I was very nervous and did not understand that the new group at the door of the restaurant was there to join the guests already seated and so I showed them to an empty table. They declined the table and told me that in fact they would join their friends already seated and pointed them out to me. Once they were seated with their friends, they ordered a bottle of white Burgundy and asked me to transfer it into a carafe (in effect decanting it) and serve it as an aperitif. I was slow to react and did not put the right glasses on the table for the white wine.

It was obvious that I was quite rusty on the service side. I realised that I was not doing too well so I decided to accelerate as I did not want to run out of time. Unfortunately, when decanting the white wine, I made a wrong move and a little bit of white wine dropped onto the decanting table instead of going inside the decanter. It was really a beginner's mistake. Not much wine had dropped on the decanting table, but still it was not very slick. I apologised and offered to compensate the guests for my blunder as would have been done in a proper restaurant. Nevertheless, I knew that it was a poor show and that there was no way that with such a mediocre performance I deserved to be in the final. I was devastated and very demoralised. My rushed preparation coupled with my paranoia had beaten me.

As Romané was still only eighteen months old, he stayed in England with my parents-in-law. Nina only joined me when we were in Montreal, the day before the final. When I met Nina in the evening, after another long excursion day, I told her what had happened and how unlikely it was that I would be in the final. Nina reasoned with me and tried to cheer me up, and I started to relax and accepted the fact that I would most certainly not be a finalist.

The day of the final arrived, and again, instead of letting the candidates relax in the morning, we had to attend a long tasting of local wines. By then, a lot of candidates had had enough; the event was too long, too packed with excursions and too stressful for the serious candidates to manage, but of course the final was going to take place that afternoon, so we needed to stay alert. After lunch, we arrived at the Hilton for the final. In front of a large audience the finalists would be announced. A lot of people were looking at me just before the head of judges gave the numbers of the candidates taking part in the final. Quite rightly there was no miracle and number one, my number, was not called. It was a huge surprise for the audience that I was not in the final. From being the top favourite, I became a big flop.

I did not show my disappointment and I watched the final with great interest, all smiles among the crowd. The French candidate, Olivier Poussier, was one of the top favourites, the Canadian, Alain Bélanger, and the Japanese, Hiroshi Ishida, were both regarded as serious contenders, so it was not a surprise to see the three of them in the final, but the last finalist, the Swiss Paolo Basso, was fairly unknown then and he was the big surprise finalist.

The final was highly disputed, but Olivier Poussier totally dominated the contest and deservedly won the world title. Paolo Basso again surprised everyone with an excellent performance and was a worthy second. Alain Bélanger and Hiroshi Ishida were up and down in their performances and finished equal third.

I congratulated my friend Olivier for a wonderful performance. Although Olivier is from Paris, he supports the same football team as me, Saint-Etienne. On the podium, once he had been given his winner's medal he put on the green shirt of Saint-Etienne.

My Canadian trip was not over, as the publisher of my book and his Canadian agent had arranged a book-signing session in Ottawa for the following day, late in the afternoon. The Canadian trip taught me that when things go wrong, they go really wrong. Not only was I not world champion, as had been hoped for when the signing session had been organised, but on the planned day of the book-signing session, our train from Montreal to Ottawa broke down in the middle of its journey. We were stopped for several hours, stuck on a freezing cold train as the heating had stopped working too. Nina and I arrived in Ottawa at ten o'clock at night instead of four in the afternoon, so the bookshop was closed, and I never did do any book signings in Canada.

The following day we went back to Montreal, dazed and mentally bruised by the past few days' events. We had one evening free before flying back to London. During this last dinner in Canada I had a long talk with Nina.

Reflecting on the competition, I was naturally very disappointed with my result. There was no point in moaning or complaining about the competition. Olivier Poussier perfectly deserved his title and my mediocre performance was my own doing. Yes, I had lacked time to prepare properly, but it was me who had chosen to write a book the year before the competition and it was me who had given in the manuscript late by several months. It was me who had chosen to devote only a minimum amount of time to train on the service aspect of the competition. It was very simple: I had screwed up with my preparation.

For weeks before the competition I had been telling everyone that whatever happened, the Best Sommelier in the World 2000 would be my last competition. Now, two days after the competition, having dinner with Nina in a Montreal steakhouse, I was thinking very differently. There was no way I was going to stop my competition career with such a miserable performance and a poor result. I told Nina that I wanted to enter the next competition. She was surprised at first, but not annoyed. She would have had good reason to be annoyed as it is a big commitment that would once again take me away from family life. She thought for a moment and simply said: 'Fine, if it is what you want to do, I will help you and support you. Now, let's not talk about it any more for this evening. Instead, let's enjoy our dinner and our evening and when we are back in the UK we can sit down and think about the strategy for the next competition.' I thanked her, gave her a kiss and as agreed we did not talk about it any more. We had a wonderful evening – one of the nicest moments of the Canadian trip!

Once back in the UK, I forgot about the competition until the end of 2000 and a few weeks later Nina, Romané and I took a holiday. My plan was to restart my preparation in the first part of 2001. The idea was to understand fully what went wrong in Montreal, even though I pretty much knew the answer to that question, and I knew I had to have a plan in order to find a new and different way to prepare. The reality was that since 1996, when I won the Best Sommelier of Europe, I had not progressed in my methods of preparation and in effect I had slipped back, while some of the other candidates had improved and had come up with new ideas. I needed to be innovative and creative for my future preparation if I was going to win.

Sixteen

The Joy of Mentoring

As the Hotel du Vin Birmingham took shape, I had to become very involved several weeks before the opening as we were struggling to fill the head sommelier position. We continued to promote within the group where possible, and to a certain extent it had become easier because this time we could take members of staff from three different hotels. I had asked the number two sommeliers of Winchester, Tunbridge Wells and Bristol, but none wanted the head sommelier position in Birmingham. I even offered a bonus, but it didn't help. Birmingham simply did not appeal to any of them.

I was starting to get worried, as the Hotel du Vin group was known for its large and excellent wine selection; it was what made us stand out, so the role of head sommelier was extremely important. One day, six weeks before the opening of Birmingham, I drove to Tunbridge Wells and spoke to the head sommelier, Dimitri Mesnard. I told Dimitri that I wanted to offer the top role in Birmingham to his number three, Corinne Michot. At first, he was very surprised, but then he said, 'Why not?'

When I spoke to Corinne, I told her that I had great news for her. She was going to be promoted to head sommelier of our new Birmingham hotel. She would create the list, set up the cellar and do the opening. She nearly fell off her chair and genuinely thought I was joking.

Corinne was then in her early twenties and quite shy, having only just started to speak decent English. She had joined us a year before as a commis sommelier in Winchester and was a lovely, charming young lady; I could also see she was very smart. I told her that Henri Chapon, who by then was working in the role of beverage controller for our group, and I would be with her for several weeks to give her all the support she needed. Corinne worked extremely hard and rose to her new challenge with great aplomb. It was becoming part of the raison d'être of Hotel du Vin to nurture and mentor young people. We trained them, not only in hospitality, but also in life skills, and Nina and I have been rewarded by watching our people grow, mature and fly, and flourish in their subsequent careers.

Hotel du Vin Birmingham was also where we started a new concept. Unlike our three other hotels, where it was easy to fill up the rooms, Birmingham was not quite like that. We did well during the week, but we had a lot of empty rooms at weekends. Therefore, I created the Ecole du Vin, a once-a-month weekend wine school. I took Henri Chapon, who by then had become a master sommelier, as my assistant for the wine school. During each weekend event we would focus on one theme, such as Bordeaux, Burgundy or California and so on. We limited the numbers to fifteen couples. The guests checked into the hotel on the Friday afternoon, with a themed welcome dinner in the evening, where Henri and I would comment on the wines. At 10.30 a.m. on Saturday, Henri and I conducted a two-hour tutored tasting of twelve wines. By one o'clock the guests were free to do what they wanted, and the final planned section of the weekend was the gala dinner on Saturday evening, with delicious wines from the themed region.

The wine school did not make us a fortune, as to attend such a weekend was fairly reasonably priced, and the wines were so top quality that they reduced our profit. Nevertheless, we still made a decent profit on the food and accommodation. They were popular and went well – except once. It was during the second year, by which time Henri and I had run more than fifteen schools. That particular weekend, the Friday dinner food was very ordinary, and I could sense that some of the guests were a bit disappointed. After the dinner, I spoke to both the head chef and the general manager of the hotel and told them that the dinner had been very average, and we needed a great performance for the next day's gala dinner. The day after, Henri and I had prepared some wonderful wines for the morning tutored tasting and we worked hard to produce a great presentation. The guests were very happy, and I thought if the food that evening was of an excellent standard then we would have recovered from our weak beginning. Unfortunately, the gala dinner didn't go as I had planned.

To start with, just before dinner, when I was greeting the guests over their aperitif, I discovered to my surprise that both the head chef and the general manager were having an evening off. At dinner the starter was again very average; it was followed by a better middle course, but the main course was a total disaster. The lamb was chewy and served almost cold. I sent it back to the kitchen. I told the head sommelier to prepare bottles of a very decent wine, which we had in good quantities, and bring them to me. I made a speech apologising for the poor standard of the dinner, gave a bottle of the wine to each of the guests and re-invited them all for a future wine event. The day after, I had both the head chef and the general manager in the office and told them that they had shown a complete lack of care and a poor level of professionalism by not briefing their team properly before they left for the day. What is more, I had specifically asked them to ensure the gala dinner went well. My saying is: when working on an important project, if you make a silly mistake it is understandable and forgivable. If you make this same silly mistake once more it is careless and arrogant, but if you repeat it again, it is stupid and criminal.

Another time I decided to do a Madeira, Port and Sherry weekend. I love all those fabulous fortified wines and I thought it would be good to be different from our regular wine weekends based on a famous wine region. However, I only had applications from two couples. Financially, it was not worth our while to run this event with so few paying guests, but on reflection I decided that I would not cancel it. I contacted two other couples who had been to most of our wine school weekends and who were also very regular at our Sunday wine dinners within the Hotel du Vin group. I offered them the weekend for free and they accepted.

With Henri and me, that made ten people for that event, which turned out to be intimate and fun.

A year and a half or so after Birmingham became operational, we opened Hotel du Vin Brighton. The building was situated in a street very close to the sea front and not far from the renowned Brighton Lanes. The hotel had thirty-seven rooms, most of them very spacious and very modern in style, as well as a large bistro, two function rooms, a large bar and a lovely upstairs lounge. It had a very small car park, but again we had access to a commercial car park nearby.

Brighton was very successful from day one and was a great addition to our collection of hotels. The Hotel du Vin group was really on a roll. By then my role was to focus almost exclusively on the wine and beverage side of the group. I was spending a lot of time organising wine dinners, as well as the wine school weekends. Since Hotel du Vin Birmingham was up and running, giving us five venues, we had a wine dinner almost every weekend in rotation. So apart from the period leading up to Christmas, and some quiet Sundays in August, within a year we were putting on around forty-five wine dinners and ten wine school weekends.

In addition, I was running monthly training sessions for the sommelier and bar teams. One week I would go to Bristol to do training sessions and then go through all sorts of issues with the head sommelier and head barman (new ideas, gross profit targets and so on), stay overnight to check on the overall dinner service and then early in the morning drive to Birmingham to do the same. The following week I would go to Tunbridge Wells to repeat both training sessions and the admin follow-up, and the next day I would be in Brighton. Winchester was our head office, and there I could do training and admin for the Winchester team a bit more often. I used to enjoy my training sessions with the different teams and also my work with the head sommeliers and head barmen, as they were all so motivated to learn and improve their skills. Many of them entered competitions very successfully, and we launched some brilliant careers.

The Hotel du Vin Group began to be seen by many in the trade as a bit of an academy for barmen and, above all, for sommeliers. Not only did it make for a fantastic working environment, where sommeliers and barmen wanted to emulate the successful performance of their colleagues, but also it helped recruitment. Many ambitious young barmen and sommeliers wanted to work with us, and I used to receive a lot of CVs.

In addition, the head sommeliers and barmen were in charge of their own lists. I gave them some guidelines on how a wine list and a bar list should look, and the products to have on it, but I also allowed them a lot of freedom. For me it was crucial that each head barman and each head sommelier had such responsibility. It made them accountable, but also made their work more enjoyable and gave them a real sense of pride in the list they had created and their overall work.

All these years later, it gives me enormous satisfaction to see how some of our barmen and sommeliers from the Hotel du Vin days have progressed well in their professional careers. To list a few, especially those we have kept in close touch and remain great friends with: Corinne Michot is a director for AXA Millésimes, a company owning several prestigious wine estates; Claire Thevenot, MS is a sales director for the thriving wine importer Wine Source; Vincent Gasnier, MS is a successful wine consultant, having written several wine books; Matthieu Longuere, MS is head of the wine department at the UK branch of the Cordon Bleu cookery school; Franck Massard owns a beautiful vineyard in Catalonia, as well as a wine company selling Spanish wines on the international wine market (Franck is also godfather of our son Romané); Dimitri Mesnard, MS is International Brand Ambassador for Jackson Family Wines, an American wine company owning a collection of prestigious wine estates; Steve Pineau owns some successful restaurants in Brighton; Xavier Rousset, MS co-owns several successful restaurants in London; while Eric Zwiebel, MS is head sommelier of the prestigious Summer Lodge Hotel, part of Relais & Châteaux, and is also a renowned sommelier on the international competition circuit.

★

From 2001 onwards, I kept my eyes open for anything that could inspire me in my preparation for my next attempt at the Best Sommelier in the World title. It would take a while for that to happen, but when it finally did, it was a revelation. In the meantime, I started to prepare as I always had, rewriting my wine and spirit files and making sure I was constantly updating them. My thinking was that I would go on preparing in my classic way and do it by building a crescendo of intensity.

In 2002 we heard that the next Best Sommelier in the World competition, planned for New York in 2003, would have to be held somewhere else, because of organisational problems. Barcelona was a possible replacement, but that fell through. Finally, it was rescheduled for Athens in 2004.

In 2003 we opened our last Hotel du Vin – in Harrogate, with forty-three bedrooms and the usual facilities: bistro, bar, lounge and functions rooms and a small gym. I must say when Harrogate opened, I enjoyed working there less than the other hotels. Nothing was wrong with the hotel or the beautiful town of Harrogate, but it was a bit far from the Winchester head office and suddenly we had become a relatively big group. It was difficult to give the same personal attention to all the teams of each hotel.

I had notified the Academy of Food and Wine Service of my intention to have another go at the world title. It turned out that the recent winners of the UK Sommelier of the Year were not hugely interested in competing. Most of them worked in famous and busy restaurants and either did not have a lot of time to prepare or did not want to devote so much time to the challenge. In addition, of all the UK candidates who had entered the latest editions of the Best Sommelier of Europe (1998, 2000 and 2002), none had reached the final, so there wasn't a candidate who had pulled away and had a strong claim to be the candidate for the Best Sommelier in the World 2004. I was ready to enter the UK selection, but after some discussion and owing to the lack of interest from other potential candidates, I was selected as the UK Candidate for the Best Sommelier in the World 2004. I knew I would have to give a great performance, as if I did not it would be the end of my dream of becoming world champion. Indeed, I would have been very unlikely to be selected again if I obtained another mediocre result.

My training was going well, and even better after I was officially selected by the AFWS.

I was starting to plan the later phases of my preparation. I wanted to build a team around me. For the first time, I wanted an official coach and a group of sommeliers who would regularly set up tough tests for me. That would not be difficult to organise as we had plenty of highly talented sommeliers at the Hotel du Vin Group.

I used to have a dog, a cross between a boxer and a beagle, called Merlot. She was lovely but strong and powerful and needed a lot of exercise, so I took her for early morning walks in the forest. During my daily walks with her I imagined that I was blind tasting some wines. Each day, I decided on the wines before starting my walk and I would describe them very precisely as if I was really tasting them. It was a very useful exercise, done in peaceful and beautiful surroundings.

In 2003, two episodes played a big part in how I envisaged my future preparation. Since my teens, I had always read the sports section of newspapers. One day, there was an article in the *Independent* newspaper about Peter Ebdon, the 2002 snooker world champion. In this interview, Ebdon explained how positive thinking took him to the summit. He referred to the book *Think and Grow Rich*, by Napoleon Hill, and described how important this book had been for him. I had never heard of the book, but I thought I must buy it without delay. I had watched the world snooker final that Peter Ebdon had won on TV, so for me his name really meant something.

The book *Think and Grow Rich* is made up of intriguing chapters on topics such as thoughts are things, desire, faith, autosuggestion, specialised knowledge, imagination, organised planning, decision, persistence, power of the master mind, the mystery of sex transmutation, the subconscious mind, the brain, the sixth sense and the six ghosts of fear. Even though it was written in 1937, a lot of it is still relevant today.

Not long after I had bought and read the book, I saw another article, about Sven Goran Eriksson. At the time, Sven was the manager of the English national football team. He had been appointed to the post in 2001, when the team was in a difficult situation. The article explained Sven's mental approach for his team for an upcoming World Cup qualifying match against Germany. It detailed how he mentally prepared the minds of the English players, with the help of a sports psychologist. To the surprise of the very large majority of football observers, England beat Germany 5-1 in Munich and would end up top of the group, directly qualifying for the 2002 World Cup.

The article also mentioned a book, *Sven Goran Eriksson on Football*, written by him in conjunction with Willi Railo (a doctor) and Håkan Matson (a journalist). Again, I quickly bought the book.

The key insight was to de-stress the players before the match, to make them believe that, for instance, the match with Germany was not so important after all – that they should go and play without worrying about the result. The book suggested that previous managers might have psyched up the English team too much, maybe by telling them to play for their country. In effect, it had put a huge sense of responsibility on the shoulders of the players.

Bearing in mind the Eriksson book and *Think and Grow Rich*, I realised I needed to work on the right mental attitude. That insight made me think about preparation in a different way. Before, I was mostly concerned about being technically ready: knowing my wine facts, being sharp for the blind tasting and assured for both the service and the food and wine sections. I had never really considered in great depth mental preparation. Of course, one could argue that if you are technically ready you tend to feel confident and therefore mentally strong. That is partly true, but a great mental attitude brings an extra element. If an unexpected event arises during a challenge, just being technically ready might not always be sufficient to deal with it and overcome the problem. In 2000 in Canada, not only was I not technically ready, but I had not dealt well mentally with having drawn one as my candidate number. Being the favourite of the competition had added extra stress. I had let my paranoia overwhelm me.

As I worked on the mental aspects of preparation, I also began to look for different ways into the technical aspects. For instance, to do well in the theory section it is crucial to memorise an enormous number of wine facts. I am not sure how it came about, but one day I heard of a competition, the World Memory Championships. I did some research about that competition and I also found books on improving memory written by some of the world champions, including Dominic O'Brien and Jonathan Hancock. I read their books and, as both lived in England, I contacted them separately for private lessons.

Dominic came to spend a whole day with me at my home for an intense session. Jonathan lived in Brighton, which was great because when I went to Hotel du Vin, Brighton, I arranged to meet Jonathan a few times. From both of them and their books, I picked up a few tricks that greatly helped me. As an example, the day I trained with Dominic, I told him I was struggling to memorise technical words about sake. He told me to take my list of sake words with me and we went outside on a little walk. He suggested that as I looked at features such as houses, trees and cars, or even invented features, I should create a memorable story and incorporate those sake words into the story. For instance, for 'Yamada Nishiki' (a very high-quality type of rice, used to make sake), I imagined sitting on a Yamaha motorbike (Yama), with a lovely woman called Dani (da Ni) being cheeky (shiki) – as in, she was topless on the motorbike; and so on for the other words. Repeating the story a few times meant that many Sake words stuck in my memory. I am no memory expert, but one aspect to help increase memorisation is that the more vivid a story is, or the more exaggerated it is, the more likely it will stay in our memory.

My training sessions with Dominic and Jonathan had taken place more than a year before the competition, so I had enough time to redo some of my wine files, incorporating some of their brilliant ideas. I made the files more 'learning friendly', with all sorts of funny or simple drawings, made bright with pens of different colours. Making the files vivid and memorable helped me greatly.

The Best Sommelier in the World 2004 took place in October, so early in the year, having in mind that my training was going to intensify considerably in the next few months, I appointed a coach to supervise and direct some aspects of my preparation. I wasn't looking for a professional coach as such, but rather someone who was smart and wise, who had time to spare and who was genuinely excited to help. I was racking my brains to find the right person when Nina suggested I asked Uncle Bob, or more precisely our Hotel du Vin non-executive director Bob Niddrie. It was a brilliant idea. I got along extremely well with Bob and he fitted the bill perfectly. He was retired, although still very active, so he could make some time for me. He was very bright and curious about life in general and I knew Bob would relish the challenge. Bob was flattered to have been asked and accepted immediately.

From the very beginning of 2004, I increased my theory revision. I began to blind-taste wines and spirits as much as I could in the Hotel du Vin outlets. With my teams of sommeliers, I practised service and food-and-wine-matching drills. I would meet Bob once a month to go through what I had done, and we would identify where I needed to focus more. The days that Bob and I met we would also try to set up some tests organised by one of my sommeliers. For those specific tests, when possible, we would invite some people either Bob or I knew from a different background, to see if they could bring some new ideas. Once we had a TV actor; another time, we had a professional magician to give us some feedback. Each came with some specific points to help, especially with my posture and demeanour.

In addition, I had some training sessions with Anne Alltimes, a very nice lady who owned a training company for people in the catering industry. I knew her well since my Chewton Glen days. With the assistance of some of my Hotel du Vin sommeliers, she set some great training sessions and gave me some valuable advice.

I also took a private course with a voice expert. It consisted of two mornings, two weeks apart. Both sessions took place in London. I met the teacher in a large, cold room, situated slightly below ground, one of those where you can still see the tops of the windows from the pavement above. The teacher was a woman in her fifties, who was polite but quite forceful and not very friendly. After a ten-minute chat about what I wanted, she asked me if I could do a short presentation of approximately twenty minutes in length. At the next Ecole du Vin weekend in Hotel du Vin Birmingham, Henri and I would be teaching the subject 'The Rhône Valley', so I thought I would present that, even though Henri and I had not prepared much yet.

I did my presentation off the cuff. I knew my facts well, so there was no problem on that side, but still it was not that easy to improvise a presentation. In addition, being alone in a large room with a woman who was looking at me in a very severe way was quite intimidating, so I could feel my performance was weak and uninspired. She stopped me after fifteen minutes by saying something like, 'I have seen enough. My God, it is so boring! You speak on the same tone in such a monotonous way, you are sending me to sleep! I now understand what we need to work on.' Harsh words, but she was right, and I was not surprised. When Henri and I presented during an Ecole du Vin weekend, we might not have been the greatest wine presenters ever, but at least we were in a familiar context and feeling very confident, so we acquitted ourselves well. Here it had been different. I had not expected to do a presentation and I was in a slightly hostile environment.

During the rest of the session the teacher made me do a lot of voice exercises, for which I had to alter the strength of my intonation. She had divided voice intonation on a scale of five, one being the lowest and five the highest. I had to talk at certain moments at level three, then five, then one and four, going to two and back to five, and all sorts of variations. It was extremely interesting and useful.

I came back two weeks later for the second session and I re-did my Rhône Valley presentation, but this time having prepared and using her voice intonation system. At the end of my presentation she told me, 'You have improved – not bad at all!' Coming from her I knew it was a great compliment.

In my monthly sessions with Bob, we had different invitees coming to be involved with my training, and of course, this included some fellow sommeliers. In one of the last sessions before the competition, Matt Wilkin, MS, a very talented Australian sommelier who was working in London, kindly travelled to my home in the New Forest to be part of the session. We did some blind tasting drills and some decanting exercises, but Matt proved most helpful on the food and wine aspect.

Thinking that if I was in the final, I needed to impress the judges with my choice of wines for the food-and-wine-matching task, I had prepared in my mind a mini wine list of around fifty wines of different styles, origins and prices – wines that I would know extremely well and so could present with flair and confidence. Furthermore, as the competition was in Greece and the final in Athens, I wanted some of them to be relevant to the area. Normally, the finalists are given a menu of five or six dishes and are required to recommend a wine with each course, selecting wines from different countries. Even though it is not explicit, the candidates are also expected to suggest an aperitif, digestif, mineral water, coffee and whatever other beverages pair well with the meal in accordance with the situation.

Coming back to my fictive wine list, I wanted some of the wines to be extremely topical. Therefore, I had selected two Greek wines and was ready to suggest them. I had also thought of suggesting one wine from the world-famous Château Margaux, as the owner, Corinne Mentzelopoulos, has a Greek background. I had also thought that as the competition would be in October 2004, which happened to be a month after the Olympic Games had taken place in Athens, it would be great to have a wine for that occasion. Therefore, I decided to have a wine linking the 2004 Olympic Games in Athens with the very first modern Olympic Games in 1896, also in Athens. The only sensible wine for me was a great Madeira. The best Madeira can last as long as that. I have been several times to this beautiful island and tasted in the wineries some stunning wines from the nineteenth century, so having an 1896 Madeira was perfectly reasonable.

Matt Wilkin set up a food and wine exercise for me as if we were in Athens. I suggested all sorts of relevant wines and of course towards the end of the exercise I came up with the Madeira 1896, giving my explanation as to why. Matt was impressed, but then gave me an even better proposition. He suggested that in addition to my Olympic Games link, I could add a football link. Madeira is a Portuguese wine and in July 2004, two months or so before the competition, to the surprise of everyone, the Greek national football team won the European Championship taking place in Portugal. I thought if I was in the final and could suggest the Madeira 1896, and link it both with the Olympic Games and of course with the football result, the Greek audience would love to be reminded of a national football victory. It was a brilliant idea!

My friend Franck Thomas was representing France. Once Franck had been selected as the French candidate and I as the UK representative we had agreed that we would help each other, but only for the theory part. As the theory plays an important part in the early round that made sense, but of course for the rest of the competition we did not want to share some of our secret ideas. We would phone each other regularly, talking about the new information each of us had found. It was very helpful in one way, but also a bit stressful. Indeed, we worked in a different way in our research and sharing some of our findings could add to the pressure. Franck tended to think I was in advance in my preparation and I thought Franck was ahead of me! Anyway, we had great fun motivating each other.

Seventeen

Another Shot at the Title

By the end of September 2004, I felt that my training had gone well, and so in early October 2004 I flew to Athens, confident that I had a reasonable chance. Nina, Romané, who was five years old then, Jean and Tony were all with me, as were Uncle Bob and his wife Maureen.

Thankfully, we did not have a heavy programme before the competition. The Greek Sommelier Association took a much more relaxed approach, for which all the candidates were grateful. We were flown to the beautiful island of Santorini, where the first part of the semi-final was going to take place. Once in Santorini, some activities were organised for everyone, but the candidates could simply rest at the hotel, enjoying the swimming pool or doing whatever they wished.

After two days of familiarisation, the competition started with the written blind tasting and the questionnaire as the first part of the semi-final. As usual it was impossible to know for sure how we did as we were not given the answers to the questions. However, I had a good feeling about it.

The following day we flew to Athens for the second part of the semi-final, which took place the day after. The first task of the second part of the semi-final was an oral blind tasting performed one by one in front of a jury. I felt I had done well for the tasting and so I was ready for the last part of the semi-final, the service task.

I entered the room and saw eight or nine people seated around a large table. The Master of Ceremonies told me that these people had chosen a Greek white wine. He pointed out a wine fridge and asked if I could decant the white wine into a carafe and serve it to them. I was not given any more indication than that. I asked him to repeat the instructions one more time and was told exactly the same thing. I put wine glasses on the table and prepared my gueridon (trolley) for the decanting. I went to the fridge; all the bottles were the same, so I took one and went to show it to the host. Once the host was happy with the bottle, I took it back to the gueridon and opened it. I asked the host if I could taste the wine to check if it was in excellent condition and at the right temperature before decanting it. The host consented, so I took a very small sample in a tasting glass. I smelt it, and to my horror the wine smelt corked. I was stunned as the cork I had just taken from the bottle was a plastic one. In theory, it is possible to have a corked wine under a plastic cork closure, as the wine could have been infected before bottling with a similar compound that gives the smell of cork taint. However, it is very rare.

I did not attempt to give any wine to the host to taste, but instead I told him I was not happy with the wine as it was out of condition and offered to open another bottle. The host did not want another bottle, but instead asked me what the problem was. I told him the wine was faulty and asked again for him to let me open another bottle. However, the host insisted on wanting to know what, very precisely, the problem was. I told him the wine smelled dirty and unpleasant and that it was defective, and again asked him to let me open and serve another bottle. I could not bring myself to say the word 'corked', even though I knew it was corked, because the wine had been closed with a plastic closure; I thought if I said the wine was corked they might think I was mad. Had it been a real cork I would have pointed out that the wine was corked straightaway.

Anyway, against my will the host asked me to decant and serve the faulty bottle. Once decanted, I gave him a small sample to taste and after tasting it he said: 'But the wine is corked!'

To which I replied: 'Yes sir, you are right, and it is why I insisted on not wanting to serve it to you!'

Then the host asked me if it was possible to have a corked wine under a plastic cork closure. I explained that although it was very rare, it was possible as the wine can become contaminated by similar cork taint compounds, and there have been a few cases the taint coming from wooden barrels, or even other wood in the winery, such as the roof beams. The host seemed satisfied with my answer and asked me to pour the wine for the guests anyway.

I left the room very demoralised. I thought I should have been firmer and said the word 'corked', not just that the wine was out of condition, faulty or defective. As this was the last task, I had completed the semi-final and so I could go to my room. When I arrived, I found Tony my father-in-law playing with Romané. Tony quickly saw that I had an unhappy look. He called my wife, who was with her mother in her room, and asked Nina to come immediately. When Nina arrived, I was practically suicidal. I told her that it was like Canada all over again. I had flunked it and I was a complete idiot!

Nina thought for a few seconds and then very calmly asked me to tell her precisely what had happened. I went through it all in as much detail as I could. At the end Nina said: 'You repeatedly told the judges that you did not want to serve the bottle because it was faulty and several times you offered to open another bottle, so I cannot see where the problem is. You might lose a few marks because you did not pronounce the word "corked" but no more than that.' That made me feel slightly better and so we all went into town to have something to eat and see the Parthenon. We had a lovely afternoon together.

In the evening, we met with the other candidates and of course I started to chat to them about the service task. To my surprise, many of them had served the wine without tasting it first, getting wrong-footed and into trouble when the host told them it was corked. I must admit that, selfishly, it made me feel much better. I realised then that the organisers had had all the bottles for the semi-final doctored in advance in an oenological laboratory with a TCA compound to give the smell of corked wine.

The day after, for the final, all the candidates were brought on stage. Once the presentation of the candidates had taken place, with a very upbeat music background, the organisers had planned a little game. Instead of announcing the finalist numbers, they had decided to announce one by one the numbers of all the candidates eliminated. It was going to take longer but they must have thought it would be more theatrical, especially when there were going to be only a few candidates left on stage. Anyway, the numbers started to be announced and at first I was not too worried as I thought they would do it from the lowest marks first up to the best marks, and I had probably not scored quite enough to be in the final. Therefore, I would only start to worry when just ten candidates were left on stage as I was convinced that while I might not be in the final, I was surely among the top ten. Well, suddenly when around thirty-five candidates were still on stage, the number of one of the big favourites, the Canadian Ghislain Caron (Best Sommelier of the Americas 2004) was called. I was stunned and suddenly got very nervous as it meant that at any moment any of our numbers could be announced. The organisers had obviously decided to call the numbers of the eliminated candidates at random! Indeed, a bit later another favourite's number, that of the Swiss Paolo Basso (second in Best Sommelier in the World 2000) was called. Again, a bit later the number of the Swedish candidate Andreas Larsson (Best Sommelier of Europe 2004), another favourite, was announced and at that point my friend Franck Thomas of France (Best Sommelier of Europe 2000), standing next to me on stage, whispered in my ear, 'It is good for us that so many favourites have gone!' He had barely said that to me before his own number was called!

Finally the last eliminated number was called, and there were four candidates left to dispute the final: Jürgen Fendt of Germany, Hervé Pannequin of the United States, Enrico Bernardo of Italy and myself.

For the final I drew number three as my order for performing. I cannot remember the exact order for the first two, but Jürgen and Hervé performed before me. After roughly an hour and a half of waiting in an isolated room, set up just for the finalists, my turn came, and I was taken to the stage.

I did an excellent blind tasting of wines and spirits and a wonderful food and wine matching. As the scenario lent itself to it, I was able to place the Madeira 1896 with the link to the Olympic Games and the football result of the Greek team in Portugal. The audience went wild and I got a standing ovation! Unfortunately, after that I relaxed too much and lost a bit of focus and while decanting a red wine I spoke for too long with the guests, which slowed me down quite considerably; so much so that I did not have time to finish serving the wine. Then I did a very average correction of the wine list with mistakes, and performed poorly in the cigar exercise. When I left the stage, I was a bit puzzled by what had happened. I could have watched Enrico perform, but I chose not to as I was dissatisfied with my performance. I just wanted to relax, so I went outside the theatre where the final was taking place. After Enrico had had his turn, the competition was finished, and we were going to know the winner in the next twenty minutes or so. In the past, the winner was always announced at the gala dinner, but this time, for the benefit of the press and the media, it was decided to announce the winner earlier, just after the final had finished. While waiting I talked to Franck Thomas, who told me that in his opinion Enrico had won, but I should be second, as while I had some ups and downs, overall I had performed better than Hervé and Jürgen.

No surprise, Enrico was named the new world champion. Later on, at the gala dinner the rest of the rankings were given. Jürgen Fendt of Germany was fourth, Hervé Pannequin of the US was third and I was second.

Reflecting on my result I had mixed feelings. On the one hand I was disappointed as I had prepared hard to win the title, but on the other hand, I was happy as I had redeemed myself from my poor performance and the result of Canada four years earlier. In life all is relative!

Robin Hutson and Anne Alltimes, the professional catering trainer, had flown to Athens to see the final and they stayed for the gala dinner. In spite of not winning, I celebrated my silver medal with them and my family.

We flew home the next day. Weeks before the world competition, I had seen an advertisement about Tony Robbins, often regarded as the greatest international motivational speaker, coming to London for a weekend event that took place the week after the competition in Athens. Since reading *Think and Grow Rich*, I was into all the motivational buzz and so was tempted to attend. I mentioned the event to Nina and told her that I was hesitating about enrolling, as after all it would take place after the competition and so would not be useful on that front. Nina's answer was: 'If you feel you have performed badly in Athens, you will need it to pick you up; and even if you had a great result, it will be fun anyway, so go for it!' So a few days after the competition, I found myself in London with my father-in-law for the Tony Robbins event. We had fun doing some of the different exercises, including the famous ritual fire-walk on hot coals!

In the midst of all my preparations for the competition, something else important and life-changing had happened.

In 2004 we had been approached by MWB, the holding company behind the Malmaison Hotel Group, our main competitors. They wanted to buy our group. The Malmaison Hotel had been created by Ken McCulloch in 1994, the same year that we had started Hotel du Vin Winchester. The first Malmaison was opened in Scotland in Edinburgh and then slowly, while the Hotel du Vin group was moving north, Malmaison was moving south, and in 2001 both groups met head-on in Birmingham.

In the early part of 2004, we had purchased the old Brakspear brewery in Henley-on-Thames, intending to open our seventh Hotel du Vin there. Soon after, we began negotiations with MWB, which progressed well – but there was a lot to do. Also, everything had to be done very discreetly, almost in secret, as we did not want to demotivate our team members and alert our customers.

Three months before we sold our group, I was writing a wine dinner brochure that would come out almost at the same time that the group sale would be completed. Among the wine events listed in the brochure there was one that was a bit special: the 10th Anniversary Party. Hotel du Vin Winchester had opened in October 1994, so the party would take place there during the first week of October 2004.

By complete coincidence, the sale of the group was signed two days before the 10th Anniversary Party, but it was going to be made public only the day after the party, on the Monday morning. Even so, Robin made a speech midway through the party to announce the sale and also to introduce the new owners to our party guests. It was a bit of a dampener on the evening. Indeed, some guests were upset to learn the news, but on the whole the anniversary party went well.

After the sale, Robin stayed as a project/site consultant until the new Hotel du Vin in Henley was completed. For my part, I stayed for a few months, working part-time to run the wine dinners and wine school weekends and other wine events. I was happy to stay a few more months as the new series of wine events was just starting and I felt it was right I was still involved. I had planned all the events and I did not want the wine professionals to feel that I had negotiated with them on false pretences and deceived them about my future involvement.

The sale itself felt surreal: the group was sold for £66.4 million. Of course, we still owed quite a lot of money to the bank, as each time we opened a new hotel it increased our overall loan. I seem to remember that we owed the bank around £25 million at the end. And Robin's and my share percentages had dropped significantly through all the different restructuring. Nevertheless, I found myself with around £2.5 million in my bank account, ten years after having put in, with a certain amount of difficulty, £25,000 to start with. Not a bad return!

The Hotel du Vin venture lasted eleven years: one year of planning and ten years of trading. Luck had been on our side to come up with a new concept that appeared at the right time.

The end of 2004 was a bit surreal for me. Instead of working five days a week, going to the different Hotel du Vin outlets for training and other duties, I was just working a few days per month consulting for the group. My sole role was to organise the next series of wine dinners and to carry on running the monthly Ecole du Vin weekends at the Hotel du Vin Birmingham with Henri Chapon. Soon, I had plenty of time on my hands.

The new owners and directors of the group were extremely nice to me, but having co-founded and co-owned the group it felt very different with new owners and leadership. If I had wanted to sit down and have dinner with a friend, or open a relatively expensive bottle of wine for a special occasion, I would now have to ask permission. I gave up my consultancy work six months after we sold the group.

What was more surreal was that Nina and I had a bank account with more than £2 million in it. It was lovely, but it was also scary, because we'd never had so much money before.

In the early days, we went out to fine dining restaurants a bit more than usual. Nina spent some money on doing things in the house she had always wanted to do, and we planned a few holiday trips for the coming months. We also changed our cars. However, we did not go crazy. Our only real extravagance was to organise a party for around 100 people, friends and some people we wanted to thank for their support, on a Saturday night at Hotel du Vin Winchester, around the same time as I stopped my consultancy work for the group. As we took the whole hotel for our exclusive use, the price was significant, but in the great scheme of things it wasn't going to make too much of a dent into our finances and we wanted to thank people who had been important in our lives up to then.

Eighteen
My Next Challenge

By the spring of 2005 I was itching to find a new challenge. Four years before, I had heard that the Bordeaux Business School, at the time called BEM (Bordeaux École de Management) and later on known as KEDGE Business School, had launched a Wine MBA in early 2000. As I had some free time and the money to afford it, I felt it was an excellent idea to consider taking the course. In addition, it was a prestigious programme as it was run by the Bordeaux Business School in conjunction with three other universities: the University of South Australia, the Pontificia Universidad Católica de Chile in Santiago and the famous University of California, Davis.

While the bulk of the study had to be done in Bordeaux, two weeks had to be spent in each of the other three universities, each of which offered a specialist module. In addition, there were some home study periods during the year to do special assignments. I studied the programme and quickly decided that I needed to do it. It was very much like a regular MBA, with modules such as marketing, finance, strategic management, supply chain management and organisational behaviour, but all the case studies would be based on wine. Thus one case study could be on the financial state of a winery in Chile, another case study could be on the marketing strategy of a winery in Australia and so on. There were some classroom exams and the special home assignments included a business plan, a marketing essay and, most importantly, a thesis that the students would need to write and defend. Finally, even though it was headed by a French university, the programme ran in English.

Over the years I had become interested in reading about the MBA programmes and rankings of the leading universities like Harvard, Stanford, London Business School or INSEAD. I was in awe of people who had completed an MBA, having met quite a few, such as my ex-business partner in Hotel du Vin, Peter Chittick, Roland de Calonne of Champagne Ruinart and Ákos Forczek, a friend and owner of Top Selection, a prestigious UK wine merchant, all three alumni of INSEAD.

I contacted Isabelle Dartigues, the programme director of the Bordeaux Wine MBA. I met her at a wine show where she was promoting the Wine MBA and I filled in the entry form. Several weeks later I was received on the programme that started in Bordeaux in January 2006; the last study session was in October 2006 in Davis, California, and then we had to complete the thesis and defend it in March 2007 in Bordeaux.

It was a great feeling to be on an MBA programme and I found the Bordeaux Business School to be a superb venue. This MBA was recognised by serious international accreditation bodies. In fact, by the mid-2010s, KEDGE, Bordeaux Business School (its new name) had a high international ranking for its MBA programmes in the *Financial Times*. To date, the directors of KEDGE are working hard to make this school a leading international university, with campuses in Bordeaux, Marseille, Paris and China.

As it was a specialist MBA and had only been run for a few years prior to our class of 2006/2007, there were not many students on the programme, just eleven of us in total, coming from different parts of the world, so it felt even more exclusive and we formed a lovely bond between us.

I learnt a lot on the programme and greatly enjoyed it, even though sometimes I struggled with certain aspects. The supply chain management module was a real nightmare for me. We were given a computer-animated programme called GISEL, representing a winery with all sorts of supply chain management issues. We had to implement some forecasts and make all sorts of decisions, and then input them into the programme. For that exercise we worked in small teams. If my team had relied solely on my input, we would have had some atrocious results and the fictitious winery we were managing would have gone bust. Thankfully, Marc Torterat, our team leader, was very savvy, resulting in us obtaining some excellent marks. Since the MBA, Marc and I have become great friends and we have worked together on some projects for Tamada, the Georgian winery of which Marc is a director.

During our study periods in the different universities, we visited some wineries at the weekends. It wasn't part of the programme, but as half the students were in the wine industry, we had great contacts and so it was not difficult to organise superb winery visits. In addition, some graduates from previous classes of the Bordeaux Wine MBA worked in great wineries. Carlos Serrano, a graduate of the 2004/2005 class, worked for Vina Montes in Chile and he set up an amazing visit and barbecue lunch for us at Montes winery during our two weeks in Chile. Also, in our 2006/2007 class we had Susan Hoff, who owned Fantesca Winery in the Napa Valley, so while we were studying at Davis University, during the weekend she took us to her Napa winery, and we had a fabulous time.

All the work I had done on essay-writing techniques for the MW did help me quite a lot, even though the style of writing for an MBA is different, but I was able to adapt. I did fairly well in the different classroom exams, and I obtained great marks for both my business plan and the marketing essay we had to do from home.

For my thesis, after talking to my MBA mentor, Lulie Halstead, CEO of Wine Intelligence, I chose to analyse the impact that different presentations of the same wine list could have on restaurant customers. I asked a friend, Lucy Townsend, who was a partner in a gastro-pub, the Peat Spade Inn in Stockbridge, if I could use her wine list for my research.

I took her wine list of around eighty references and wrote it in three different ways: one very classic, by geographical headings (France, Italy and so on); one by food-matching headings (delicious with delicate fish, wonderful with roast meat, exceptional with game and so on); and finally with descriptive headings (light and crisp, lively and fruity, rich and full and so on). Even though the list was written in three different versions, each version had to have exactly the same wines, the same number of pages, the same font, and look identical to the others, the only difference being the grouping of the wines under the different headings. I organised some small focus groups at home with some of our friends and at our son's prep school with some of his teachers, where I gave each group the three versions of the list and a questionnaire to fill in to see which wine list was preferred. In addition, three Mondays in a row, I worked at the gastro-pub. One Monday, I gave the classic list to the guests, another Monday the descriptive list and the last Monday the food-matching list. Each time when handing the list to the host of the table, I would give him/her a questionnaire (different from those given to the focus groups, as this time only one wine list was used each time) and to motivate the person to fill in the questionnaire I would give them a pocket wine book as an incentive. With the help of a special computer program and the guidance of an expert, I analysed the results of the different questionnaires. The results of my research proved that most customers interviewed preferred a wine list with descriptive headings.

I handed my thesis to the Bordeaux Business School and prepared for its defence, which would take place a few weeks later.

After the defence of my thesis in March 2007 in Bordeaux, as it was the very last part of the MBA programme, we were given our results that same afternoon. The enormous amount of time and effort I had spent during the whole year of 2006 on the MBA programme paid off, as I obtained the top prize for the marketing essay, the thesis and as the overall student. To be fair, I was at an advantage as I had very little else to do during that year, unlike most of the other students, who had to work during the out-of-class periods. In addition, Nina was running the show on the domestic front, so I had plenty of time to study and focus fully on doing my assignments – but I was still proud of my excellent results.

In the evening, all the students and their families had a celebratory dinner at the famous restaurant of Les Sources de Caudalie, as Florence

Cathiard, the owner of the very prestigious Smith Haut-Lafitte winery, was the Honorary President of our 2006/2007 course. Nina and my son Romané were with me and we had an enjoyable evening meeting the other families of my alumni.

A short time before considering whether to enrol on the Wine MBA, around the spring of 2005, Nina and I had started to think what we should do next. We were too young to retire, but more importantly we wanted to take on another exciting venture. After contemplating a few projects, such as one where we would buy run-down houses, get them restored and then sell them for a profit, we decided instead to create a new hotel. After all, hotels and restaurants were what we knew well. When in October 2004 we had sold Hotel du Vin, Robin, Peter and I had signed a clause forbidding us to start up a similar business for a year, but as the time restriction was soon going to elapse, we could start planning a new hotel.

We became very taken by the idea of doing a small hotel in our region. To start with, the New Forest is a very touristic area, with great potential for hotels, and there are big and medium-sized towns around it, so a lot of prospective customers for restaurants. We understood the area well as we had lived in the region for many years. Furthermore, through my time at Chewton Glen and Hotel du Vin, especially when I was spending most of my time at the nearby Winchester outlet, I had built up a good following of local customers, which would be extremely useful if we went ahead with our project.

We did a lot more thinking on the pros and cons of opening a hotel in the New Forest and we completed business exercises based on what I had learned in my Wine MBA. We also contacted several estate agencies to see what local hotels were on the market. To our surprise there were quite a few available. Of course, many of them would not be on the open market and we could only find out about them if we were prepared to sign a non-disclosure agreement.

One day, while Nina, her mum and Romané were away on a relaxing holiday in Menorca, I received a brochure from an estate agent about a small hotel, not too far from Lyndhurst, called the Busketts Lawn Hotel. I looked at the brochure and the hotel looked as if it had great potential, although estate agents' brochures always manage to make hotels look nice. It seemed about the size we wanted, and the price was within our budget.

Strangely, I had never heard of this hotel, even though I had been living in the New Forest for more than twenty years at that time. Actually, when I did some more research, it was not so surprising that I did not know about this hotel. It was situated in a small hamlet in a very quiet area away from the main New Forest roads. It was a very simple hotel, which I discovered had two main types of clientele: forest walkers were the core of the weekly business and weddings and parties formed the most important revenue stream at weekends. The hotel had a very simple restaurant that was mostly only used by the residents and so hardly anyone not staying at the hotel would have a meal there. As I had never been invited to a wedding or a party at the Busketts Lawn Hotel, I had no reason to know about it.

Through the estate agent I arranged to visit it and liked what I saw. It was not a big hotel, but still of a decent size. It had fourteen bedrooms, as well as the owner's apartment, a medium-sized restaurant, a kitchen, a small lounge, a long bar area incorporated within a spacious function room, an outdoor swimming pool, a large car park and, crucially, an underground cellar. Of course, it needed a lot of work to transform it into what we wanted. In fact, it was not too different in size from the Southgate Hotel, the first one we purchased with Robin to create Hotel du Vin Winchester.

I phoned Nina in Menorca and gave her my report, and she was excited to see it on her return. With Tony, my father-in-law, who like me was at home, I drove by the hotel to understand the area better. It was on the edge of the New Forest on the Southampton side. I drove on several days at different times from the hotel to Southampton centre to see how long the journey took. Southampton is the largest town around and I knew that we needed a lot of people from Southampton to use our restaurant in order for the business to work. Therefore, it was important that the journey was not too long. On the many test drives I did it was often less than twenty minutes, so that was encouraging.

On her return, Nina went with me to see the hotel and, like me, she liked it. Having a site in mind, I could now start a proper business plan and make an estimate of the costs of renovating the property as we wanted.

We met with different bankers, but quickly established an excellent rapport with Lloyds Bank and David Binding, who was the bank manager. We were prepared to put in £1.4 million of our own money and we wanted the bank to match that, giving us £2.8 million to play with. As we were in the middle of 2005 and the UK economy was going well and had been doing so for around twelve years, it was relatively easy, with a decent business plan, my Hotel du Vin track record and our own money to convince the bankers at Lloyds to back us up.

After Nina and I had done a few drawings and later, after several discussions with the architect (the same one we had used for all the Hotel du Vin projects), we reached the following conclusions. The existing fourteen bedrooms and the owner's apartment would be transformed into eleven modern bedrooms. The architect suggested that we create more bedrooms within the existing space, but we rejected this proposal as the bedrooms would have been extremely small. The existing kitchen at the back would be renovated and would become a prep kitchen and used for functions, thus not impacting on the second, main kitchen. The medium-size restaurant would become our function room, capable of seating thirty-six people for an event, or catering comfortably for a business meeting of around twenty people. The lounge would only require redecorating. The function room, with the long bar inside, would be changed into a restaurant with a visible wine cellar and an open kitchen. The very small terrace would be enlarged and fitted with a roof so we could serve al fresco meals in the summer, even when it rained. In front of the restaurant and the terrace we would keep the large plot of grass, adding some tables and chairs. The swimming pool would be kept more or less the same, just with a few repairs where needed. Finally, the simple cellar would be restored and turned into a magnificent wine cellar. Just as we would have two kitchens, we would have two cellars (I was in heaven at the idea!): one underground one, to keep our stock, and one in the restaurant, to have at least two bottles of each wine ready to be served.

The hotel was owned by a Mrs Hayes who, with her late husband, had bought it in the 1970s. It was for sale at £1.3 million. We offered £1.1 million but finally we agreed on £1.2 million. I was fairly confident that the building work and all that was needed to make the hotel ready for trading would require another £1.2 million, making the total costs around £2.4 million, so well within our budget.

As we were starting the purchase formalities, we had another meeting with Mrs Hayes. It was at the end of 2005 and she asked Nina and me what our plans were for the hotel. We explained that once it was ours, we were going to close it immediately and start a six-to-nine-month transformation period and then reopen it with a new name and a new style of offering. Mrs Hayes looked at us and said: 'I am afraid you cannot do that. I have around fifty weddings booked for 2006.' For a few seconds we were stunned by the news. We did not wish to cater for those weddings and certainly did not want to run the hotel as she was doing, so we came up with a proposal. She would keep her hotel for the whole year of 2006 and do the fifty weddings. We would sign the official papers and pay her an advance of 10 per cent on the agreed price, and we would take over the hotel at the beginning of 2007. Mrs Hayes and her family were happy with our proposal and the deal went ahead. To be honest it turned out best for me, as otherwise it would have been difficult for me to do the Bordeaux Wine MBA.

For me the year 2006 was devoted to the Wine MBA, with Nina planning our new business project. Having been the co-founder and a business partner at the Hotel du Vin Group I had learnt a lot on the one hand, but on the other, we were a great team of directors at Hotel du Vin and we trusted each other unreservedly.

While we were going to create another hotel with a strong wine theme, our idea was not to redo Hotel du Vin. Of course, as I was known for my wine expertise it would have been strange not to play the wine card. I had a real affinity and legitimacy with wine, so using another theme could have looked a bit artificial. In addition, for a restaurant serving excellent food, wine is a natural element of it, so the wine theme would not be perceived as a gimmick.

At Hotel du Vin, the restaurants were all decorated in a slightly retro, 1930s French bistro style, and in fact we called them bistros rather than restaurants. They had nicotine-stained walls, some lovely 'trompe l'oeil' décor and a lot of pictures on the walls with wine memorabilia. We did not want any of that at the new hotel. Not because there was anything wrong with that type of décor, but we felt that it was important we were seen doing something different, not merely replicating Hotel du Vin.

Nina and I had enjoyed visiting California and so that would be our inspiration. We wanted to have a very airy restaurant. The open kitchen would add a modern take and the terrace would make the restaurant very bright and open with plenty of natural light.

Nina and I carried on planning the hotel until the end of 2006. We met with several building professionals in preparation for early 2007, when we would take over the hotel and start the transformation.

During my last MBA class session, in October 2006, at Davis University, California, Nina came to join me at the end of the session, and I stayed in California with Nina for another two weeks to do some market research for our project, coupled with a bit of a holiday break. We visited several hotels and restaurants to get some ideas. One hotel in Healdsburg, a small town with great character in Sonoma County, California, simply called the Hotel Healdsburg, gave us a lot of inspiration.

We needed a name for our future hotel. Our inspiration came from the wine regions of California, and in that part of the world a large number of trendy restaurants had Italian- or Spanish-sounding names. For instance, on our first trip to California we had been very impressed by a restaurant in St Helena that had recently opened called Tra Vigne.

We had some simple but truly delicious food there and remembered our meal with delight.

One day, in the car, Nina and I were talking of wine-related films like *Sideways*, which happens to be set in California. Suddenly, another wine film sprung to mind, *Mondovino*, and we played with the name. The Mondo part was transformed into Terra, as in French, Monde is a synonym of Terre, and Vino became Vina. We put the two transformations together and came up with TerraVina. We liked the sound of it and thus we had found the name of our new hotel: Hotel TerraVina.

With my time taken up doing the Wine MBA and planning Hotel TerraVina, I was not sure if I would ever re-enter the Best Sommelier in the World competition. But during 2006 as I progressed with the Wine MBA, my competitive streak began to fire up again.

Around September 2006, the AFWS began looking for a UK candidate for the Best Sommelier of the World 2007, which would take place again in Greece, in Rhodes.

Of the eligible sommeliers, some had not competed for years and weren't interested. Others had left the on-trade, while some still simply felt they didn't have the time to devote to the preparation. So, once more, the AFWS selected me as their UK candidate.

I was delighted, although, once again, I had only a short time to prepare: roughly six months. Not only that, but I was full of energy, as I wasn't working. My Wine MBA thesis was well advanced, and in early 2007 Nina would take charge of the Hotel TerraVina development, so I could devote almost every day to preparation.

I went back to long hours of revising and learning the theory, incorporating the memory techniques I had learned in 2003. For example, I created a lively fantasy story involving Chewton Glen Hotel, where each part of the hotel corresponded to one of the fifty-one Alsace Grand Crus. I blind-tasted countless bottles of wines and also liqueurs and spirits, using miniature bottles, while my friend Bob Niddrie, Uncle Bob, agreed to be my coach again. Several sommeliers from the Hotel du

Vin group volunteered to help with setting up both some regular service practice and food and wine exercises.

But as I was no longer part of the Hotel du Vin Group, and Hotel TerraVina was not yet trading, I had to find a way to work the floor regularly. I contacted Andrew Stembridge, managing director of Chewton Glen, and asked him if I could work, unpaid, at Chewton Glen two evenings a week as a commis sommelier, to make sure I was consistently practising wine service. Andrew kindly accepted. It was ideal, as Chewton Glen has a fine dining restaurant with a superb wine list.

Two months before the competition I had two short tests in London. One of them was at Tom Aikens' restaurant and it was organised by his head sommelier Gearoid Devaney, MS, with the help of Sophie Brown, the talented general manager of the AFWS. The second test was at the office of Wine Intelligence and it was run by CEO Lulie Halstead. Lulie is not involved with the on-trade but she gave me some different ideas. Both tests proved most valuable. In early March 2007 I had to go to Bordeaux to defend my thesis for the Wine MBA. Once that was out of the way, I felt totally free to focus on the Best Sommelier in the World competition.

Three weeks before I was due to go to Rhodes for the competition, Alan Holmes, the head sommelier of Chewton Glen, kindly set up a mock exam at Chewton Glen one afternoon. Alan Holmes won the UK Sommelier of the Year in 1999 and is a very talented sommelier, so he knew what to prepare.

On that same day, I arrived at Chewton Glen around three o'clock and Sergio Dos Santos, one of Alain's assistants, took me to a small room. He told me to wait there and that it should not take long for the test to be ready. He had prepared a tray with twelve small glasses of liqueurs and spirits and with it he gave me a pad and a pen and said, 'In the meantime smell these and write what you think they are!'

Ten minutes later I had completed the blind tasting of liqueurs and spirits and was ready for the test. Thirty minutes later I was still waiting and started to get agitated. Forty-five minutes later I was still waiting, and by then I was getting really annoyed. An hour later, Sergio reappeared and asked me to follow him to the main restaurant, thirty seconds' walk from the small room I had been waiting in. When we arrived at the restaurant, unusually, the sliding door was closed. Sergio told me to wait and said that he would double-check if everyone was ready before I could enter. Then he said, 'Excellent, you can come in, Gerard!'

I entered and saw three tables, two with two guests each and one with six guests. I did not know everyone, but I recognised a wine merchant, Julian Rigotti of Berkmann Wine Cellars, at the table of six. Alain had obviously invited outside people for my test to make it more real. In addition, Alain was going to play the Master of Ceremonies for the test. There was also a service table with all sorts of equipment, such as decanters, wine baskets, glasses, plates, napkins, trays and so on, as well as some bottles of wine.

I felt very uncomfortable. I had expected to be going through a series of exercises with Alain and his team, but instead I had waited an hour and when I came into the room, I was confronted with a tough set-up. I did not do a great job at all. I was slow and made quite a few mistakes. In addition, I was very nervous during the test. If I was to perform like that in Rhodes, then I would not get into the final.

I thanked Alain and everyone who had given up their time for the test. Alain had done a brilliant job as he had recreated real competition conditions. Even the hour wait in the small room was very well done as such a long wait does happen in sommelier competitions, even though I think the wait was not intentional on Alain's part, as it was more a question of Chewton Glen having had a busy lunch that day that delayed the test. Nevertheless, it was perfect.

I went home and Anke Hartmann, another of Alain's assistants whom I had befriended during my evening work at Chewton Glen, came with me as she was off work that day. We went through my performance again and constructively criticised it (there was a lot to be criticised) and then we debriefed and explained to Nina what had happened. I was very concerned. As usual, Nina calmed me down and suggested I called a lady called Beata Nilska, a professional theatre director, based in Paris. I had met her recently and we had become quite friendly.

The next day, I phoned Beata and explained to her what had happened. Her explanation was that I was exhausted, almost burnt out, as I had been preparing for the competition seven days a week, ten hours a day for the last few months and that had taken its toll. She suggested I should relax and have some fun. She was right and in the last three weeks that is exactly what I did. I spent only three to four hours some days preparing for the competition, but also I had a few days of not preparing at all. I watched a lot of funny films with Romané, who was eight years old. We enjoyed the Pink Panther series with Peter Sellers, including the 2006 film with Steve Martin, and a few French films, with the comic actor Louis de Funes, and we had great fun together. That was a magical time for me to spend time with Romy, just him and me together.

By the time I flew with the family to Rhodes I felt much better. Again, as in 2004, we did not have a heavy pre-competition programme, which was perfect. The competition was set up in the usual way and I was relatively satisfied after the early part of the semi-final. I felt that I had done a decent written blind tasting and similarly for the written exam.

The day after, for the service task, as my candidate number was fairly high (I think I was number thirty-eight out of just under fifty candidates) I waited around five hours before being called for the tasks. I remember that when number thirty-seven was called I started to stress quite a bit. I had done a lot of breathing exercises in the hours coming up to that moment, but because it would be my turn next, I was really tense. Suddenly the Bulgarian candidate, whose number was higher than mine, looked at me and said something like, 'Relax, Gerard, it is only a bottle you are going to have to serve!' Of course, neither he nor I knew what the scenario would be, but that made me laugh.

In fact, I thought the second part of the semi-final was fairly straightforward. We had an oral blind tasting with some food and wine recommendations and then the service and decantation of a magnum of red wine for a table of eight people. I did fine in the different tasks and that was the end of the semi-final.

In addition, for the first time in the Best Sommelier in the World competition, there were two extra assessments. For the two additional mini exams, each winner would receive a prize. One exam was a questionnaire on mineral water, sponsored by Acqua Panna and San Pellegrino, and the other was also a questionnaire, but on the grape Syrah/Shiraz, sponsored by the Australian winery Peter Lehmann Wines. These two extra exams were not compulsory but all candidates chose to take them. As we were told a few weeks before about them, I made sure I had revised the topics of mineral water and the Syrah/Shiraz grape. We did them in between the two parts of the semi-final.

On the day of the final I was fairly relaxed, but not overly confident that I would be in the final. On stage the numbers of the finalists were announced and Paolo Basso of Switzerland, Andreas Larsson of Sweden, Eric Zwiebel of France and I were in the final.

The final started with the blind tasting of wines and then of some liqueurs and spirits. When it was my turn to perform, I was not really nervous, but I cannot say I was on fire or in the zone either. In fact, I was slow and did not finish the last wine of the blind tasting, and while I did a reasonable performance for the liqueurs and spirits, that was not brilliant either. I knew I had to change gear and so I did just that for the service task. The scenario was that I was working in a restaurant that had just opened and as the head sommelier I had to train a commis sommelier, show him how to deal with the guests, serve and decant a bottle of wine and also suggest some wines to complement the dishes. Having trained many sommeliers in my life I felt very at ease with this scenario and I did a great show. When it was over, there was some loud applause from the audience. Then we had the dreaded wine list with mistakes, and I missed a few so lost some marks there.

Waiting for the results and talking to some sommeliers who had seen the four finalists perform, there did not seem to be a strong consensus of who the winner would be. Some thought Paolo had won, others believed

Andreas had done it, some thought Eric might have had the edge, and some thought the title was mine. The impression I had was that all four finalists had some ups and downs.

Before we discovered who the new Best Sommelier in the World was, the head of the jury announced the winner of the Acqua Panna & San Pellegrino prize and then the winner of the Peter Lehmann Syrah/Shiraz prize. I was called as the winner for both prizes, which of course I was delighted with, but then I started to think that it was unlikely that I would win all the prizes and the biggest prize was yet to be declared. A few minutes more to wait and finally Andreas Larsson of Sweden was announced as the new Best Sommelier in the World. It was a very fair result, as friends of mine who saw the whole final told me that Andreas had been much more consistent than the other finalists.

At the gala dinner, Eric, Paolo and I were given equal positions so really we could all call ourselves runner-up, vice-world champion or equal second. I was disappointed, but deep down I knew that I had started my preparation too late. Six months to prepare for such a competition was still too condensed, even preparing full time.

I was already considering the Best Sommelier in the World competition in 2010 in Santiago de Chile and I was wondering when to break the news to Nina . . .

Nineteen

New Beginnings

Once back in England, I had little time to reflect. The opening of Hotel TerraVina was just a few months away and that required all of my and Nina's energy and focus.

Mrs Hayes had kept the hotel until the end of January 2007. After the final legal papers had been completed, we got the keys at last and by early February we could start the transformation of the hotel in earnest.

By the end of 2006, we had appointed a builder introduced to us by our architect. He was young and inexperienced, but his enthusiasm and the personal recommendation from our architect persuaded us to go with him.

From the first day of the building work, Nina was on site every day from eight in the morning until seven at night to supervise what was happening, but also to ensure there was someone there to make the decisions that kept cropping up unexpectedly on a daily basis. At the beginning I would come at least once a week to see the progress, and then much more frequently in the latter part of the building works. In the evenings, Nina would debrief me and if, during the day, a major decision had to be made quickly, Nina would phone me so we could talk it through before deciding.

The building work was progressing nicely, but as is usual on a construction site we encountered some unexpected, unplanned-for and un-costed problems. We had been told before the work started that the roof was fine and did not need attention. However, once we advanced into the renovation the opinion of the experts changed and we were told that not doing anything to the roof was a risky option. In the budget, I had estimated that the cost of the building work would end up at least 25 per cent more than the amount quoted by the builder at the time of starting the work. That meant we had a bit of a margin, but still any additional spending quickly adds up and it is very easy to fritter money away.

In addition to being on site, Nina was also setting up meetings with suppliers for fabrics, furniture and equipment and any other materials that would be needed for the hotel. We had in mind our Californian theme and so we wanted some bright, sunny colours. Nina went for an orange theme, quite different from the green of Hotel du Vin. There was reasoning behind the choice of orange as it is a warm, welcoming colour and is apparently proven to put people at their ease.

By the end of April 2007, we were confident that we could open the hotel around July/August. We needed to think of creating a team around us. We did not want to employ people too early, but we thought it would be useful to have a general manager and a head chef with us three months before the opening. I wanted the head sommelier with me four weeks before the opening and then the rest of the team in the last two weeks before trading.

We put an advert in the *Caterer* magazine for the recruitment of the general manager and the head chef. It did not produce many results for the head chef position, but we received four or five promising résumés for the general manager.

After some initial phone conversations with our preferred candidates we whittled down the number to two and arranged to meet them. The first one was a woman; her interview turned out to be disappointing. The second contender was a young man in his late twenties. He was assistant general manager in a good hotel, and we were quite impressed with him. At the end of the interview we told him to think about our potential offer and to let us know if he had any more questions, and we would do the same. He came back with his wife to show her the hotel (it was still very much a building site then) and the area as they lived an hour and a half away.

We were almost ready to finalise the deal with him when we received a last-minute application from a woman living in the county of Norfolk. Her résumé read very well and so I phoned her to arrange an interview as soon as possible. She had been working in excellent hotels and for the last few years had been general manager of a small hotel of a similar size to the one we would be opening. We were still convinced that we would go for the young man, but as we had not finalised it with him and her résumé was excellent it was worth seeing her.

The following day, I went to collect her at Southampton Central station around ten o'clock and took her to the hotel to show her around, then we interviewed her on the lawn, as far away as we could from the noise of the building work. Her interview went very well and after almost two hours I took her back to the station. I thanked her for having come to see us and wished her well on her journey back, explaining that we would let her know either way as soon as possible, and she said: 'Thank you very much for showing me around. I greatly enjoyed meeting you and your wife. I know your hotel will soon be a flourishing business and even if you don't select me, I wish you great success.'

Later on, during the day, Nina and I discussed our impression of her. We had both enjoyed meeting her and thought she had an excellent personality and seemed extremely professional. For me the clincher was her last, unselfish remark, that even if we did not go for her as our choice, she was wishing us success. We had obtained her permission to contact her current boss (in fact, she had resigned a few weeks earlier from her present job and had just completed her notice period) and the previous boss before that, but we already knew that unless we got negative feedback from either of them, she would be our general manager. Our impression was confirmed by her former employers and so we offered her the position and she duly accepted. Suzi Glaus would become our general manager and would start working with us in late May.

The head chef position was much trickier, as the *Caterer* advert did not bring us any suitable candidates, so we contacted some recruitment agencies. Very quickly, we were looking at several CVs and one caught our attention. The chef's name was Rory Duncan. He had worked for four years in Cornwall in a small hotel with a highly rated restaurant. He had left that hotel just a few weeks previously and was temporarily working in a gastro-pub while considering his next move.

Nina, along with her parents and Romané, went to Gloucestershire for Sunday lunch in the gastro-pub where Rory was cooking at the time. As I had a lot of commitments that week, I could not go with them. The gastro-pub was nearly three hours' drive from home. Rory had been made aware by the recruitment agency that Nina would be coming, so they managed to have a quick chat. When Nina debriefed me, she was very enthusiastic about his cooking and his personality. Rory was from Jamaica and had been in England for a few years. Prior to his head chef position in Cornwall, Rory had worked as *chef de partie* (catering jargon for a chef in charge of a section of the kitchen) in some famous restaurants in London.

As Nina had liked Rory and his cooking, we arranged a formal interview at our hotel. The interview went well, and we offered him the head chef position. As Rory was just doing some temporary work, he did not have much notice to give, so two weeks later he was with us. He started at about the same time as Suzi. Having Suzi on board early was very helpful. She started to set up all sorts of systems with folders for health and safety, food hygiene and restaurant bookings.

It was a bit of a luxury to have Rory so early on, but still it was helpful to have him for finalising the purchase of the kitchen equipment. He also had plenty of time to create all the different menus we would need: restaurant menu, function menu and even menus for special times of the year, including Easter, Mother's Day and even the Christmas period. As we got closer to the time of opening, Rory got involved in the recruitment of the chefs for his kitchen team too.

Nina and I took Suzi and Rory to eat in some local restaurants that we wanted them to know. We also spent two days in London going to eat in some trendy restaurants and we stayed in a very stylish town-house hotel. It was all valuable market research, useful exercises to get some inspiration for our new venture. Furthermore, Suzi and Rory would be our key people, so it was crucial that we established an excellent working relationship of trust, respect and support with them.

As the weeks went by, we started to employ a few more people. Lin Howe, Nina's aunt, was looking for a job at that time and, talking to her, we found out that she was interested in the head housekeeper position. Knowing how pristine her own house was, we thought that if she gave the same attention to the role, she would be the perfect candidate.

Obviously, as our new hotel was called Hotel TerraVina and wine would play an essential part, the position of head sommelier was a critical one. However, I did not need to advertise for the position, as even before we started the renovation work, I had found the right person. A young English woman called Laura Rhys was my choice. She was working at Hotel du Vin Winchester, but she had started there a few months after we had sold the group, roughly at the time I stopped my consultancy work with the group, so I had never been involved in working with her professionally. Despite this, even though Laura had never worked with me before, I knew of her as I had had a few meals at Hotel du Vin Winchester after I had cut my ties with the group and I had found Laura to be very professional and to have a very endearing, charming personality. Thus, when she came to see me at home in 2006, the interview went extremely well. We agreed that we would regularly keep in touch on the progress of the hotel development and that roughly ten weeks before the opening she would give her notice and start with us a month before the opening.

As to the wine list, I took ideas from the findings of my Wine MBA thesis and applied some of them. Our list would be compiled (or 'curated' as people say now) by styles (light and crisp, rich and smooth and so on), but unlike the gastro-pub I had used for my research, our list wasn't going to be a small one. It would have between 400 and 500 references on it and under each stylistic heading the wines would be classified geographically.

As soon as Laura started with us, I got her involved with the wine list. She had never been a head sommelier before, but I wanted her to be very much part of the selection process and to decide with me under which stylistic headings we would put each wine. We contacted several wine merchants who sent us or brought us samples to taste. All those tasting sessions were very useful for me to understand Laura's palate. I was quickly satisfied that with just a bit of guidance Laura could do a great job and fairly soon she would be able to look after the list on her own.

The rest of the employees started working with us between two weeks and a week before the opening. Some of them did not stay with us more than a week, but this always happens with a new venture.

In the meantime, the renovation was advancing with some ups and downs. Nina and I were happy with much of the work, but less happy with other aspects. Our relationship with the architect and the builder started to deteriorate in the last few weeks before the opening. Until June 2007, we were under the impression that we were on budget. Not the initial budget, but the budget we were revising regularly with the builder's input. Suddenly we were told that we should expect a much higher bill.

We could not understand why, out of the blue, the final cost should be much higher. All the costs for the changes that had occurred along the way had been accounted for, discussed and agreed, so it did not make sense to us that we should need to pay much more. Likewise, the builder kept promising the building would be handed back on time, and then just as the invites were sent out with the opening party date on them, he panicked and said there was no way it would be completed by then! Several fierce discussions ensued. It is a great shame when a situation like that arises because there is rarely any winner. On reflection, mistakes were made on both sides and neither side was helped by the architect, who we had trusted due to our longstanding relationship from our Hotel du Vin days. With a frank and constructive discussion, we could have probably found a reasonable compromise, but sadly it wasn't to be.

Several months after the hotel's opening, we were still wrangling with the builder, which was both stressful, costly and time-consuming, and took the excitement away from the new hotel. The case went to arbitration. We ended up having to pay more than we thought we should, but much less than the builder had wanted. Of course, there were hefty legal fees on top too. All that tarnished slightly the special feeling that we should have had in creating a new and exciting hotel and there were definitely no winners in such a sad and messy affair.

At the beginning of July, we fixed the opening date. We would have the two dry run evenings on Wednesday 15 and Thursday 16 August, and the opening party on Saturday 18 August. We would be closed the following day and then open properly for trading on Monday 20 August.

The team was taking shape and we worked hard to get the hotel ready in time. Nina's parents, Jean and Tony, were on hand to help with all sorts of jobs. It was at once stressful and yet exciting too, but because of our Hotel du Vin background it was not a totally new experience. No two openings are the same, so we had a few surprises. In addition, when we opened Hotel du Vin, we were two main players, Robin and I, with our respective families as vital support. Here it was just me and Nina.

In the last two weeks, all sorts of equipment and materials were delivered, and a security guard was on site during the night. Nina and Suzi looked after organising the allocations to all the departments concerned. On my side, with the help of Laura, I looked after the cases of wine that we had ordered. The wood and cement racking that I had ordered for the cellar was not yet installed, so we could not put the wines away. This was understandable as the builder focused on the most important elements still outstanding, so that we could receive the hotel guests, but that did not help me with the set-up of the wine cellar. A week before the opening, on Sunday 12 August, some workers outside in our garden were cutting the cement slabs to be installed in the cellar. The noise made by the cutting was extremely loud and as there were a lot of slabs to cut, the neighbours went mad. Nina's phone was lit up like a Christmas tree with neighbours calling her to complain, as well as the builder phoning to say he was inundated with furious people at the hotel telling him to be quiet. Not the nicest of ways to start a relationship with the neighbourhood and in fact we never did manage to win over some people living near to the hotel.

We had two evenings of dry runs before the opening party. For those evenings we had invited a mixture of family members, friends, some of the building workers and contractors and some former guests from Hotel du Vin with whom we had kept in touch. In total we had around thirty-five people each evening, with some of the invitees staying in the rooms. Both evenings went relatively well. The only major problem was a certain lack of understanding between the restaurant and the kitchen in regard to the timing of sending the food for the guests. Rory, our head chef, did not want to start preparing the food until the guests were sitting at the tables. That meant that if the guests had already spent thirty minutes in the bar, enjoying an aperitif, and they then went to the tables, they might have to wait another twenty minutes before any food was in front of them. After reviewing it all in a constructive way, the negatives and positives of those two dry run evenings proved to be very helpful and we changed the way the food was 'called away'. In fact, very quickly Nina imposed her own concept that worked brilliantly for us. As we had an open kitchen in the restaurant, anyone standing at the 'pass' (kitchen jargon to indicate the place from where the food is sent from the kitchen) could see what was happening at once in both the kitchen and the restaurant. Thus, to ensure a smooth service it was decided that we needed one of the management team to run the pass. It is normally run by the head chef, but not at TerraVina; for ten years we ran it with Nina mostly at the pass and it worked very well. The chefs got used to not having to worry about the dynamics of the service and just enjoyed the service and their cooking.

Also, as the wine was such a crucial element of our restaurant, we worked hard to ensure that the wine was always served before the food. Nina, or the manager at the pass, would only allow the waiters to take the food if the wine had already been served. It makes sense because if there is a problem with the wine – it's corked, or at the wrong temperature – the wine team have time to rectify the situation before the food is served. It seems obvious, but even in some top restaurants I have witnessed the food being served before the wine, because the owner is a chef and he or she is concerned before all with the food.

The opening party on Saturday went well. We had just under 100 people, and the weather was on our side. Overall, it was a very successful event.

Once all the invited guests of the party had left, and as we were not yet open for trading, Nina, Romané and my parents-in-law, Jean and Tony, took advantage of the empty hotel. Nina and Romané drove to a local pizzeria and came back with different pizzas for us to enjoy and I opened a lovely wine. Taking advantage of the warm August weather, we ate on the terrace in a calm and relaxing environment. That evening was to be the most calm and relaxed we ever experienced at TerraVina.

Monday 20 August 2007 was our first day of trading and we had just one couple booked in for lunch. I was expecting that we would have a few extra customers who would come unannounced, so I was quite disappointed that this did not happen. The two people who had lunch were very happy and in fact would become regulars of our restaurant.

In the evening we were much busier. We had a few rooms booked, which meant residents were eating in the restaurant, and some outside bookings, of which one was a large table of eleven people. The evening was going well, until the main courses for the large table were delivered to the guests. A minute after the guests had started eating their main courses, I went to check on them. Most of them had ordered our rib-eye steak and they all complained that the food was cold. I could only apologise, and we organised for new steaks to be cooked. That meant that the guests waited quite a long time for the new rib-eye steaks to be ready. The kitchen team were a bit disorganised and so the outcome was quite disappointing. It was a fiasco financially as we wasted some food and had to compliment a large part of the bill to compensate the guests for their poor experience. Not the resounding success I was hoping for on our first day of trading, and a PR disaster.

The month ended up slow in terms of bookings, and I knew we had to change gear on the PR front. Nina and I thought about all the lifestyle journalists we knew, and we contacted them directly, telling them about Hotel TerraVina.

The first one to respond was Brian St Pierre, at the time reviewing restaurants for *Decanter* magazine. He phoned me and told me that he had looked at the train timetables and could arrive at Ashurst New Forest station, the little station closest to our hotel, at 6.40 p.m.; if I could come and collect him from the station, he would have an early dinner and take the train back, hoping to catch the train departing before 9 p.m., if possible. I did collect him on time, but it was not easy as that evening Laura was off, and I was looking after the bar and the wine. While we were not really very busy that evening and the station is only five minutes by car from the hotel, I had to make sure the few customers already in the bar had their drinks and then jump in the car to collect Brian. As he did not want to travel back late to London he ordered quickly in the bar and sat down in the restaurant on the dot of seven, when we opened the restaurant. In an hour he had eaten his meal and again I had to make sure all the wines were served before I took him back to the station. A few weeks later when the magazine came out the review was excellent.

We had plenty more reviews in national newspapers such as *The Times* and the *Telegraph* and some leading magazines, and that helped us tremendously, especially as the reviews were very positive. I would like to highlight two for special mention.

The first one was a review by Sally Shalam, at the time writing for the *Sunday Express*. It was an important review for two reasons: firstly because it was the first review of Hotel TerraVina in a national paper, just four weeks after we had opened; secondly because Sally was not only very complimentary, but she underlined the fact that Hotel TerraVina was very different from Hotel du Vin and congratulated us on not having done the same thing again. Her only quibble was that the price of breakfast was not included in the price of the room, which she thought was not right, as the hotel was in the countryside and so, unlike in a big city, guests did not have a choice as to where to have breakfast. We took notice of her comments and soon after we did include a full English breakfast in the price of our rooms.

The second review, of which I have extremely fond memories, is the one that came out in *You*, the supplement magazine of the *Mail on Sunday*. At the time, it was read by an enormous number of people. Paul Levy, a wine writer on the magazine, had come to stay. A week later, Angela Mason, the Associate Editor (Food) for *You* magazine, sent a photographer to take several pictures of the hotel and many of the dishes. A month later, when the review came out, it was unbelievable. Not only was it extremely positive, but we had five full pages in the magazine, one page with the review and four pages of pictures. From that Sunday morning and for the next ten days the phone never stopped ringing and we obtained a great number of room bookings on the back of it.

The first few months of trading were slowly improving and by December 2007 the hotel was becoming established. The early life of a hotel is always a voyage of discovery, learning what works and what doesn't, and learning about the clients, too.

Rory, our first head chef, had been working very hard, and he produced some really stunning dishes; his crab lasagne was divine. However, it is fair to say that he was not the most organised of chefs. It was his second head chef position, but Hotel TerraVina was much busier than the hotel where he had stayed four years as head chef. One weekend he came to see me and told me that he was worried as we had very little fish in stock. It was actually Easter weekend, so a very busy weekend to boot! I don't know what he had done with his ordering, but we could not have managed the busy weekend with so little fish. I took my car and spent the whole afternoon of Good Friday going to most fishmongers I knew, buying some fish. Two weekends later, I went through the same experience again, as once again Rory had messed up his fish orders. I even called Chewton Glen Hotel to ask Luke, the head chef there and a friend of ours, if I could have some seabass from him, to which he kindly agreed. Another weekend followed with us having to shop around to compensate for Rory's lack of organisation.

Sensing that I was not very impressed with his lack of kitchen management, Rory handed in his resignation, which we accepted, and we parted on good terms. Rory was succeeded by another head chef who proved to be skilled, but slightly inconsistent, so less than a year after he had started, he too resigned. The third chef didn't last long, and it was only when we got to the fourth head chef that we got the level of consistency and regularity we were looking for.

Looking back, our chef dilemmas were really quite small. One day in early 2008, I heard an economist on the radio saying that we were heading for a recession. A few days later, our bank manager was having lunch at the hotel, so I caught him before his guests arrived and asked him what he thought about the likelihood of a recession coming any time soon. 'No, Gerard, not a recession, just a mild downturn in the economy!' he reassured me.

By September 2008, of course, the whole world economy was on the verge of collapse. It was a very serious time and small businesses like ours felt it immediately. We lost a lot of business from local firms, who became very cautious and either reduced their spend or did not come to visit at all. Business lunches and away meetings were cancelled, and we began to suffer.

For all the planning we did before we bought the hotel, the one business scenario we didn't envisage was the likelihood of a worldwide recession. Nina and I had to work very hard to adapt to this new economic environment. We increased our marketing efforts and came up with all sorts of offerings for people staying at the hotel. As the general public swung from being easy spenders to bargain hunters, we had to come up with answers fast.

Luckily, I had a great network of friends in the wine trade, which, coupled with my wine credentials, would prove extremely useful. We did a deal with Jason Yapp, co-owner of Yapp Brothers, a very reputable UK wine merchant. We created a very attractively priced package for couples staying at Hotel TerraVina that included the room, full English breakfast for two, dinner for two and a bottle of wine that we bought from Yapp Brothers. In exchange Jason put our special offer on one of his yearly mailings; as Yapp Brothers had a strong mailing list, it proved hugely successful and we gained many bookings from it. Some of these guests would become regular visitors to the hotel.

A few months later, we repeated the same type of reader offer with another extremely powerful UK wine merchant, The Wine Society. I wrote a wine article for one of their newsletters and, in exchange, The Wine Society advertised an attractive overnight package at Hotel TerraVina. Again, we received excellent results from that campaign, with guests returning time after time on the back of it.

We also managed to put a Hotel TerraVina reader offer in the hugely powerful supermarket Tesco's newsletter and on their website. In exchange, I tasted a huge range of their wines, selected my favourites and wrote the reasons for my choice and some tasting notes. Again, that offer brought us a great number of customers and was very successful.

Of course, it was important to have the different reader offers at different times, so they were well spread out. Normally, a reader offer would last for three months and we would not run one during the busy summer months when we had enough tourists visiting. It was vital to run them in the quiet months. In addition, those reader offers clearly specified that they would not be valid on Fridays and Saturdays, when we had a high demand for our rooms.

We also created some special packages on our own website. One of them proved to be very popular – an all-inclusive price for dinner, bed and breakfast for two people sharing a room, with an added cellar tour and two glasses of Champagne. As we had a lovely cellar, the idea was that one of my sommeliers, or myself, if I was at the hotel, would lead the residents who wanted to visit our cellar and tell them stories about our role, the hotel and about special wines we had in the cellar. Again, it proved very successful.

Hotel TerraVina was marketed and portrayed as a California-inspired hotel/restaurant, but none of our head chefs had ever been to California. Nina and I wanted the cooking to be in the same vein as the wine counties of California – simple but delicious dishes, made with great products and with brilliant colours on the plate. We gave our chefs books of Californian recipes and told them all about our eating adventures in California, but it is not quite the same as going over there. Nevertheless, over the years we had a few Californian visitors, and the good thing is that often they would say things like, 'You really succeeded, your food is so Californian!' or 'It is like being back home.'

On the wine front, we had some great reviews about our wine list in some trade magazines. Also, Laura was competing in the UK Sommelier of the Year. In our first year of trading it was difficult for her to prepare, but she only missed the final by a whisker. She did, however, win the Young UK Sommelier of the Year competition and finished second in the International Final in Vienna.

By 2009 we were more organised at the hotel and she had an assistant. Laurent Richet, a very talented French sommelier, had worked in top restaurants in France, as well as an exclusive resort in Palm Beach, and wanted to work with me to prepare for his Master Sommelier exam. Between the two of them, we had a great study atmosphere, similar to the Hotel du Vin days.

I had watched Laura perform during the 2009 UK Sommelier of the Year competition, and during the second part she was brilliant. I have been privileged to have had many talented sommeliers working for me over the years and several of them went on to win the UK Sommelier of the Year and/or became Master Sommeliers. I would not want to say who my best pupil was, because they all had different qualities. However, one thing I can say about Laura is that, while like many of my past sommeliers she was an excellent all-rounder, she definitely was the best for wine service. I used to call her 'The Ballerina' as she was so quick, seemingly floating over the floor between tables and serving people at an incredible speed, but with so much grace that no one ever felt rushed or hurried.

In the second part of the competition, Nina and I watched as she served with an abundance of charm, grace and panache and I was not surprised when Laura Rhys was declared the winner. The day after, Jancis Robinson reported the event on her Purple Pages website: 'A young English lady who beats two French men in a sommelier competition – that is brilliant!'

I was really happy and so pleased with Laura, she had performed wonderfully all day. I have always been intensely proud of the number of talented sommeliers who have worked with me and have not only gone on to win major competitions, but have had exceptional careers. It has been a joy to work with them.

A few months after Laura won her title, we had completed our second full year of trading. The effects of the recession were still very much felt but we had learned to cope with them.

Twenty

One More Shot

It was only in early 2008 that I started to think that doing the Best Sommelier in the World one more time was feasible. I knew that it was probably my very last chance to enter. I would be fifty-three years old in 2010 and although there is no age limit to participate in the competition, it tends to be more difficult as you get older. By the middle of 2008 my mind was made up: I would enter the Best Sommelier in the World 2010. I told Nina and she gave me her full support. She might not admit it, but I think secretly she enjoyed coaching me for all those wine exams and competitions.

Looking back at my Best Sommelier in the World competition track record, one thought came to mind. During a professional career spread over the 1960s and 1970s, French cycle racer Raymond Poulidor finished third on five occasions and second on three during the Tour de France, always just missing out on the big prize. Throughout the 1980s and 1990s, Jimmy White, one of my favourite snooker players and one of the most exciting players ever, reached the final of the world championship six times, but sadly never won it. I was determined not to be the Raymond Poulidor, or the Jimmy White, of the Best Sommelier in the World competition.

I notified the AFWS in 2008 that I would like to participate in the 2010 competition. I was told that, unless I was the only one to put my name forward, there would be a UK selection in 2009.

Towards the end of 2008 I had put a lot of thought into my upcoming preparation. I wanted to refresh my approach compared with how I had prepared for the 2004 and 2007 contests. Uncle Bob had done a great job coaching me for the last two contests, but to get a different approach and view, I needed a new coach.

I knew a business coach called Nick Twyman, so I asked him to be my manager for the Best Sommelier in the World 2010. I contacted two of my ex-Hotel du Vin sommeliers, Dimitri Mesnard and Xavier Rousset, and asked them to be part of my team. Nick and I would decide on the main aspects of my preparation and after each important stage he and I would review my progress and decide what we needed to modify or amplify. Dimitri and Xavier would be in charge of organising a few tough tests, similar to those I was likely to experience during the competition. Some of these tests would take place at Hotel TerraVina, but others would take place in unfamiliar surroundings.

My two wonderful Hotel TerraVina sommeliers at the time, Laura Rhys and Laurent Richet, regularly set up countless blind tastings of wines and spirits for me. They were both preparing for sommelier exams or competitions at the time; Nanda, Laurent's future wife, was our restaurant supervisor and she would often set up a service exercise, such as decanting, at six o'clock before the restaurant service. Nina supervised everything, as she had so much understanding of sommelier competitions.

For my preparation I also needed to consider the financial aspect. Some members of my team, like Dimitri and Xavier, very generously donated their time for free. Obviously if they wanted to stay and enjoy an overnight stay at Hotel TerraVina that would be with our compliments, although they offered their time and expertise spontaneously, without expecting anything in return. Others quite logically had to be remunerated. Several bottles of wine, many liqueur and spirit miniatures and some training equipment needed to be purchased. New outfits for the competition were bought and of course a lot of activities would take place away from home or our hotel, which also created some costs. Therefore, as I had done before, I raised some money through sponsorship. This time I did not ask Le Creuset, but a spirits company with offices not far from Hotel TerraVina and an international wine company that I knew well. Between the two companies I raised £10,000, which Nina and I matched from our own finances to make sure I had a sufficient pot of money for my training.

In 2009, a few past winners of the UK Sommelier of the Year decided to enter the UK selection. I knew that I had to be very sharp, as Matthieu Longuère, who had worked for me at Hotel du Vin, was among the candidates, and was a very talented and serious contender.

The selection took place in a hotel in London, and was run by Nick Scade, MBE, director and president of AFWS, Paul Breach, OBE, director and vice-president of AWFS, and Brian Julyan, MS, CEO of the Court of Master Sommeliers. I cannot say that my performance was brilliant that day, but I was consistent. Also, my long competition experience greatly helped me in terms of knowing when to take risks and when to play it safe. After a long questionnaire, a written blind tasting and some service exercises I was declared the winner of the UK selection process and this ensured that I would be in Chile in 2010. The final phase of my preparation could start now in earnest.

With just a bit less than a year left before the competition, I first spent two months redoing all of my wine files. The last time I had completely revised them was in 2003 when preparing for Athens 2004; I had simply updated them for Rhodes 2007. I now felt it was important to have some new material and I redid them from scratch. Next, I restarted my training routine.

Nick, my coach, with the help of Dimitri and Xavier, set up a tough test in London, in a private club in Sloane Square. The idea was to recreate what Alan Holmes had done three years previously at Chewton Glen, but in an even more alien environment.

On the day of the test, I made some mistakes, but on the whole, technically I did reasonably well, both on the blind tasting and in the different service exercises. However, my performance was a bit laborious. I was not very inspired and there was a lack of dynamism. It was worrying.

As people who take part in hard and difficult challenges know, the months leading up to the big moment can be tough and testing. We experience all sorts of feelings. One day we are on top of the world, believing that nothing can stop us, and another day we can feel extremely low, convinced that we will never make it. After the test at the London club, I felt that perhaps my best days as a competitive sommelier were behind me.

Following the test, I talked a lot with Nina, and in her very rational manner she reassured me about my sommelier ability. We came up with the idea that for the last two months I would work 'on the floor' at TerraVina and be the sommelier. From the opening of Hotel TerraVina I had always been involved with the wine service, but rarely fully, as I had some talented sommeliers working for me. Indeed, my role was to greet guests and work with Nina to supervise the overall service.

Therefore, I told my two sommeliers, Laura and Laurent, that each evening I would do the wine service at Hotel TerraVina and they would be there just to back me up during very busy periods in a reversal of the roles. It turned out to be a great idea, as I put myself under a lot of pressure. Regular guests wanted to talk to me, but I had to find polite ways to keep the conversations with them short and not get behind, in order to accomplish the wine service with minimum help from Laura and Laurent. On the whole I managed well, and in fact I really enjoyed it.

In addition, I did two very short stints in top restaurants. Diego Masciaga, the managing director of the three-Michelin-starred Waterside Inn, the restaurant owned by Michel and Alain Roux in Bray, kindly let me spend two days working as a commis sommelier there. I explained to Diego that it was important that I was treated no differently from any of his employees. Those two days were extremely beneficial as I was serving at the top end of fine dining, which I had not done since working at Chewton Glen.

The second restaurant was the three-Michelin-starred Restaurant Gordon Ramsay, in Royal Hospital Road in Chelsea. Jean-Claude Breton, the managing director, and the then head sommelier João Pires,

MS were extremely kind too, in allowing me to work as a commis sommelier for a whole day in their wonderful restaurant. These two short stints made me experience a stress level very similar to the one endured in a sommelier competition.

I also had some practice tests at Hotel TerraVina, organised by Dimitri and Xavier. In one of them, Brian Julyan, the CEO of the Court of Master Sommeliers, came to assess me and give me some constructive criticism. Brian had organised the UK selection the year before and he would be the representative of AWFS in Chile; he also had a very long experience of judging sommeliers for the Master Sommelier.

Roughly two months before the competition, I was having a chat with Nina and I was telling her that I didn't know why but I thought something was missing from my preparation. Nick Twyman, my coach, was doing a great job in checking I was following our plan and he was giving some precious advice. Dimitri Mesnard and Xavier Rousset had set up some really excellent tests and I was getting some useful advice from Brian Julyan, Nick Scade and Paul Breach and a few other people. However, suddenly I felt I was not moving forward any more, but instead going around in circles.

I asked Nina if she knew someone who could think 'outside the box' as the saying goes, and unblock me. Nina thought for a moment and then she said: 'Actually I do know someone. There is a young mother whose children are at the same school as Romané. She is called Rebecca Williams. She is very friendly and very smart. She works in PR and she could be just the person you need. I will ask her if she would be happy to meet with you for a chat.'

A few days later I met Rebecca and straightaway I liked her, just as Nina had predicted I would. We got on well and she agreed to spend two or three hours with me each week up to the competition. I would be telling her my doubts and she would come up with some original ideas to spur me on.

For instance, she would explain some of her points to me by using analogies with characters found in the book *Gulliver's Travels*, and getting me to think of my situation as a voyage of self-discovery. Rebecca wanted me to see myself from different viewpoints. She made me imagine showing more of my inner core and being almost vulnerable, to connect with people at a deeper level. We spoke about this as we likened Gulliver's journey to that of the voyage of discovery of the competition. The characters within those discoveries gave me a new perspective and the confidence to come at the competition in a new way by losing the hurtful or difficult experiences that I had previously had. It was very different to my usual thinking patterns and very liberating.

I had set up a great team from early on with Nina, Nick, Dimitri and Xavier as the main players, but Rebecca's addition to the team was the cherry on the cake.

On Sunday 28 February 2010, I was up early, revising, when Nina called me from our bedroom. She was watching the news and there was a special report on the severe earthquake that had happened hours before in Chile. It was a widespread earthquake and the damage was significant. Sadly, around 500 people died, and thousands of homes were damaged. We felt extremely sorry for our friends in Chile. We knew quite a lot of sommeliers and wine professionals there and we sent them some messages of support. In fact, we had known of a Hotel Terra Viña in Chile that had opened not long after we had started our own Hotel TerraVina, so we emailed them too to send our best wishes of support for the difficult time they were facing.

I was convinced that the competition would be postponed, or perhaps relocated. The following week the candidates heard from ASI that, having spoken with the president of the Chile Sommelier Association, Hector Vergara, MS, they had decided the contest would go ahead at the planned time, in April 2010. I was extremely surprised, but so full of admiration for the Chilean people and their bravery, courage and determination to carry on regardless. I would discover in April, during the competition, that although some modifications had occurred from the original programme, the event would be run extremely well, with great professionalism, warmth and kindness by the Chilean organisers.

As in 2007, Alan Holmes, the head sommelier of Chewton Glen, set up a test for me at Chewton Glen two weeks before the competition. It would be my very last test before going to Chile. For that test, Nina and Rebecca came with me, to watch and take notes. Alan had organised a different test from the one he did for me in 2007, but it proved extremely useful too. I was given a short questionnaire first, then a written blind tasting of liqueurs and spirits and after that a service exercise.

The service exercise took place in the large function room of Chewton Glen. Nina and Rebecca were invited to sit down and watch in a corner of the room. A few minutes later, I was brought into the room and there I discovered three tables with two people per table. Each table had a different request. I had to suggest and serve a bottle of Champagne for the guests of the first table – but one of the two diners was a diabetic. At the following table I was supposed to advise the guests on wine for their chosen menu. For the final table I was required to decant and serve a bottle of red wine for the guests.

I had done well with the small questionnaire and the blind tasting of liqueurs and spirits. Concerning the service, I made one serious mistake and for the rest I did fine, even though I did not perform with great panache on that occasion. My serious mistake was in relation to the Champagne I selected and served for the table with a diabetic guest. I served them a Brut that had a small amount of sugar, when I should have served them a Brut Nature, with almost no sugar at all. (Although I am not sure what the scientific view is regarding someone diabetic drinking Champagne . . .)

Back at home, Rebecca, Nina and I went through my performance. Regarding my lack of panache, we came to the conclusion that it was, in part, due to the occasion. It doesn't matter how well a training session is set up, it can be difficult to forget it is only a training session and to feel fully enthused. Many top sportsmen and sportswomen behave very differently in a real competition than they do in training. The adrenaline is so much stronger when it is for real.

What we all thought was far more concerning was that I had completely ignored the diabetic person's requirements and thus lost vital points. Dissecting how it happened with the guidance of Rebecca, I had a *Eureka!* moment. The reason I did not record the diabetes issue was because when Alan told me the scenario, my mind was only half focused on what he was telling me. The other half was looking at the set-up in the room to see if there was anything that I should be aware of. It was a mistake I had made a long time ago and seen done by so many sommeliers in competitions. As all the tests are under very strict time conditions, some competitors imagine it is possible to anticipate potential traps or prevent mistakes by having a careful look at the set-up while being told what to do. Except by doing that, not all of the important instructions are taken in and the outcome can be devastating. Indeed, the few seconds supposedly gained by examining what materials and equipment are available can prove to be of little benefit when compared with the possible misinterpretation of the instructions.

I knew that was what had happened. Alan had explained to me in great detail my tasks and what the issues were for the different tables, but I was too busy thinking of what decanter I should use and what size glasses I should put on the table and so my mind did not register that one guest was diabetic. It was a great lesson, and a great reminder that it doesn't matter how much experience one has, it is easy to fall back into bad habits.

Nina, Romané, my parents-in-law and I left London to arrive in Santiago de Chile on Saturday 10 April. What should have been a very relaxed journey to Chile turned out to be quite stressful, owing to mix-ups at Madrid airport that saw us shuttling and running between terminals, while juggling heavy, book-laden hand luggage. We got to the flight just as they were about to close the doors. Another couple of minutes, and my competitive career would have been over. Finally, we landed in Santiago and were taken to the W Hotel, a large, deluxe hotel where the competition would take place. The presence of so many colleagues and friends at the opening gala, plus the friendliness of our welcome, made me relax. Better still, I did not have to attend all the activities organised for the next day, so I didn't have to waste energy before the contest.

I was one of fifty-one candidates, the largest number there had ever been at a Best Sommelier in the World contest until then. Because of the sheer numbers, the technical committee introduced an extra round before the final; everyone would do the first part, then the twelve best candidates would go through to the semi-finals, and the top three candidates would reach the final.

On the Monday, the competition started with a long questionnaire, followed by a written blind tasting of wines and a written blind tasting of liqueurs and spirits. The first round was concluded with a restaurant service exercise. I had a good feeling. I hadn't been brilliant in the service part, but I'd done what was required; the next round was going to be the semi-final, and I was confident I would be one of the twelve.

As indeed I was. Most of the other favourites had qualified too. It was an interesting mix of heavy-hitting international winners and talented outsiders.

The questionnaire for the semi-final was aimed at judging our reasoning, and one question asked us to create and price a menu to match some very specific wines for an imaginary, highly rated restaurant in Paris. As I rarely eat in top Paris restaurants, I wasn't completely sure that my menu pricing was realistic.

In the afternoon, we went into two rooms, one by one. The first room involved an oral blind tasting of wines, and then one of liqueurs and spirits, in front of a jury.

In the second room we had to serve a bottle of Champagne to seven guests, but the bottle of Champagne was not closed with a traditional Champagne cork wire, but instead by a cork attached to the bottle by a big staple. As it was not common, it demanded a bit of adjustment, but I handled it fine and my service of the Champagne was excellent. For the next task, we were given a classic Chilean dish, a ceviche, and two glasses of two different wines. Candidates were given an exact time to taste the dish and the wines and then we had to say which wine was best with the dish and explain why.

On Thursday morning, I relaxed as much as I could. Around mid-morning I went outside and met my friend Paolo Basso, and we went for a walk and a coffee. The more we sat and chatted, the more we convinced each other that we hadn't done enough and couldn't possibly get to the finals. By the time we walked back to the hotel, we were both quite depressed. Still, we turned up to the function room as required.

At 3.30 p.m., in front of a large audience and a few television crews, the twelve semi-finalists were introduced to the audience. After the presentations, the three finalists were called – and my number, 33, was one of them. Paolo Basso of Switzerland and David Biraud of France were the other two finalists. We then drew our numbers to decide in which order we would go on stage for the final; I drew number three and Paolo drew number one.

David and I were taken to a room on a different floor, to ensure we were completely isolated. We had someone from the competition babysit us, and our mobile phones were confiscated. David chatted for fifteen minutes just to kill time, but for the last thirty minutes or so he kept to himself, as he wanted to concentrate.

Some competitors like to go first and get on with it, others like to be in the middle, so as to have some time to regroup, but not to wait too long either, and a few, like me, like to be last to go on stage. Indeed, for me it was the perfect draw, as I could focus and work on relaxing. As well as the official Chilean TV crew, there was also a TV crew from the Japanese channel NHK, because the Japanese like following sommelier competitions. Prior to the competition, an NHK crew had come to see me at Hotel TerraVina and filmed me doing all sorts of preparation work. Of course, they interviewed me too. I knew that when I was on stage, one of their cameramen would be filming the reactions of Nina and Romané. I did not want that to affect and stress me, so I applied the principle I had learned reading the article about Sven-Goran Eriksson and his sports psychologist: I blanked Nina and Romané out of my mind and told myself that I was there to give the audience a great time and also to enjoy myself.

Finally, someone came and took me to the stage. I was shown the different tables, each of which had several judges, and I was told in which order I should tackle each table. The first task was to serve a bottle of Champagne to three guests and make a Negroni for the fourth guest, in four minutes. I relaxed and enjoyed it, because the classic Negroni cocktail (one-third Campari, one-third Martini and one-third gin on ice, with an orange peel as garnish) is one of my all-time favourite cocktails.

The second task was a food and wine matching exercise. I had to create a menu around some very special bottles, in six minutes. The hours of practice paid off and I came up with some delicious dishes to complement the superb wines, making sure that each dish logically followed the one before.

The third task was the decanting and service of a magnum of red in six minutes. Before the competition, I had decanted countless bottles and magnums of wine with Nina timing me. She would note very precisely my timing for each small operation of the decanting. I did well in that task, and I enjoyed it.

I also had to correct a wine list that had mistakes on it, in four minutes. The wine list was projected on a large screen so the audience could follow along, but they had been told by the MC to keep quiet. This was normally my weakest point, and I was never able to find many mistakes. What I had done this time was ask several sommeliers to write and send me some wine lists with mistakes, with the corrections listed separately. Over the year I had collected around forty such wine lists and in the last six months I would correct one or two a day. The preparation certainly helped – my performance wasn't flawless, but I received an excellent score.

Then came a blind tasting of four wines and a series of liqueurs and spirits, to be done within fifteen minutes. There was a three-minute quiz – pictures of famous estates and well-known personalities were projected onto the screen and I had to identify them.

Fortunately, I knew a lot of them.

Finally, there was a question about the profession itself. I had two minutes to give my perspective on the role of sommelier. I had plenty to say, as I had written articles tackling this very topic for trade and consumer magazines over the years.

Then it was all over, and I left the stage. I felt empty and exhausted. This was my last chance to win, and I'd given it everything. If I didn't win today, then I would join the ranks of the also-rans, those who could never quite break through. But at least I knew I'd given it my all.

I walked as far away from the function room as I could.

Fifteen minutes later, a few people came to find me, including Nina. 'Where were you?' she said. 'They are waiting for you on stage!' Then she gave me a kiss and said: 'Good luck, *mon amour!*'

I climbed on stage and took my place next to David and Paolo. We listened to a short speech given by Kazuyoshi Kogai San, the president of the Association Sommelier International. He was an extremely nice man – he has sadly passed away since – but he spoke quietly, and it was difficult to hear what he was saying. The audience began to get restless and the room became noisy. That meant that when I heard the president pronounce my number, 33, I wasn't really sure what he meant. Was I third?

I sat in confusion, wishing he would repeat himself, but then I heard the applause and the cheers – and I realised they were for me.

I had just been named the Best Sommelier of the World.

A sterling silver Moët & Chandon bottle was placed in my hands, engraved with all the names of the past winners. The next few moments were a blur of photographs being taken and speeches being made. I called Nina and Romané to join me on stage and gave Nina my heartfelt thanks for everything she had done – without her, I wouldn't have been standing there.

That was also the day I realised that only first place counts. When I had come second in 1992, 1994 and 2007, journalists had been kind, but had kept the post-competition interview short. Now I watched as Paolo and David were perfunctorily interviewed, and then asked to leave the stage. (I also learned, of course, that life offers second chances – Paolo was named Best Sommelier in the World in 2013. Curiously, he was candidate number 33, as was the Best Sommelier in the World 2016, Arvid Rosengren of Sweden.)

After my own interview was over, it was time to go back to our rooms to change. Romané was in charge of the silver trophy, and he dropped it in front of the lift, giving the crowd a good laugh. It wasn't damaged (the tiny dent doesn't count . . .).

I was in such a cloud of happiness that I hardly remember anything about the superb gala dinner we had at a castle in Santiago de Chile.

The title was mine until April 2013, and the benefits of winning were amazing – as the competition was sponsored by Moët & Chandon, the prize included a weekend for ten couples of my choosing at Château de Saran, the private chateau belonging to the Moët & Chandon and Dom Pérignon Champagne company. Of course, I took along the people who had been so instrumental in my win. The weather was wonderful, we had a superb time and I was glad I could repay everyone for the tremendous support they had given me.

They had helped me achieve my dream: the dropout from Saint-Etienne had achieved something that no other person in the whole world of wine had done before. I was a Master Sommelier, a Master of Wine, a hotelier who had helped create a ground-breaking series of hotels that had been sold for a tidy sum, and a graduate of the Wine MBA. And, at last, I had been named Best Sommelier in the World.

It was an extraordinary moment.

There is, of course, a price to be paid for everything. The day after the gala began with some stress, because it was difficult getting out of Chile. An eruption in Iceland had thrown clouds of volcanic ash in the air that had the potential to damage aircraft engines; the result was the biggest shutdown of aviation space since the Second World War. We did finally manage to get to Madrid, but everything was in chaos, with flights cancelled, hire cars overbooked and not enough trains.

Robin Hutson's wife Judy and her friend were also stranded in Madrid and so we met up and had an enjoyable few days dining and exploring the city with them. Thanks to Robin's great organisational skills, he eventually managed to have a father-and-son team of drivers travel to Madrid to collect us in a minibus and after a two-day trip, with some driving worthy of Formula 1 at times, we eventually all arrived home safely.

Although we enjoyed the week in Madrid, it feels, looking back, as though the ash clouds in the sky were an omen.

Twenty-One
Dark Clouds on the Horizon

My win made me so euphoric that it took a few months before I noticed there was something wrong.

Hotel TerraVina was now two and a half years old. It was doing well in terms of revenue, but my intense competition preparation had distracted me, and we weren't watching the details as we ought to have done, so we didn't notice that our profits weren't as high as they should have been.

The problem was that the head chef wasn't getting his food margins right. Not by a long way. His food was good, and the customers were happy, but he was paying too much for food and wasting quite a lot of it.

We had, of course, noticed the problem and mentioned it a few times to the chef, but I hadn't paid enough attention to whether the situation was improving or not. In any case, the hotel was very busy and making a small profit, so we weren't feeling the urgency of the problem.

We should have been stronger on the issue, and also helped him find a solution. But by the summer of 2010, we made it clear that he couldn't carry on like that and we offered to help him find a mentor who could teach him how to buy better, control spending and minimise wastage. He wasn't interested and gave us his notice.

Our young sous-chef, Neil Cooper, held the fort while we looked for a replacement. Having just lost our third head chef, we didn't want to rush this time. In any case, the weeks passed as we struggled to find someone. Neil was doing a great job, not only maintaining the food quality, but getting the costs right, too. We asked him if he wanted the position and he promptly accepted.

Soon, Hotel TerraVina was doing very well again. In addition, the economic situation in England and in fact in the whole of Europe seemed to have greatly improved since the terrible 2008 recession.

Having great hoteliers in close proximity is a double-edged sword. It can bring interest to the area and help you fill your rooms, or it can mean you are no longer the new place to stay. When I learned that Robin was opening a new hotel very close to ours, the Pig Hotel in Brockenhurst, which was to be aimed at the mid-level segment of the market, just as we were, I felt nervous. Robin had partnered with a local billionaire, Jim Ratcliffe. Knowing Robin's great talent for creating innovative and stylish hotels, coupled with the enormous wealth of Jim Ratcliffe, I knew the competition would be fierce.

In life you have to accept competition and there are definitely positive aspects to being challenged. I'd always known that a strong competitor would pop up one day. The Pig Hotel did hurt our business, but I have to take full responsibility for that. We had done a great job of setting up Hotel TerraVina and marketing it, which had helped us get through a tough recession, but I'd failed to develop a vision for growth.

From the moment Nina and I had the idea of starting the hotel, I should have found one or more wealthy business partners and created a strong business plan for developing Hotel TerraVina as a brand with several outlets. I should have envisaged other outlets that would be bigger and situated in slightly better locations in terms of footfall than the original Hotel TerraVina. It would have been feasible to expand Hotel TerraVina and make it a national brand like Hotel du Vin. In the first two years we received an incredible amount of coverage in many newspapers and several magazines and they were very complimentary, so we would have had a great opportunity to capitalise on such wonderful goodwill.

But what I had learned from the Best Sommelier of the World competition is that life offers you second chances, if you have the courage to take them. So maybe I was looking for a second chance when I took my next decision.

After I won the Best Sommelier in the World in April 2010, I'd begun receiving proposals. People offered me consultancies and brand ambassador jobs, and I was pleased to take some of these opportunities. They meant a lot of international travel and I enjoyed them. Hotel TerraVina was going quite well, so Nina and I began discussing selling it. We knew that we wouldn't get all of our money back, but we could get enough back to be happy. Discreetly, we put the hotel up for sale, but no offers came in. Not even after we changed estate agents.

In the second half of 2011, the chairman of a small group of four restaurants paid us a visit, on the pretext of buying the hotel. He looked the part and talked a good game. His restaurant group was quite well known in the trade, so I was delighted by this opportunity. But after a few weeks of discussion he told me that his group did not have the funds available right now, but perhaps at a later date . . .

Our discussions had been friendly, and he was charming, so we kept in touch. Gradually we began to believe that both sides could profit from the expertise of the other. Eventually the word 'merger' hung in the air. We also talked about starting a new wine business, where I would bring my reputation and wine expertise, and he would bring his business acumen.

Nina and I considered it. Could this be our path towards growth?

In May 2012 we exchanged shares in both businesses. Nina and I now owned shares in their business, and they owned shares in ours. The chairman of the restaurant group became a director of our hotel, while Nina and I joined their board of directors. Nina became managing director of the whole group.

Of course, our lawyer and accountant had done due diligence before we merged – but as it turned out, not enough.

We did get one big hint that there was something very wrong. Early in the merger period, we discovered that the restaurant group owed a lot of money to HMRC. The chairman told us that it was a huge mistake and they had been unfairly dealt with by the tax department, and we believed him. We gave him the contact details of a friend of my father-in-law Tony, who is a goldmine of useful contacts. Tony called Hennessey Thompson, an accountant specialising in complex tax issues. A long time ago he had helped Tony to come to an arrangement with HMRC regarding his small welding business and they had been great friends ever since.

Hennessey is a lovely, kind man and highly talented at what he does. He not only took on the case, but also won it – not because the group did not owe money, but more because the tax inspector dealing with the case had made several mistakes in the way he proceeded with his investigation. It was wonderful news for the restaurant group. Hennessey had saved them a lot of money and almost certainly stopped them going bust.

The case did embarrass Nina, me and Tony, however. Despite Hennessey's fee being very reasonable, the chairman resisted paying it. I felt awful, as I was the one who had put him in touch with Hennessey. Fortunately, Hennessey is extremely successful in business, and he was less bothered by not being paid than he was by the chairman's attitude and lack of respect. It was a symptom of what was to come.

Then we made the truly dreadful discovery that the restaurant group we now had shares in was laden with huge debts. Our shares were worthless. Their shares in our business, however, were not.

Twenty-Two

A Disastrous Time,
but One to Learn and Grow From

I thought it was a mistake. It felt like falling in love with someone, and hearing a friend warn you that the person you're infatuated with isn't someone you should be with – you don't listen. I convinced myself that there was an explanation for all this debt and that we would find a positive solution.

The first thing we suggested was a restructuring of the restaurant group. By selling two restaurant leases, we could get things back on track. The next step would be to make the remaining two restaurants perform better.

But they weren't interested. In any case, the restaurant group was in such a mess financially that it would have been extremely difficult to get back on track, regardless of what we did.

By December 2012, Nina and I were in partnership with an ailing business and I was potentially involved in a new wine business with the chairman of the restaurant group.

In January 2013, I called my lawyer and arranged to see him at our home. I went through it all and his advice was to cut all ties with the chairman and his associates. It was what I was thinking, but much easier said than done. I was starting to be very concerned that it could all unravel, and we would lose Hotel TerraVina in the process.

Two weeks later, a meeting of our restaurant group took place at Hotel TerraVina. Very early on in the meeting, Nina and I told our associates that we were not happy. We had not been told of the real situation before the merger and we wanted to demerge the two businesses and go our separate ways. They were surprised and not very pleased. The chairman looked at us and told us that we had hijacked the meeting.

A moment later he asked me if he could go to the office, so that he could make an important phone call in private. When he came back, he told us that he'd spoken with his personal financial adviser and arranged for some money from an overseas investment to be put through the business. It would be available by the end of the week. I knew it was pure fantasy, as by then I was used to him and his imaginary stories. He always did this, pledging all sorts of things that never materialised.

As predicted, the end of the week came and the money failed to arrive, so both Nina and I resigned as directors of the restaurant group. Of course, the chairman did not resign from his position as a director of Hotel TerraVina.

One good thing is that when we set up our new business, we'd designed it so that both businesses were relatively independent from one another, legally speaking. Further, there was a clause that said if one of the businesses went bankrupt, the directors of the remaining healthy business could buy back the shares in their own business.

As they did not want to demerge, Nina and I had only one choice: to have the restaurant group go bust and then negotiate with the appointed liquidator to buy back the Hotel TerraVina shares retained by the restaurant group. The group owed a lot of money to trade suppliers, so on paper it looked easy: an unpaid supplier simply had to take the group to court, at which point it would go bankrupt.

Except it wasn't so easy in real life. Directors who are owed money rarely take the business to court – after all, what's the point of incurring legal costs if there's no money to be had?

We had a legal battle on our hands and needed a lawyer. The one we used was the partner of the lawyer I'd used for a long time, who had looked after the sale of Hotel du Vin, and who had come to my home to advise me when the fiasco first started.

It turned out that just as we had no experience with con men, so we had no real experience with lawyers either – but we were about to get it.

As it was a new experience for us, we listened carefully to our legal advice. On the advice of the lawyers for both sides, a conciliation meeting was organised, with all the directors and lawyers present. The meeting was to take place at two o'clock in the offices of our lawyer, so Nina and I met with him in the morning. We went through some ideas and were surprised to find our lawyer wasn't very interested. I made a few suggestions and the lawyer turned to me and said, 'I have twenty years of experience, so I don't need to be told how to go about it!' I was shocked. I wasn't trying to tell him what to do but was simply brainstorming ideas to prepare for the meeting. Oh well, I thought, he will amaze us when the time comes.

But he did not.

The meeting lasted around three hours but achieved nothing. The directors of the restaurant group came up with some silly demands, suggesting that we could buy back our shares for an extortionately high price. Our lawyer was a complete lamb during the meeting. He said very little and did not once put our opponents in difficulties. Eventually the other side stormed out with no resolution or progress made. Nina and I sat there, stunned and disappointed.

'That went well,' said our lawyer.

Nina and I looked at each other. 'You think the meeting went well?' I exploded. 'We must have been at a different meeting. I cannot believe what I have just witnessed. Your twenty years of experience for that! I am so disappointed!' His colleague, the lawyer we had worked with for so many years, had joined us after the others left, and was shocked by my reaction. But I told the lawyer there was little point in carrying on and dismissed him with immediate effect.

Two days later we received an invoice. I called his office and pointed out that in my view we had already paid him a not inconsiderable sum of money, so I could not see why we should pay more for such a poor job. He accepted my request that the final invoice be waived, and it thus went unpaid.

The next lawyer we appointed was chosen on the advice of a very dear friend who meant well. We went to London to meet the new lawyer and told him clearly what our budget was and asked him if it was sufficient. We also wanted to know what the best strategy was to reclaim the shares of Hotel TerraVina. He took us on.

Very quickly, however, it was obvious to us that he was used to dealing with big corporate businesses for which money is no object. Not only did he make us feel as if we were small fry, but he would answer my emails by filling them with lots of legal jargon and many obscure Latin quotes. I once sent him an email asking him for his opinion on an idea I had and wrote, 'No jargon and no Latin please!' He did try to temper the Latin words and jargon a little thereafter but after a few months we stopped using his services. It was all very frustrating and extremely expensive, because dismissing a lawyer means that the next lawyer has to read everything from the beginning. By then there were hundreds of existing emails and all sorts of papers, which instantly added a layer of costs.

The chairman of the group then launched a legal case against me relating to the supposed wine business that had never taken off. In his opinion I owed him money because I had never paid him for his time. Originally, we had agreed that I would give him some wine as payment when we first started to meet, because at the time his role was supposed to be that of adviser. I did give him some wine and some very nice bottles at that! However, when the idea changed and moved to a possible wine business partnership, we agreed that there was no reason for me to give him wine any more. For the rest of 2012 and the first part of 2013, he never once asked me or sent me an email claiming wine or payment. I wasn't worried about his claim, but of course that was adding to the overall legal costs. And we still didn't have a replacement lawyer.

It was Nina's dad Tony who came up with the answer, as he had so many times in our career. Tony loves flamenco guitar and was taking some lessons with a local flamenco guitar teacher. There happened to be a lawyer in his class, who told Tony he would be happy to talk to us.

Dennis Cuff was a young lawyer and straightaway we liked him. He listened to us with great attention and made us feel that he wasn't in it just for the money, but because he wanted us to win. He is a strategic thinker and working with him felt as if we had joined a team. Nina and I had the legal battle on our minds for most of the day, every day, and we talked about it non-stop. It was an annoying position to be in, but I must admit that part of me – and Nina, too – sometimes enjoyed the challenge. It was exhilarating to consider the next move and make plans to create difficulties for our opponents and perhaps even inflict the 'killer blow'. It felt like playing a chess match at a significant level. I would even go as far as to say that it would have been great fun if we hadn't had to pay our lawyer's fees and other related legal costs.

Of course, Dennis was not a magician and so the case was not resolved immediately. It carried on for several months after he had started working with us, but in that time a few positive things happened. The chairman of the restaurant group resigned as a director of Hotel TerraVina, which was satisfying, even if it didn't change the overall situation.

Months had passed when we had a lucky break. Hennessey Thompson, the wonderful accountant who had sorted out the restaurant group's tax problems, heard about the problems we were having. He announced that, if it would help, he would be happy to take the restaurant group to court for his unpaid fee – and he did. I was convinced that the directors would be smart enough to pay his fee so they would avoid court proceedings but, amazingly, they weren't.

The case was heard at the High Court in London and Nina went with Hennessey. She had to go twice as the case was not resolved the first time round. At the second hearing, the restaurant group was declared bankrupt. Soon, we began dealing with a liquidator to get back our shares in Hotel TerraVina.

Dealing with the liquidator was no picnic either, but eventually we were able to buy back our missing shares. It annoyed us to have to pay for them as they belonged to us in the first place. However, as we still owed a significant sum to the bank on the initial borrowing and we had not done so well with the hotel in the last eighteen months, the valuation of our business was not high, which meant that the value of the remaining shares was not great either. Hotel TerraVina was back in our hands – but at a terrible cost. We had to sell a flat we had bought after selling Hotel du Vin and I had to work very hard abroad during that time to pay all the legal costs. It was a horrible time and we were grateful to emerge from it bruised but not beaten.

On the wine business issue, the case continued and the chairman of the restaurant group, through his lawyer, started making some offers. The first one was for me to pay him £25,000, plus his incurred costs, for him to abandon the case; of course I refused. A few weeks later, a revised offer came for me to pay him £15,000 and costs, which again I rejected. A third offer came very close to the trial date for me to pay him £10,000, but this time with no costs to be paid by me; again I rejected the offer. I was determined not to pay him any money as I owed him nothing.

I had prepared a strong defence that would demonstrate in court that his accusations were laughable, so if we had to go to court, I was ready. A few days before the hearing we heard that the chairman of the group had abandoned the case and so no hearing would take place. I could have sued him for the legal costs I had incurred defending myself against his claim, but I had had enough.

If we thought that having recouped all our exchanged shares in Hotel TerraVina was going to make our life easier, we were in for a bit of a surprise. In our minds we were out of the woods, but our new bank manager did not see it that way at all. In December 2014, literally the day after we had officially received the exchanged shares in Hotel TerraVina back from the liquidator, we had a meeting with this new bank manager. Although 2014 had been a below-average year for Hotel TerraVina, the situation was not dramatic.

Our new bank manager did not see it that way and gave us a real telling-off for not meeting our targets. It was true, we hadn't, but while Hotel TerraVina was not making much profit, our hotel was still a sound business. The hotel was paying all its bills on time and was never in breach of payment of staff wages, VAT, suppliers, banking or bills. The only people who were not getting much were Nina and me, having no salary paid to us, but simply receiving a very small reimbursement of the initial monies we had put into the hotel.

We thought the news of us having recouped our missing shares would have pleased him and he would show some understanding for the tough situation we had been through, but that seemed irrelevant to him. He had a strong disagreement with Nina, and I had to calm her down, as she was getting very irritated – I thought at one point she was going to slap him. In all our years of marriage, I had never seen her so angry.

I pointed out to him that taxpayers had rescued the banks from bank-ruptcy back in 2008, including the one he was working for, and so part of the mess the country was in was the fault of people like him. Of course, it was not very diplomatic on my part, but I was very annoyed too. The meeting ended and he told us that he would come back to us by email very soon.

The week after, Nina and I were in Saint-Etienne for my mother's funeral. She had died a few days earlier at the age of ninety-eight. It was just four days before Christmas. While waiting to go to the church ser-vice, I looked at my emails and saw one from the bank manager. He wrote that, owing to the sad circumstances, he would send his email relating to the hotel the following week. Realising it was probably bad news, I asked him to send the email immediately.

After the funeral I checked my emails again, and there it was. The bank manager was changing some conditions, including putting up the interest rate on the floating part of our loan from 2.5 per cent to 6 per cent, plus adding some monthly penalties and a few other nasties. We were devastated. We felt like a drowning man struggling in the sea, seeing someone on land and hoping to be rescued, but instead being pushed further into the water.

After a few days, I contacted a different manager at the same bank, but higher up the ladder, whom we knew well. He was much more understanding and cancelled the new directives. We were very grateful to him and his intervention on our behalf. Ironically, we still work with the same bank manager that Nina was so angry with and I am pleased to say that we get along more harmoniously these days, although I am always wary when he and Nina meet!

Thus, we started 2015 with renewed energy and were determined to turn the business around. We could now focus solely on the hotel, without having to worry about the activities of unwanted associates. We were free, and as both legal battles were coming to an end, it felt great. Even better, 2015 proved to be one of the best years for Hotel TerraVina in financial terms and so we were back on track, which pleased the bank manager.

It was also a great year on the wine front as my head sommelier, Tanguy Martin, who had taken over from Laura Rhys, won the UK Sommelier of the Year 2015. It was wonderful to have another winner after Laura's win in 2009. Hotel du Vin had had several national winners, but we'd had six hotels and a lot of sommeliers, whereas Hotel Terra-Vina was just one small hotel. To have produced two national winners in just a few years at Hotel TerraVina made me as proud as when I'd won my own titles.

Things ticked along, gradually improving. In the first quarter of 2016, we beat the figures achieved in 2015 for the same period.

Then came 23 June 2016. The Brexit referendum. The campaign had begun in May and was very negative on both sides, dampening the general mood. After the shock of the Brexit side winning, business confidence dropped dramatically. Local businesses became very cautious and we lost a lot of functions and business meetings at the hotel.

Perhaps because we'd experienced a rollercoaster from the first day we opened Hotel TerraVina, Nina and I didn't immediately grasp the impact of the situation. So, we told ourselves it was just a blip and it would be fine in the end.

Twenty-Three

Blue Sky Thinking and a New Direction

As 2016 came to a close, it was clear we were just breaking even – and that was thanks to both the excellent start of the year and a new arrangement with the bank. In the summer of 2016, we had had to renegotiate our loan with the bank, which meant that instead of having only six years left to pay them, we were back to fifteen years of repayments, although they were much smaller monthly repayments than before.

The year 2017 was challenging too, and maybe it was because Nina and I didn't do everything necessary to reverse the curve. We implemented several marketing actions, but nothing ground-breaking, and I was travelling a lot for wine activities, and didn't spend enough time focusing.

But we were also tired. It wasn't just that the overall business mood in the country was tense, or that we were under fierce competitive pressure from other hotels, or that we'd just come out of a bruising and protracted legal dispute. It was also as if we had been plunged into a semi-sleep, with little energy or appetite to fight the difficult business situation we found ourselves in. We felt very weary, like a boxer who has just suffered a series of strong punches and is losing control of the fight. For the first time since we had started Hotel TerraVina, we could not really see a way to redress the situation and we had lost the drive, impetus and motivation that we needed. Hotel TerraVina had been an exciting journey, but also a hard one at times, and it had taken all our strength. We had nothing else to give.

Nina and I used to take a modest sum of money from Hotel TerraVina each month, as a monthly reimbursement of the considerable monies we had originally invested in the business. To help the business survive, we stopped taking any money at all from January 2017. Once all the bills, VAT, wages and bank repayments had been paid there was nothing left. At least we could pay everyone, but it's not a situation any business owner wants to be in. It is understandable and acceptable to struggle in the early months, but for a mature business such as Hotel TerraVina was by then, we should have been growing and not regressing!

Towards the end of spring 2017 we knew that unless we had an amazing summer (and being in a tourist area, the summer months are usually our best months), we would need to take serious action.

The summer of 2017 went by and there were no miracles. In spite of a fair amount of marketing and continuously high ratings on Trip-Advisor and elsewhere, trading was fine, but certainly not busy enough to change the curve and put us back into a healthy financial situation in readiness for the quieter autumn and winter trading months.

For the last five years, Nina had been taking a break during August in Norfolk with Romané and her parents. As I was often travelling abroad for wine activities, I had never been with them. However, in 2017 I decided to join them for a few days. One thing Nina had noticed during her Norfolk vacations was that there were a lot of places in the county that served simple but excellent food, locally sourced and of great quality; these cafes were attached to a shop, usually a delicatessen, a life-style store, a plant shop or all three together. Nina was very impressed, as all the ones she had visited were normally extremely busy. She had mentioned them to me before and had always stated that if Norfolk could offer such a great one-stop venue, maybe there was room for something similar in Hampshire too. Until the second part of 2016 we were not yet in a difficult situation with Hotel TerraVina, so we had not thought much about it or even considered that we could do something similar with our own business.

In the early part of August 2017 I travelled to Norfolk, to the village of Docking, where my family always stay in the same lovely rented cot-tage. During the days I was there we went to have breakfast or lunch in many of those different places Nina had mentioned. We did a lot of market research and we even talked to the owners of one of the businesses we were most inspired by, Thornham Deli. It had a vibrant kitchen/café, a deli and some bedrooms. By coincidence the owners, Janie and Jeanne, had been hoteliers like us. They were extremely friendly and along with their great general manager, Denise, gave us some very useful advice and urged us to stay in touch.

Thus, the more we thought about it, the more it became clear to us that we needed to change Hotel TerraVina radically. For the first time in an age we were both excited that there could be a future for the business. August 2017 marked exactly ten years that Hotel TerraVina had been open and we felt that it had had its day. It needed reviving, updating and a new purpose. We had missed the opportunity to grow the business in the early years when we had a great following and a positive image, but now it needed a change.

Selling it wasn't an option, because our hotel was small and not generating huge revenues. Even in the days when it was doing well, it wasn't enough to attract potential buyers, and those days were past. Perhaps because the reputation of TerraVina had been largely based around wine, it might have scared the few potential buyers away, as they did not feel capable of following our vision, and did not have the vision or courage to create a concept of their own. If nobody was interested in buying Hotel TerraVina, we had to find another solution.

Once back in the New Forest, Nina and I started to write a business plan for a new concept. Nina focused on the look, the offering and the running of the new concept and I worked on the financial side. It was great because for the first time in a long time we started to feel excited again about our own business. Of course, we were not totally sure it was the right thing to do, but as Hotel TerraVina was struggling, we could not just take half measures. We had to be bold!

Therefore, inspired by the different businesses Nina had seen in the last few years on her holidays, and more recently my experiences too, our new concept idea was to transform Hotel TerraVina into something similar to what we had seen in Norfolk. Our existing restaurant and its separate bar would become one single unit as a kitchen/café, serving tasty, simple food from eight in the morning non-stop to five o'clock in the afternoon, but then close for dinner. The look would be very different from TerraVina, being more modern and more relaxed. The lounge would become a lifestyle shop, selling lovely craft items, many made locally, and the function room would become a delicatessen, selling some of the food we served in the kitchen/café, but other food items too, principally from local artisan producers, preferably organic ones. The bedrooms would stay the same, although we would not advertise ourselves as a hotel any more, but instead would market ourselves as a bed and breakfast. Our wine-related image would disappear, and we would have only a few simple wines and no sommelier to serve them or explain them, very much unlike Hotel TerraVina.

It was going to be a big change and really it was like opening a brand new business. In fact, we changed the name as it would have been strange to keep the existing Hotel TerraVina name, and even detrimental to the new business. We needed to come up with a completely different name to send the message that our new venture was a complete break with the past. After some brainstorming within the family, Tony came up with Spot in the Woods.

For a few weeks we carried on doing a lot of research and refined our business plan. We did not mention our intentions to anyone, so no one in our team at Hotel TerraVina knew of our plans, except for Neil Wilson, who was working for us on the marketing side. But as Neil was freelance and not on the payroll and we trusted him implicitly, we felt it was sensible to share our ideas with him. In his Hotel TerraVina work Neil worked principally and directly with Nina and me. We took him into our confidence because we knew he would be excited to work on this project, plus he would bring some ideas, and we trusted him to keep it confidential. We had known Neil for a long time, from when he was working for the Rose Road Association, a local charity organisation helping children with complex disabilities that we supported; we are ambassadors for the charity.

In the middle of this renewal and excitement, I began suffering from back pain. Nothing unusual, as I had suffered from back pain for many years, but fortunately I had learnt to cope with it and manage it quite well. Every two or three years, when I've moved the wrong way or somehow cricked my back, I go and see my local chiropractor, Guy Blomfield, he applies some gentle treatment and then I'm back on track.

As soon as I felt the pain, I went to see him, and he carried out the usual treatment. However, a week later I was still having the same problem. While it was not extremely painful, it certainly did not feel like the normal pain and I understood that this time my back problem was not within the range of my chiropractor. I contacted my GP, who organised a blood test and an X-ray at the local hospital in Lymington. A few days later I had the results – my X-ray had shown an infection. This was bad news, as I was about to fly to Hong Kong on a tasting mission for *Decanter* magazine, and then on to Tokyo for some masterclasses. But I dutifully collected the prescription for antibiotics and began taking them as instructed.

The Asian trip went well, but the antibiotics didn't make me feel better. The back pain was still there and so, I guess, was the infection, so I went back to see my GP. This time he arranged for me to have more serious tests: an MRI and a CT scan at the Spire Hospital in Southampton. I had three weeks before my appointments, so in the meantime I continued with my wine-related activities, spending a week in Bordeaux, a week in Champagne and two days in Lyon, where I took some time off to see my sister.

I came back in mid-October and had the scans two days later, and then went home, back to planning Spot in the Woods. When I came back from my French trip it was 16 October 2017 and the two scans were planned for the morning of 18 October. On that day, I had the scans and went back home. A couple of hours later, I was contacted by the Spire Hospital asking me to come back the following morning as I needed to have a gastroscopy urgently.

I knew it wasn't going to be great news, but I checked in without fuss, was sedated and had the gastroscopy.

When I woke up, Nina was there waiting for me. She and I listened as Mr Kelly, a renowned surgeon, broke the news: I had cancer of the oesophagus and my tumour was 8 centimetres long. If it could not be operated on, I had no more than a year to live.

To my surprise I did not panic or have a meltdown. I was sixty years old and I thought, 'Well, if my time is up, then so be it.' I reasoned that as the English cricketing expression says, 'I have had a good innings.' Nina too was philosophical, and we were determined to remain positive and upbeat and fight it together with all our combined force.

I believe that if I had been ten years younger, I would have reacted differently and probably thought it was very unfair. Of course, I was not happy, just philosophical. However, I am a competitor, so my mind turned to finding solutions and not just accepting my fate without doing all I could to overcome the issue.

It was a tough period for our close family unit, as just two months before my own diagnosis, my mother-in-law Jean had been diagnosed with a non-Hodgkins lymphoma and she had already started on a tough chemotherapy treatment. Romané had just started university at King's College in London, studying French with English literature. He was processing the news of his Nana's illness, who he is very close to, and so we did not tell him over the phone that I too was ill. We waited until he came home at the weekend to explain the situation. As both Nina and I were calm and positive when talking to him, he did not have a bad reaction and bravely took the news in his stride.

In late October I had a PET scan at Southampton General Hospital and a few days later we had a meeting with my doctor, Dr Bateman. While the scan showed there was also another concerning spot close to my adrenaline gland, he and Mr Kelly believed that an operation was possible, so that was quite encouraging. Now it was a question of planning the process. Dr Bateman suggested a strong chemotherapy treatment called FLOT, a relatively new treatment to the UK, during November and December, followed by an eight-week period of rest and recuperation to build up my strength, followed by a major operation to remove part of my stomach.

Strangely, I was quite relaxed and extremely positive in my mind. I almost saw it as having to replace a part in a broken-down car; the mechanic does the work and then you can drive the car the same as before. I would follow the advice of the medical experts and let them do what they had to do, and it would all be all right.

Having said that, my thoughts turned – inevitably – to Nina and Romané. It was crucial that I left them in the best financial situation that I could.

Nina and I had been working hard on perfecting our business plan when we received the bombshell news of my cancer diagnosis. As I could no longer travel, at least for a while, I would have more time at home to work on the business plan. That was the silver lining, such as it was.

So . . . the concept was not enough. We also needed financing and timing. We decided to contact several banks and present the project to them. We thought that with a new bank we could start a new relation-ship and also raise the extra bit of money needed for the transformation, plus they would view it as a new business, something that we were unsure our current bank would do.

We met bank managers from different banks, but although some were fairly enthusiastic to begin with, ultimately they all turned us down, so the only route was to stay with our existing bank. Months later, as we reflected on that fact, Nina and I would be glad to have been rejected by the banks we contacted. Indeed, if a new bank had given us more money than our existing loan, we would probably have been less careful and might have spent a bit more than necessary.

Staying with our existing bank was going to be tough, but we had no choice. We would need to be extremely frugal. As we knew that our bank would not let us increase our existing loan, we needed to raise some funds from outside. Part would go on refurbishment and new equipment, part on buying new stock, part on reimbursing TerraVina gift vouchers and advanced booking deposits, especially functions, and part of the money would be kept for the potential redundancy payouts, even though we would not put many people out of work. Finally, as the new concept, like most new businesses, would not produce huge revenues from day one, we needed a bit of money to sustain salaries and all the other costs.

We were prepared to put our own money into the project, bearing in mind we were already working full time within the business for no financial recompense. We contacted some clients, friends and people we had known for a long time and offered to sell them a small number of shares. Two such family friends, along with their lovely wives, had been some of our initial shareholders at Hotel du Vin in 1994 and we had kept on great terms with them all ever since. Between them and some other great customers who agreed to participate, we raised just over half of what we needed. So, adding our own funds we had just enough to implement the new concept. It was going to be tight, but we had no other way.

Once we had raised the money, we had a meeting with our bank manager in December. He was pleased that we had come up with a radical idea and studied the figures I had assembled with the help of my accountant; he was happy enough to give us a bit of support by increasing our existing overdraft facilities for six months.

It helped to ease what had been a fraught time. I had begun chemotherapy in early November, after having a PICC line (a tube) inserted. Every two weeks I had to go to hospital to be injected with drugs, one of them through a pump I had to keep on for twenty-four hours, with a nurse coming to my home the following day to take off the pump.

Between the treatment and the new concept, I had to cancel most of my professional activities and rumours about me began to circulate. Nina, who wrote a blog for Hotel TerraVina, used it to announce both my condition and the new concept:

> As many of you are aware, Gerard has been very ill in recent months and while the chemotherapy treatment has gone well, he now faces a major operation in early February, with a very lengthy recovery period.

During recent months we have had cause to reflect, reconsider priorities and re-assess our lives and the work/life balance, not just for us, but also for our wonderful team. To that end, we would like to let you all know that we have made the decision to change the concept and style of the current business.

Her blog was picked up by local newspapers, as well as the catering and wine press and in response we received an outpouring of love and support from friends, colleagues and many people I didn't even know. I was overwhelmed by people's kindness.

Some of the support was practical. Tim Atkin, MW, a famous and well-respected journalist and friend, generously offered to run a wine auction to raise money for me, understanding that I might be short of money as my professional activities had come to a halt.

For the same reason, Michèle Chantôme and Andrés Rosberg, respectively general secretary and president of ASI, offered to organise wine events to raise money. Andrés even took the time to quickly fly to see me. I declined all their very kind offers, not because I am a proud man, or because I am wealthy, but because I received a lump sum of money from a critical illness policy that Nina and I had contracted into many years before. It seemed to me that it would have been wrong to let friends raise money for me when I was not in immediate need of it.

Many people I did not know who heard of my illness, who were suffering the same disease, also got in contact. One effect of so much care and concern was paradoxical – it meant I was talking about my cancer all the time, when I didn't want to. The side effects were very obvious – I'd lost my hair and my sense of taste had changed, along with some other (miserable) problems – but I didn't want to live in a cancer world. Besides, Nina and I had our new project and that needed all of my health, time and attention.

Now that we had the finance in place, we could decide on a timetable for the changes. We decided that we would tell our team at the beginning of the second week of January as there were a lot of legal aspects to follow through with our employees, especially those who would not have a position in the new business. We needed to reduce the number of chefs by one, and the number of waiting staff by one. Luckily one of the chefs and one of the waiters had given their notice in December anyway. The only people who were going to be affected were my three full-time sommeliers and the part-time barman. Our executive chef, Gavin, would lose his title and become head chef, as a kitchen/café didn't need an executive chef. He also kindly agreed to take a pay cut to help the business find its feet. Luckily, the sommeliers had been with me for more than a year and most of them were already thinking to move on during the coming year. In addition, they were all relatively young and none of them had family responsibilities; none was married or in a long relationship, or had mortgages and other commitments. Still it is never easy to have to tell people that they are not needed any more. They all took it very well and each of them found a new sommelier position very easily.

Having known from early December that we were going to change the business, but only telling the staff a month later, proved complicated. Nina and I wanted to have as few bookings as possible for Hotel Terra Vina functions for the year 2018, as we did not want to have to reimburse many deposits or have to honour functions that would delay us implementing our new concept. To stop our Hotel TerraVina management team taking future function bookings was completely against our ethos and so Nina told our team that we were going to refurbish the function room in early 2018, so any booking enquiries should be referred to her. The team probably found this a bit strange, but nevertheless no onereally suspected anything and most enquiries were passed on to Nina.

When, in the first part of January 2018, we made our employees aware of the news about the restructure, we asked them not to say anything as we wanted to announce it to the public on 28 January at the occasion of our very last Hotel TerraVina wine dinner. That wine dinner, which we called the Protégés Wine Dinner, was really special; it was with six of my past head sommeliers, four from my Hotel du Vin days, including the first two head sommeliers of Hotel TerraVina. Each came to present a wine and tell a funny story of working with me. We had a full house and it went extremely well. My ex-sommeliers (Corinne Michot, Laura Rhys, MS, Claire Thevenot, MS, Tanguy Martin, Dimitri Mesnard, MS and Xavier Rousset, MS) did a brilliant job that evening with great humour. It was my first big public outing since I had undergone my chemotherapy treatment and our guests were very pleased to see me giving the welcome. At the end of the evening Nina and I made a speech and after thanking all our staff and our six 'protégés' we announced the news about Hotel TerraVina changing to become Spot in the Woods.

It was five days before my operation. The chemotherapy had ended in late December and I was really tired. That year was the first year I did not work the Christmas period at the hotel. But I needed the time to recover before my January operation.

And recover I did. It helped that I had so many people to offer moral support. I spoke to my friend Christelle Guibert about surviving chemo-therapy and now preparing for a major operation. 'Well,' she said, 'it's like you're racing in the Tour de France. You have come top after the Alps and now you have to do the same going through the Pyrenees!'

The person who had a really tough time of it was Nina, who was supervising the closing and re-opening of the hotel, while driving me everywhere, and also looking out for her mum, who also had cancer.

It helped that we live in such a beautiful area. The New Forest is ideal for walking, and luckily for me I had Malmsey, our boxer dog, to keep me company. Malmsey is a dog full of energy and she made me walk much further than I had intended – it turned out I was stronger than I believed.

We told the public that we would close Hotel TerraVina on Sunday 25 February 2018 and reopen exactly seven days later on Monday 5 March 2018 as Spot in the Woods. Of course, Nina and Neil had planned and organised a big campaign on social media for the day after this last wine dinner and the news was sent to all the people on our database. At the same time, a special offer to come and stay at Hotel TerraVina before the closing date was made available.

This special February offer proved very popular and the hotel occupancy was high that month, delivering a decent revenue that was very welcome after a fairly grim January.

Twenty-Four

Moving Mountains Is Impossible but Climbing Them Is Sometimes Achievable

Nina and I had done several openings with Hotel du Vin and of course Hotel TerraVina, but this one was a completely new experience. It was so much more difficult than a classic opening. When we had done these before we had closed existing businesses we had just bought – indeed, in some cases, they were just empty buildings – and then we had months in front of us to prepare to open the new business. This time, there were only five weeks from the time we made the new project public on 28 January 2018 to the opening of Spot in the Woods on 5 March 2018, and only a week between the closing of the old business and the opening of the new one. I had also just come through gruelling chemo treatment and was preparing for a major operation, so the timing really could not have been worse.

We had to make sure that all the people who had bookings at Hotel TerraVina after 25 February, when the hotel closed, were informed that after that date it was shut for a week and then it would be reopened as a new concept. We offered to either refund their deposits or transform their bookings from the old business to the new one. Fortunately, we did not have too many bookings, and most were easy to deal with; they either cancelled, as they did not like the idea of staying in a place not serving dinner, or they simply kept their bedroom bookings, and were pleased about the new, reduced rates.

The more delicate issue was with people who had booked our function room for a business meeting or a lunch or dinner party. Ideally, we would have liked them to cancel their event as we needed to transform the function room into a deli. However, we left them the choice and offered each person who had organised a business meeting, or a party, the option to retain their booking, if that was their wish. A few people kept their function bookings. On the one hand it was useful to have a few guaranteed revenues with those function bookings, but on the other hand, it was a nonsense as we could not implement the opening of the deli. We had to wait until mid-June to open the deli and even then we created it once and then had to strip it again for a breakfast meeting, so all that hard work was for very little financial gain. However, the delay in opening the deli did give us time to focus on the kitchen/café.

In the early weeks of the new concept, I was slowly recovering from my operation, so Nina had to orchestrate what was happening on the ground by herself. Of course, when Nina was back home at the end of a long day, we would discuss the new business, or occasionally Nina would ring me during the day for advice on an important impromptu decision, but it was not quite the same as being physically involved.

During the closed week, despite three days of heavy snow, loss of electricity, tradesmen being unable to get to us due to the weather, and me just out of hospital and very weak, Nina and the team managed to transform the existing bar and restaurant into a beautiful kitchen/café. The place looked completely different, and all achieved without spending very much at all.

Nina had bought a few inexpensive tables and chairs of different shapes and colours and we also kept a few of our existing tables, repainting them in all sorts of colours, with a mish-mash of chair styles added to them. The place was also painted with a different colour scheme from before and so, all in all, Spot in the Woods kitchen/café did not look anything like the restaurant of Hotel TerraVina. It looked refreshed, clean, modern – and absolutely brilliant.

The kitchen/café proved immediately successful with a lot of people coming through the doors from day one. It was lovely to have many locals embracing the new concept, many of whom had shunned Hotel TerraVina because it was perceived as too posh and expensive.

On the bedroom side it was much more complicated. Because we did not have a bar any more, nor a lounge (which had been transformed into a lifestyle shop) and we did not serve dinner either, our offering was completely different. We had become a B&B. There was nothing wrong with that at all, but we needed to build a new clientele, as most of the people who stayed at Hotel TerraVina before had enjoyed using the bar and having dinner in situ. Neil, our marketing consultant, and Kayleigh, one of our managers at the time, did a brilliant job at addressing this problem by working intelligently (by which I mean not giving too high a commission percentage) with a few online travel agents. Neil also worked hard on social media to build a database of new customers. Within a few weeks the results for the number of bedroom bookings had improved significantly.

Indeed, the occupancy was running from 46 per cent in March, our first month of trading, to 54 per cent in April. By May, the occupancy went to 72 per cent, dropping to 62 per cent for June, but with fewer discounted room rates. In July, the occupancy really took off and ended up at 86 per cent overall with some excellent room rates.

The lifestyle shop located in the former lounge of Hotel TerraVina was open from the start, but it did not perform that well financially. Aside from the fact that Nina had stocked it well, everyone was too busy working in the kitchen/café to give it much attention. To be honest, in my business plan, the lifestyle shop and the deli were treated as one single unit. Thus, the lifestyle shop was not really to be looked at on its own, so it would have to wait for the deli to be opened to be judged.

Nina had done a superb job of stocking the deli with interesting and predominantly local products such as jams, chutneys, cheeses, pasta and sauces, eggs, artisan breads, chocolate, fudge, beer, cider, gin and much more, including a good selection of wine at exceptionally great value. Much of the food and drink comes from local artisans and much is also organic. Overall, the deli looks enticing. Nina had used the existing banqueting tables, but covered them with hessian, and she dotted lots of rustic-looking shelving, sacking and crates about the room too. With the simple lighting, the overall look is very rustic.

By coincidence, the day we opened the deli, in mid-June, we had a meeting with our bank manager. He was happy with the way the business was moving but annoyed with the fact that we had not quite achieved the figures we had shown in my business plan. To be fair, it was not surprising; when you write the figures for a business plan, there is always a certain amount of guesswork involved. In addition, as much as I hate being overly enthusiastic with financial predictions, if I had been too cautious the bank might not have agreed to support us. It is a difficult balancing exercise.

Overall, financially the business had taken pretty much exactly what I had predicted in March, April and May, increasing well each month, but it had stagnated in June, taking less than predicted, and in addition we had overspent on staff wages.

There was worse news to come. Around mid-June, my back pain returned, which meant another PET scan. Dr Bateman explained that my cancer had returned – and it was incurable. I would have between six and twelve months left.

Of course, the diagnosis sent us into a tailspin. But, once again, friends from the world of wine rallied round, with introductions to a renowned French oncologist who has had very promising results with cancer patients such as myself. Nina and I began to do what we do best – strategise. New diet, new approach, and regular visits to France to see the oncologist.

But, of course, Spot in the Woods still needed our attention. The first priority was to tell the bank manager about our situation. We sent him an email to tell him and asked him for a meeting. On 23 July we met him in the morning at Spot in the Woods. Our bank manager was very sympathetic and as July's figures were excellent, the meeting went well.

In the end July proved to be a really good month, beating the revised figures, and at the time of writing in August, the business is doing well. There is always room for improvement, and we are certainly not complacent as it needs to continue to perform well and get better still. The kitchen/café is almost at capacity, beating my expectations. For the month of August the room occupancy will end in the high 80s to even 90 per cent and while the shop is not reaching the projected figures yet, it is getting close. We will see what the coming months bring in terms of revenue, occupancy and further developments for the business. I hope I will be able to play a part in the business's continued success as time goes by.

Epilogue

I never played professional football and I never crushed all the other competitors in the Tour de France. But I did hit the premier league when I won Best Sommelier in the World 2010. Although there were many serious life challenges still to face, winning that title changed my life.

One big award brings others in its wake. *Caterer* magazine gave me the Special Catey Award 2010; the International Wine Challenge made me Wine Personality of the Year 2010; *Harpers Wine & Spirits* magazine made me Wine Personality of the Year 2011, and *Imbibe* magazine named me Industry Legend 2011.

New professional opportunities opened up that I could never have imagined. In the middle of 2011, I was contacted by Arnaud Christiaens, a hedge-fund manager who had started a wine project in Bordeaux called SGC (le Secret des Grands Chefs), and wanted me to come on board. He had identified some small, hidden-away parcels of land in four prestigious appellations, and had begun producing very high-quality wine. I became a partner, which took me on wonderful adventures through Asia, running prestige SGC events.

The opportunities kept flowing. I became an international brand ambassador for Lehmann Glass, an international glass maker head-quartered in Reims, Champagne. With them I created a range of wine glasses called the Oenomust and then went on to create other glasses, some in partnership with famous restaurateurs.

I became wine ambassador for Shangri-La hotels for three years, which I enjoyed a lot. There was a mineral water deal with Ogen too. Businessmen approached me, wanting me to join their enterprises. There were so many offers that I had to turn many down.

Even with so much happening, I could still be surprised and humbled. In November 2012, I returned from a trip to Asia. 'You have a letter you should open,' said Nina.

When one of us is away, the other opens the correspondence, to make sure nothing important is overlooked, so I knew Nina must have read the letter. But she wanted me to discover for myself what it said. I felt some trepidation, because at that time all the letters were bad ones. I reached for the pile with a heavy heart – but Nina couldn't resist a hint. 'It's not bad news!' she said.

I opened it. It was a letter from Sarah Kemp, the managing editor of *Decanter* magazine, Britain's – and Europe's – most prestigious wine magazine. She was writing to tell me that I had been named *Decanter*'s Man of the Year 2013, to be announced in the April 2013 issue. I had to keep it a secret until then.

It was an extraordinary moment. The *Decanter* Personality of the Year list had begun in 1984 and over the years its laureates had become a Who's Who of the international wine scene. Being awarded Man of the Year was an induction into wine's Hall of Fame, standing alongside the great pioneers. No sommelier or hotelier had ever won this award.

In May 2013, Nina and I travelled to London to the *Decanter* offices for the Champagne and canapés party, where I received the trophy. Later that evening, my friends Arnaud Christiaens and Fred Zantman, invited everyone to dinner at the Blakes Hotel. My dear friend Raymond Blanc, the famous two-Michelin-star chef, came along to keep everyone entertained with his impromptu speeches and we all had a fabulous evening together celebrating.

At that moment, I could have hung up my uniform and simply concentrated on Hotel TerraVina, which might have been sensible. My calling card had become my qualifications – my MS, my MW, my Wine MBA. I was the only person in the entire wine industry to have achieved the trifecta, as well as carrying off the ultimate title of Best Sommelier in the World. I had to go for the last qualification to round it off.

The OIV (the International Organisation of Wine and Vine), created in 1924 in Paris, is the United Nations of wine. It's an intergovernmental organisation that provides a forum for the members to collaborate, co-operate and harmonise on key issues. The OIV also collects important data such as per capita wine consumption and the area of land under vine.

In 1986, some of its directors had decided to create a Master of Science in Wine Management (OIV Msc in Wine Management), a fifteen-month course where students have to attend modules in twenty-five countries. There are five exams – economy, finance, law, marketing and strategy – and a memoir that has to be written and defended. I wrote mine on iconic wines: 'What factors determine an iconic wine?' I finished the programme in July 2017 and received a distinction.

Finally, there were no more exams to take, no more competitions to win.

I had received an OBE, and in 2016 I received the Freedom of the City of London. In 2017, the French Ambassador in London made me Chevalier de l'Ordre du Mérite Agricole (Knight of the Order of Agricultural Merit).

Looking back, there was a price to pay for my competitive streak. Nina and I were so caught up in training and the excitement of winning that maybe we sometimes took our eye off what was happening in front of us. But nothing great happens without a cost.

And, of course, going into hotels and meeting Nina brought me my biggest achievement of all: my son Romané. He has brought nothing but joy, happiness and pride to Nina and me. I write this knowing that I will not watch him grow still further into the fine young man I know he will become, and I feel a sense of sadness. However, whatever lies ahead, he will embrace the adventures, the opportunities and challenges with strength and passion and I will always be the proudest papa of a talented and special son.

He is living proof that being so deeply immersed in wine and hospitality opened doors to a world I couldn't have imagined. My efforts to serve other people, to choose wines that would take their meal to another level, to make them comfortable and give them a night, or a holiday, that they would remember for the rest of their lives, repaid me many, many times over. I would do it all again.

Reflections

I don't really know how to qualify my life as it has been made up of a mixture of some perfectly normal sections, sprinkled with many boring moments, but fortunately it has also been peppered with plenty of exciting events too. Yes, I have been down many times, but I have also experienced plenty of really wonderful ups and joyous occasions and even momentous times.

When I analyse myself, I can say that as a person I was not blessed with the strength and skills of the great athletes or sportsmen I admired, such as some of my teen idols, Bruce Lee or Johan Cruyff. I did not enjoy the stunning good looks of the likes of Paul Newman or Brad Pitt. Equally, I did not have the brilliant and sharp intellect of Gary Kasparov or Stephen Hawking. However, one feature I have been privileged to possess, and that has served me extremely well, is a rock solid determination that made me highly resilient and totally focused!

Over the years I built on this determination and many times, when I felt humiliated and completely defeated, relatively quickly I would stop crying and feeling sorry for myself. Instead, I would turn my attention wholly to finding a solution, often leading to a magnificent recovery.

In fact, on many occasions, in a very strange way, I have enjoyed being at the bottom and fighting my way back. It was often a very bizarre feeling that when all seemed lost, I could sense that after all it did not have to be that way. Indeed, once I sensed the situation could not be any worse, I felt liberated and in my mind it was the beginning of the climb towards a much better horizon and a truly exciting outcome. Suddenly,

I could plan, prepare and act for a future triumph and most certainly it felt electricfying, exciting and so exhilarating!

I can look back to the numerous occasions when I was told I would never achieve anything in my life. However, and in spite of my rather average natural attributes, I managed to become the most titled person on the planet in my chosen profession of sommelier. There is no doubt that there is a vanity aspect in my character, which makes me feel very happy and quite proud about that, but then just like a sports champion, I wanted to win as many titles as possible, so why not – I have earned that feeling of pride and my moment of vanity.

Of course, I fully appreciate that in order to achieve all that I have, I have been extremely lucky in my life. I have a lovely sister who did a great deal for me when I was young, and later on I was privileged to meet Nina, my wonderful and loving wife who has given me so much true love and unconditional support. Thanks to her, we created a very close-knit family; we have an amazing son, Romané, and together they have made my life complete. For me, having the gift of such a happy home life as an adult means so much and is very special and I cherish it dearly. In addition, I have been fortunate to be surrounded by some extremely caring friends who have been there for me when I needed them. Finally, on occasions, some people who I hardly knew have, without hesitation or question, offered to help me without asking anything in return – to all of them I am truly grateful.

Thank you all, you have helped me to make my life very special and it's been a great adventure!

Afterword

Now I have to take up the story. Sadly, not only did my dear mum lose her battle with cancer in early December 2018, but Gerard's cancer returned with a vengeance. Despite his will to fight, along with the sterling efforts of his doctors in the UK and also in France, the cancer was the one challenge that even he could not beat.

Gerard passed away peacefully on 16 January 2019. My darling husband has left a void in our lives.

But he would have been so amazed, bewildered and humbled by the many thousands of messages that appeared on social media. He even trended on Twitter. How amused he would have been by that. Likewise, the outpouring of love and the vast numbers of people who travelled from all around the world for his memorial service at Winchester Cathedral, in June 2019, would have astonished and humbled him. It is hard to sum up everything that was written about him, but one sentence perhaps catches it best: 'The industry has not just lost a leading light in Gerard's passing, it has lost the very brightest, burning beacon.'

This book is now an important part of Gerard's legacy and that tribute is a fitting end.

Nina Basset, August 2019

Unbound is the world's first crowdfunding publisher, established in 2011.

We believe that wonderful things can happen when you clear a path for people who share a passion. That's why we've built a platform that brings together readers and authors to crowdfund books they believe in – and give fresh ideas that don't fit the traditional mould the chance they deserve.

This book is in your hands because readers made it possible. Everyone who pledged their support is listed below. Join them by visiting unbound.com and supporting a book today.

Silver Supporters

Nigel Bevan
Ferran Centelles
Christopher Coad
David & Sally Cole
Cultural Communications
Estonian Sommelier Association
Rebecca Gergely
Lulie Halstead
Kisvin Vineyard & Winery
Caroline Lestimé
Mike & Kathy Martin

Paul Michael
Michael Palij MW
Jancis Robinson
Lynne Sherriff MW
Sommelier Guild of the United Kingdom
Sopexa
James Tidwell
Wine Guild of the United Kingdom
Wines of South Africa

Bronze Supporters

Annette Alvarez-Peters
Jaime Araujo
Essi Avellan
Scott Bailey
David Baldwin
Wayne Belding
Phil Belton
Laurent Bergmann

Simon Binder
David Bird MW
Barbara Boyle MW
Ian and Amanda Brown
Graham Buckton
Kathleen Burk
Carol Cheyne
Ian Davies

Josh Dear

Richard Dear

Decanter Magazine

Sergio Dos Santos

Oliver Pieter Ellinger

Philippe Faure-Brac

Gareth Ferreira

Doug Frost

Filippo Mattia Ginanni

Nicolas Goldschmidt

Michael & Karen Goodman

Paul Grieco

Christelle Guibert

Ian Harris

Anke Hartmann

Rob Hirst

Dan Jago

Brian Jamieson

Sue and Roger Jones, The Harrow at Little
    Bedwyn

Robert Joseph

Yohann & Ildiko Jousselin

Neil and Béatrice Joyce

Sarah Kemp

Mariya Kovacheva

Cecile Lavaud-White

Natalie Leggett

Pascaline Lepeltier

Lin Liu

Edijs Locmels

Angela & Antony Lowther

Yang Lu

Stephen & Jennie Mack

Simon McMurtrie

Debra Meiburg

Tony Milner

Nicholas Mobbs

Franck Moreau

Fiona Morrison MW

Antony MossAndrea Nicholson

Diarmid O'Hara

Lindsay Oram

The Oxford Wine Club

Tony & Carol Pearson

Piotr Pietras

Joao Pires

Stephen Raducki

Hoffmann Rathbone

Nahaboo Réza

Roy Richards

Elaine Rose

Xavier Rousset

Richard Sagala

Alexandre Sampaio

Ronan Sayburn

Nick Scade

Jane Schillig

Mash Shiokawa

Andrew Smith

Simon Smith

Tim and Robert

Andy Tonkin

Paul van Maaren

David Vareille

JC Viens

Timothy Wells

Tony & Judi Woolven

Fred Zantman

Elvis Ziakos

Eric Zwiebel MS

Supporters

Heather Agnew
Daniel Airoldi
Angie Alexander
Nicholas Allen
Tracy Allen
Jean-Baptiste Ancelot
Nick Anderson
Igor Andronov
Nick Angelou
Jane Anson
Vincenzo Arnese
Tjalfe Arnstrup
Chris Ashton
Andrew Ashurst
Eric Asimov
Tim Atkin
Adalynn Austin
Mimi Avery
Sandra Aw
Martyn Backshall
Aaron Bader
Lucia Baldassi
Paul Baldwin
Richard Bampfield
Stuart Barford
Susie Barrie MW & Peter
  Richards MW
Carol Bartlett
Angela Bawtree
David Beckett
Fiona Beckett
Karen Bekker
Belvin vinska šola
Krister Bengtsson
Yannick Benjamin
Alice Bernigaud
Igor Beron

Jake Berry
Randall Bertao
Carla Bertellotti
Mike Best
Dheeraj Bhatia
Paul Billett
Richard Billett
Sally Bishop
Samuel Bisson
Nicola Blanchard
Beverley Blanning
Mark Bolton
Jeroen Boom
Ana Borges
Romain Bourger
Jane Boyce MW
Fabia Bracco
Vicky Bramley
Paulo Brammer
Mark Braund
Jerre Bridges
Rosemary & Roger Brighton
Liz Brown
Neil Bruce
Rob Buckhaven
Jim Budd
Anne Burchett
Christopher Burr
Martin Burt
Richard Burton
Joel Butler MW
Michael Camps
Tom Cannavan
Sam Caporn
Lisa Cardelli
Tim Carey
Felicity Carter

Benjamin Chan
Guy M Chatfield
Christelle Chédeville
CheeK
Nick Chisnell
Clifford Chow
Shu Hui Chua
Elaine Chukan Brown
Anna Clark
Peter Claydon
Nicolas Clerc
Lucy Clitherow
Gordon Coates
Matthew Cocks
Steve Cole
Lucie Coleman
Chris and Jane Collinson
Harry Cooke
Andreja Corokalo
Armando Maria Corsi
Igor Costa
Gregg Coull
Paul Courtney
Julie Coutton-Siadou
John Crawford
Susan Croon
Mark Crowther
Ronnie Culshaw
Nick Culver
Charles Curtis
Tim & Aimée Curtis
Rachel Davey
Richard Davies
Yolanda O. de Arri
Gavin Deaville
Brie Dema
Dave & Jan Denholm
Erica Dent

Philip Denton
Gianluca Di Taranto
Jean Marc Dizerens
Simon Doggett
Lei Dong
Pye Dorothee
Colin Dourish
Fabien Duboueix
Simon Dupaquier-Green
Julie Dupouy-Young
Sarka Duskova
Teresa Eiland
Jane Elizabeth
Symon Elliott
Michael Ellis
Ashley Ely
Tomas Eriksson
David Evans
Sarah Jane Evans MW
Michelle Ewing
Xavier Eyraud
Guntram Fahrner
Owen Farr
Pierre-Marie Faure
Danny Fay
Colin Fell
Hicham Felter
Moyra Ferguson
Eugene Ferrara
Adrian Filiuta
Joanne Finkel
Peter Foley
David Forer MW
Vivienne Franks
Jerusha Frost
Katsuhiro Fukuda
Linda Galloway
Silvia Garatti & James Lloyd
Kirsten Gates
Tim Gee

Rosemary George MW
Jim Gerakaris
Jonny Gettings
Ben Gibbins
Patrick Gijsemans
Robert Giorgione
Steve & Jan Glynn
Sally Goble
Edward Goddard
Gill Gould
Nayan Gowda
Ingo Grady
Jacob Gragg
Richard Graham
Stuart Gray
Lindsay Greatbatch
Kleanthes K. Grohmann
Robert J Grover
Karen Groves
Scott M Gruenke
Pawel Gruntowski
Paris Hadjiantonis
Noelle Hale
Gary Hall
Keith Hammond
Irene Hannah
Luke Harbor
Julia Harding MW
Janet Harmer
Jane Harrison
Peter Harrison
Edward Harvey
Barry Hasler
Mia Hayes
Joseph Haynes
James Healy
Simon Heape
Peter Helena and Peter
    Carabi
Eric Hemer

Richard Hemming
Caroline Henry
Ben Henshaw
Szilvia Herbak
Darren Hesketh
Will Hillary
Thomas Hirsch
Ed Hobbs
Stephanie Hocking
Susan & Duane Hoff
Mike Holley
Sorcha Holloway
Peer F. Holm
Alan Holmes
Mark Horton
Carl & Rina Housbey
Justin Howard-Sneyd
Chris Howell
Phillipa & Ed Jackson
Birte Jantzen
Martin Jennings
Simon Jerrome
Laura Jewell MW
Daniel Johansson
Phil Johnson
Lowri Jones
Janet Kampen
Stella Kane
Klearhos Kanellakis
Daniel Keller
Elizabeth Kelly
Olga Klukas
Emin Koh
Han Yew Kong
David John Koob
Anne Krebiehl MW
Martin Lam
Rupert Lang
Marc Lashly
Champagne Lavergne

James Lawther
Patrick Lecan
Olaf Leenders
Steve Leow
Paz Levinson
Mark Lewis
Andrew Licudi
Peter Liem
Limm Communications Ltd
James Lindner
Tim Livingston
Angela Lloyd
Matthieu Longuere
Wink Lorch
Claire Love
Gerald Lu
Richard Lukins
David Lusby
Alexander Lushnikov
Dan Lystad
Ken Maitland
Heidi Mäkinen MW
Aaron Mandel
Ali Mann
Elliott Mannis
Lucy Marcuson
Joëlle Marti
Chris Martin
Tanguy Martin
Nicola Masa
Victoria Mason
Franck Massard
Jane Masters MW
Ashika Mathews
David McCarthy
Michelle McCarthy
Cynthia McCreadie
Judith and Andrew McKinna
John McLusky
Robert Mcnulty

David McWilliam
David Mears
Slim Mello
Daniel Mellor
Lynne Mendoza
Szabolcs Menesi
Dimitri Mesnard
Jan Messing
Charles Metcalfe
Simon Milroy MW
Patrick Miyamoto
Stephan Mohr
Matt Monk
Alan Montague-Dennis
Mark and Charlotte
Moorhouse
Eric Morlot
Alistair Morrell
Kate Muir
Asim Mullick
Michele Munro
Robert Murphy
Ewan Murray
Suzanne Mustacich
Alistair Myers
Sharon Nagel
Filip Nagy
Claire Kyunghwa Nam
Tiffany Nash
Naturally Norfolk
Carlo Navato
Olga Negalho
Daniel Brian Neo
Stefan Neumann MS
Claire Newman
Stephen Nisbet
Chris Nixon
Anna Nonciaux
Aaron Nother
Philippe Nusswitz

Mark O'Meara
Katharine O'Callaghan
Mick O'Connell MW
Ray O'Connor
Fernando Okubo
Gregory Olver
Ervin Ong
Ryan Opaz
Laura Painting
M. Eleni Papadakis
Michelle Paris
Christine Parkinson
Karin Parkinson
Carlos Parrodi
Adam Pawlowski
Beth Pearce
Bridget & Caleb Pearce
Lionel Periner
Lisa Perrotti-Brown
Kim Peschier
Astrid & Pierpaolo Petrassi
Jacqui Pickles
Rachael Pogmore
Stuart Porter
Jeff Prather
Jean-Marie Pratt
Jakub Pribyl
Tim Pride
Mark Pryor
Ilaria Ranucci
Christina Rasmussen
Alexander Redfern
Amanda Regan
Nick Reynolds
Laura Rhys
Andre Ribeirinho
Andrew Richards
Phil Richardson
Laurent Richet
Jane Roberts

Jim Rollston
Nick Room
Anne Roque
Stephanie Rouse
Mei Ling Routley
Dylan Rowlands
Alessio Rozzi
Ann J Samuelsen
Claude Sassoulas
Masaki Satou
Ronan Sayburn
Marco Scarpelli
Eveline Scheren
Mike Scully
Robert Sedgwick
Rodrigo Sepúlveda Schulz
Albert Sheen
Paul Sheppard
David Shoemaker
Richard Siddle
Hugo Silva
Giuseppe Simonini
John Simpson
Fiona Sims
Stephen Skelton MW
Luke T W Smith
Peter Smith
Robin Smith
Raymond W P SO
James Spence
Ruth Spivey
Tom Stevenson
Nigel Paul Stickland
Joy and John Stokes
Patrick Strange
Anthony Swift
Dr Orsi Szentkiralyi
Max Tamagna
Siân Tattersall
Jo Taylorson

Cyril Thevenet
Claire Thevenot
Jaeson Thieme
Tara Q. Thomas
Jo Thompson
Mark and Victoria Tilling
Zsuzsa Toronyi
Stephen Towler
Lucy Townsend
Anne-Laure Trioulaire
Julia Trustram Eve
Effrosyni Tsournava
Anna Tuckett
Paul Tudor MW
Kevin Turner
Siobhan Turner
Takato Uematsu
Geoff Uglow
Kate Underwood
Cemil Urganci
Michael Urquhart
Yannis Valambous
Pascal & Louise Vallee
Sophie Vallejo
Kathleen Van den Berghe
Jan-Willem van der Hek
Gabrielle Van Neste
Dim Verbenko
Pauline Vicard
Jerome Villani
Dominique Vrigneau
Jonathan Walkden
Geoffrey Warde MBE
Mark Warwick
Becky Wasserman-Hone
Margaret Watmough
Andy Way
Peter Webb
Philip Weeks
Martin Wells

Richard Wells
Lynne Whitaker
Tim White
George Wickham
David Wicks
Teresa Wighton
Martyn Wilkins
Sarah Williams
Wine lovers in Hong Kong
James Witty
Silven Wong
Richard Woodard
John Worontschak
Tina Xie
Kaori Yamada